Digging for the Disappeared

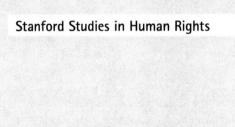

Stanford Studies in Human Rights

Digging for the Disappeared

Forensic Science after Atrocity

Adam Rosenblatt

Stanford University Press
Stanford, California

Stanford University Press
Stanford, California

Printed in the United States of America on acid-free, archival-quality paper.

Library of Congress Cataloging-in-Publication Data

Rosenblatt, Adam (Adam Richard), author.
Digging for the disappeared : forensic science after atrocity / Adam Rosenblatt.
pages cm
Includes bibliographical references and index.
ISBN 978-0-8047-8877-9 (cloth : alk. paper)—
ISBN 978-0-8047-9491-6 (pbk. : alk. paper)
1. Forensic anthropology—Moral and ethical aspects. 2. Dead—Identification. 3. Mass burials. 4. Human rights. 5. Atrocities. I. Title.
GN69.8.R67 2015
599.9—dc23

2014039062

ISBN 978-0-8047-9488-6 (electronic)

Typeset by Bruce Lundquist in 10/14 Minion Pro

For my grandparents:
Jean and David Bialer, who rebuilt the world
David and Frances Regenbogen, beloveds on and in the earth

Contents

Illustrations

Foreword

ADAM ROSENBLATT'S *Digging for the Disappeared* is a rare and moving work of scholarship. His study of what he calls the "darkened corner of human rights practice" is critical in the very best and most lasting of ways. In bringing a variety of methodological tools to bear on the history, practices, and dilemmas of forensic science after mass atrocity, his book reveals new, even radically new, possibilities for reconciling the tensions between the different constituencies that are deeply involved with investigation, justice-seeking, meaning-making, and politics after gross human rights violations. At the same time, Rosenblatt is himself deeply embedded in the fiber of the book, not only as a scholar, but as someone whose life history and research experiences in the field shape his incisive analytics into a broader ethics of engagement. This ethics is expressed in Rosenblatt's clear and jargon-free writing; in the questions he feels compelled to pursue; and, ultimately, in the lingering, even haunting, effect that the book has on the reader.

As Rosenblatt argues, the interdisciplinary yet immersive account he develops is a necessary orientation for telling the story of how a "small scientific revolution"—the use of innovative scientific techniques to sift facts from the painful complexity of mass atrocity and its aftermath—became a global project. His field experiences with the Physicians for Human Rights, which played a central role in the global development of forensic human rights investigations gave him a unique vantage point from which to observe the coalescing of what he describes as the four moral principles that distinguish this "networked field" from all others. The observation that science is the practice of a particular, and privileged, form of truth has been made before. But in Rosenblatt's hands, we are shown how this practice is shaken when it confronts collective grief, spiritual insistence, and the culturally diverse practices of death. Second, his insider's perspective as a "critically generous" researcher opens up the tight world of forensic investigations and demonstrates that practitioners bring a much-needed insistence on political autonomy to often tragically politicized processes. Third, Rosenblatt's groundbreaking synthesis reveals the surprising fact that forensic human rights investigators are, in their own way, and in quite different terms, as concerned with the universalist implications of their work as the humanitarian political and legal activists against whom their scientific investigations have been seen to starkly contrast. And finally, the book shows how forensic investigations after mass atrocity are focused on victims in elemental, immediate, and absolutely unique ways. It is one thing to file a case in court seeking accountability for victims of atrocity. It is quite another to spend hours and days amongst the decaying remains of the victims themselves in a single-minded quest to establish a factual record of perpetration and consequence that cannot be credibly refuted.

And it is here, when *Digging for the Disappeared* takes up the seemingly obvious, but often overlooked, question of the function, meaning, and materiality of dead victims that Rosenblatt's study transcends the genre of academic analysis to takes its place among literature that similarly teaches us new ways to understand and care about the mortality of those amongst us who have been broken, violated, tortured, thrown away. In many ways, Rosenblatt's book does for human rights what Drew Gilpin Faust's elegiac and award-winning *This Republic of Suffering* did for our understanding of the American Civil War. Like Faust, Rosenblatt too reveals the troubling yet often denied fact that the dead are at the center of history—in this case, at the center of histories of mass violence. But in many ways Rosenblatt goes further than Faust. Because the dead victims of mass atrocities are still with us, just under our feet, they continue to speak to us if we are only willing to listen. And if we listen, if we go to them and treat them with the care they were denied in life, we make them, in Rosenblatt's words, "precious again."

Mark Goodale
Series Editor

Preface

MY GRANDFATHER DIED when I was fourteen. After his funeral service, following Jewish tradition, family and friends went from the funeral home to his gravesite, said some blessings, and began placing stones on the lid of his coffin. Once he had been lowered into the earth, they took turns shoveling dirt into his grave. Jewish burial is a community affair. As Samuel Heilman observes in his ethnography, *When a Jew Dies*, "the [Jewish] funeral repeatedly affirms that, in the midst of death, life still goes on and we are not alone. The mortality of one person does not presage or guarantee the death and disintegration of all."[1] By having the mourners themselves begin the work of burial, the ritual is meant to foster a sense of fellowship as well as to drive home the physical reality of death: the coffin, the body, the earth. Like many other Jewish customs, it is a strange mixture of human warmth and stark realism.

I couldn't do it. At the time, to a teenager losing his first close family member, shoveling soil onto my grandfather's grave seemed morbid. After the ceremony, though, my mother offered this explanation of what the ritual meant to her: "I wanted to help make the blanket that would cover him." Seeing it in this light, I immediately regretted the chance I had missed to send one last little message of tenderness to the man who had let me crawl onto his bed on early mornings, wake him up, tell him stories, and sing him songs.

My grandmother died more recently, when I was twenty-nine, and this time I didn't miss the chance to help put a blanket of earth over her. It was moving to see the dwindling numbers of her friends, many of them frail and shaking, exert themselves to shovel even the smallest bit of dirt over her grave. Before the funeral and the graveside ceremony, and unlike at my grandfather's funeral, immediate family was invited to view my grandmother's uncovered body in its casket—a departure from Jewish custom.[2] My instinct, just as when I was offered the shovel at my grandfather's funeral, was to want no part of it. My grandmother was a woman intensely concerned with her dignity, who went to the "beauty parlor" (she was the only person in my life who used the term, and I imagined it as being much different from a mere salon) before every visit with us. She was always a perfect hostess: even in the rooms she occupied in hospitals and rehabilitation centers toward the end of her life, she would offer my wife and me the little tins of cranberry and orange juice that came with her meals. I thought she would want my last memory of her to be of a living woman, not a corpse—and in fact, this assumption about the dignity of the dead is precisely what some rabbis invoke when explaining why Jewish funerals do not feature open caskets.

This time, however, I was conscious of the regret I might feel if I later reconsidered, of the feeling that at my grandfather's grave I had missed a chance that could never be repeated. So I went in to see my grandmother. She had been embalmed (another departure from Jewish custom), and looked relatively normal, if a bit sunken, thin, ashen. The problem was that when I went to touch her forehead, she was cold. Of course she was. But what the brain knows to be logical can still shock the body, and I felt the tips of my fingers recoil from flesh that wasn't the temperature flesh is supposed to be, that felt more like fabric than skin.

A decision I had taken fearing regret wound up feeling like a betrayal. I had done exactly what my grandmother wouldn't have wished: given myself a last memory of her as a passive thing rather than the fierce, warm, wisecracking woman she had been—the force of nature in a pint-sized body.

In the time between my grandfather's and my grandmother's deaths, I had worked for an organization, Physicians for Human Rights, that investigated mass graves after massacres, genocides, and enforced disappearances. I was thus even more conscious, upon losing my grandmother, of what a miracle all the little markers of dignity and identity—a funeral, a plot of one's own, a tombstone and a name to mark it—were for the bodies of my grandparents.

Both of my grandparents were Polish-born Holocaust survivors (I have three Holocaust-survivor grandparents, but never met my biological grandfather, who died young from heart disease related to the rheumatic fever he contracted while imprisoned in Treblinka). The grandfather I knew, Grandpa David, had been separated from his first wife and his three-year-old daughter, Miriam, as the Lödz ghetto was "liquidated." Though he never spoke about this to his children or grandchildren, my grandmother told me that David's wife and Miriam were shot right in front of him. He eventually wound up in Germany, in the Sachsenhausen concentration camp, using his engraving skills to help the Nazis counterfeit foreign currency—and that was how he survived the war.

My grandmother lost her first husband and entire large family except for one brother. She passed through a number of Nazi concentration camps, including Auschwitz, where Josef Mengele, the Nazis' "Angel of Death," pointed her toward the line for the functioning showers, rather than the gas chambers. Mengele, an icon of racist pseudoscience, would have his own remains identified decades later in Brazil by a team of expert scientists that included Clyde Snow, a founder of the forensic program at Physicians for Human Rights and giant in the field of forensic anthropology, who died just as this book was being completed.[3]

I grew up knowing that my grandparents had suffered things I could never imagine. But it was only much more recently, and after my time at Physicians for Human Rights, that it occurred to me to consider, among those sufferings, the fact that my grandparents could never visit any graves of the family they lost. Their loved ones weren't only murdered, they were *gone*. These are my family's "disappeared."

But for a few twists of fate, the bodies of my grandparents could easily have been ashes over Poland, or could have joined the thousands of other Jews still lying in mass graves all over Europe. But instead these two people had survived, come to the United States, been parents and grandparents, and died in a place where they would be individualized, mourned, and cared for.

. . .

My interactions with forensic science have all been characterized by these same two, equally strong reactions to the work forensic experts do: fear, on the one hand, and admiration, fueled in part by my own family history, on the other.

When I became the research assistant for the International Forensic Program at Physicians for Human Rights, in Cambridge, Massachusetts, in 2004, I had experience in human rights organizations but no exposure to forensic investigation. At first, my work kept me insulated from the material reality of graves and bodies: I monitored security reports on behalf of my supervisor, Bill Haglund, who was traveling through Iraq collecting information about mass graves while the war there was still raging. I edited his hastily written communiqués and organized file cabinets full of photographs of contorted bodies in muddy pits, labeled with strange but soon-to-be familiar names: Ovčara, Nova Kasaba, Kibuye, and so on.

I finally entered the physical world of the forensic scientist on a trip to Ciudad Juárez, Mexico, where I accompanied Bill and a forensic pathologist on an assessment of local forensic capacity. The impetus for the trip was controversy over the investigations into the "femicides," brutal rapes and killings of women in Juárez and elsewhere in Mexico. Some of these victims were being stored and autopsied in a morgue we visited outside the city. As we followed our fast-talking tour guide through the labs, closer to where I knew the dead bodies would be, I looked for a chance to make my exit, an empty desk where I could write an e-mail to the home office while Bill and the pathologist surveyed the bodies. But I was the only fluent Spanish-speaker in our delegation, and Bill wanted to do some impromptu teaching demonstrations for the young forensic anthropologists working in the morgue. So I wound up translating while Bill and the other anthropologists examined a set of remains. It was a skeleton, a man—not one of the victims of femicide. The smell would stay with me: mostly it came from the chemicals used to clean the body and strip away its remaining flesh, but just underneath those smells I caught the odor of death. Throughout the next few weeks, back in Cambridge, every time I went into the bathroom at work and smelled the janitor's cleaning fluid, I had little panic attacks. I could smell the death again.

I also knew, standing over the skeletal remains and translating for Bill, that right through the set of doors in front of me, in a refrigerated room, were the fleshed remains of the women and girls who had been killed in the femicides. After school, or after taking the bus home from their jobs at the border factories called *maquilas*, with their cassette tapes and their doodle-filled notebooks in their backpacks, they had been raped, brutalized, murdered, left like trash in the empty lots and sewage drains of Juárez. Their bodies, on the trays in the morgue, would have recognizable faces, bruises, cuts. They would be naked, as vulnerable to my gaze in death as they had been to their rapists in life.

That's where I drew the line: the pathologist's mediocre Spanish would have to do. I hadn't had any pre-departure training, any preparation, to face the bodies in that giant refrigerator. I was that fourteen-year-old at my grandfather's funeral again, refusing to shovel dirt on a grave, thinking, *I know this might be important, I know everyone else is doing it, but I just can't.*

Throughout this book, I explore this darkened corner of human rights practice: these experts who gather in places of death and devastation to search for dead bodies and, along with the bodies, their stories, as well as whatever hopes are left in this world for some kind of justice on their behalf. In the United

States, we are in the midst of a long-running cultural fascination with forensic science. We can take our pick from *CSI*, *Bones*, or a host of other forensic-themed television shows and novels. We also live in what many observers of international politics agree is "the age of human rights," with an ever-growing awareness of human rights causes (I teach at a college where a semester-long human rights course is required of all undergraduates) and a sometimes dizzying proliferation of human rights organizations, legal instruments, and invocations. Strangely, however, few people seem to know about the intersection of these two fields: human rights forensic investigations.

Forensic science is both the past and the future of human rights. It plays a major role in documenting the mass graves and atrocities, from Argentina to South Africa to Bosnia, that have fueled the global human rights movement and the rise of human rights discourse. The unique ways in which forensic investigation blends new technologies with international activism also put it on the cutting edge of human rights practice.

Along with making this type of human rights work more visible, I also wish to make it better understood: for the general public, scholars, human rights advocates, scientists, and for myself as someone both haunted and touched by my encounter with it. Forensic scientists and the organizations within which they work do not all necessarily share the same vision of human rights activism, scientific ethics, or international politics. They work around the globe in settings torn apart by conflict, mired in corrupt governance and in ethnic and political factionalism. Not all of these locations are in the "Global South"; in New York City after the attacks of September 11, 2001, and New Orleans after Hurricane Katrina, among other places, sudden disaster has exposed the gaps in a wealthy democracy's preparedness to deal with large numbers of missing people, or to treat all of those missing people as equally significant. Forensic experts also have contact with cultures whose attitudes about the dead body may differ radically not only from one another but also from the standard procedures and assumptions of forensic science. International forensic investigation is, in other words, not a pure scientific search for truth and justice, but a form of humanitarian assistance that, like any other, is political all the way down.

I tell the stories about my grandparents and about my morgue visit in Juárez to register a sense of awe that none of my research has taken away from me. Most of us possess neither the skills nor the stomachs to sort through decaying flesh and bones to find names, evidence, and stories. Those who carry out this work are doing something profoundly ethical: reaching into history and making contact with those who have suffered some of the worst things that can be suffered in this life and the passage out of it. Yet I have now spent enough time around these experts to know that most of them wish neither to be put on a heroic pedestal nor left to inhabit an unexamined underbelly of the international human rights project. They want to talk, tell stories, solve problems, and think together.[4] In the pages that follow, I seek to provide information and reference points that invite new people into this conversation, while also offering approaches from my own field of expertise, the humanities, that practitioners can use to reencounter their own work through a different lens.

Studying mass graves changes how one sees the world. I have come to perceive the earth as a place dotted with legacies of violence just below its surface, but also as a dynamic repository for *beloved bodies* and the compelling, urgent questions they pose to us all. No technological breakthrough, no amount of concerted effort, will ever render completely transparent and comprehensible this space which is itself in a constant process of decay, absorption, shifting, and regeneration. I'll allow myself one comparison between my own occupation of professor and the work of forensic investigators: like good classroom teaching, good forensic investigation is an ongoing cycle of asking questions, discovering answers, and using those answers produce new, better, and often harder questions. Until that hoped-for day when bodies are no longer abandoned in mass graves, and all of the mourners searching for lost loved ones have found what they are looking for, these questions remain there, right beneath our feet.

Acknowledgments

IN THE YEARS I spent working on this project, people often asked me how I could spend day after day thinking about mass graves, human rights violations, and other horrors. The answer is that when I finished work at the end of the day, I could return to my joyous and beautiful family. No one has been more supportive of this book than Amanda Levinson, my wife, who brightens every corner with her lucid intelligence, tireless love, and the world's best wide smile. And nothing could dispel thoughts of death as quickly and thoroughly as a "walk out together among the ten thousand things" with my beloved boys, Leo and Sal, enchanters of the ordinary, voices that talk and sing, heads that must be kissed.[5]

I am thankful to Michelle Lipinski, an extraordinarily thoughtful and conscientious editor, and to Mark Goodale for believing in this book and working to improve it, as well as to the two anonymous reviewers for Stanford University Press. Elaine Scarry planted the seed for this book long before I was fortunate enough to meet her, when I read *The Body in Pain: The Making and Unmaking of the World* and, through it, acquired a new sense of what was possible for scholarship in the humanities. My friend and colleague Sarah Wagner has been another of my most generous and respected interlocutors. Jay Aronson, Marguerite Bouvard (whose collected papers on the Madres de Plaza de Mayo, at the International Institute of Social History in Amsterdam, were a prized resource in the writing of this book), Joshua Cohen, Zoë Crossland, Antoon De Baets, Ewa Domanska, Daniel Engster, Terry Karl, Adrienne Klein, Tshiamo Moela, Celeste Perosino, Lindsay Smith, and Helen Stacy have all influenced this book both personally and through their scholarship.

Much of this book is about listening to, synthesizing, and occasionally contrasting the voices of forensic experts themselves. I am indebted to Physicians for Human Rights for hiring me on to the International Forensic Program and introducing me to this topic, with its many layers of complexity and possibility. Bill Haglund, the longtime director of the International Forensic Program at Physicians for Human Rights, was my first personal connection to this field and continued to share information and reflections with me throughout the writing of this book. Clyde Snow, the beloved and brilliant founding figure of international forensic investigation, allowed me to visit his home and talk for hours over home-roasted coffee and (for him) many cigarettes. Cristián Orrego and Eric Stover, both of whom have spent long and storied careers intertwining scientific expertise with human rights work, have also been tremendously helpful. Clea Koff, author of *The Bone Woman*, has been extraordinarily generous with time, encouragement, and willingness to hash out ideas that were important to both of us but difficult to articulate; Derek Congram also offered crucial insights. Other experts from Physicians for Human Rights and colleague organizations who contributed their perspectives include José Pablo Baraybar, Andreas Kleiser, Thomas Parsons, Stefan Schmitt, and Susannah Sirkin. For multiple perspectives on the forensic identification of *desaparecidos* in Chile, I am indebted to Eugenio Aspillaga, Iván Caceres, Luis Ciocca, Viviana Díaz, Elias Padilla, Pamela Pereira, Isabel Reveco, María Luisa Sepúlveda, and to my longtime friend and mentor, Pepe Zalaquett. Members of South Africa's Missing Persons Task Team, Claudia Bisso, Kavita Chibba, Kundisai Dembetembe, and Madeleine Fullard, allowed me to participate in an exhumation in a Soweto cemetery, a memorable experience. For their help understanding the incomplete forensic investigations in Jedwabne and the religious objections that were raised there, I am grateful to Joanna Michlich, Rabbi Joseph Polak, Antony Polonsky, and Jonathan Webber. Last but not least, the organizers and attendees of the 2011 "Ethics of Post-Conflict and Post-Disaster DNA Identification" meeting at Carnegie Mellon, the American Academy of Forensic Sciences 2012 Annual Meeting, and the 2013 "Disasters, Displacement, and Human Rights" symposium at the University of Tennessee, Knoxville, have provided me with invaluable opportunities to share my research and learn from other scholars and practitioners.

This project has received important support, at various points, from the Modern Thought and Literature program at Stanford, a Mellon/American Council of Learned Societies Dissertation Completion Fellowship, a Ric Weiland Graduate Fellowship and research grant, an Andrew W. Mellon Fellowship in Humanistic Studies, and the U.S. National Institutes of Health for my research in Chile. I am also thankful to Dean Betsy Beaulieu of the Core Division at Champlain College for her active support of my scholarship.

Among the many dear friends who buoy me with their affection and broaden my intellectual horizons, Thomas Bacon, Colin Cheney, my "hermano chileno" Robert Alejandro Correa Cabrera, and Julie Weise have left especially deep marks upon these pages. In Vermont, Erik Shonstrom and Mike Kelly make me a happier and more thoughtful scholar, teacher, and parent.

Last but not least, I thank my own parents, Patty and Mike Rosenblatt, my sister, Mia Rosenblatt Tinkjian, and her wonderful family, and my in-laws, Kay, Rock, and Lisa Levinson. My mother's artistic and personal devotion to the tactile and material, and to the ethics of care, inspired the argument I make at the end of this book. As for my father, without him I doubt I would have spent these years studying a particular group of scientists and the powerful, life-changing and death-changing work that they do.

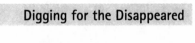

Digging for the Disappeared

Born at the Graves

A Human Rights Movement Takes Shape

From the Grave to the Cradle

The grandmothers needed science.

The early 1970s were a period of explosive instability in Argentina, exacerbated by the return from exile and third presidential term of the charismatic populist Juan Perón. Perón, in ailing health, proved unable to control the increasingly violent opposition between different groups on the right and left, each side claiming to be the ideological heirs of "Peronism." Perón died in July 1974, and his third wife, Isabel, assumed the presidency, giving right-wing paramilitary organizations even freer reign in her attempt to reassert order. On March 24, 1976, a military coup swept Isabel Perón out of power, with the support of much of the "exhausted" public.[1] As in neighboring Chile, Brazil, Uruguay, Paraguay, and other countries in the region, the new junta of military leaders cast itself as the defender of national security against armed leftist groups, but also against a much more vaguely defined "subversive" cancer that had supposedly taken root in society. One document from the "constant torrent of speeches, proclamations, and interviews" that the Argentine junta released explains, "The social body of the country is contaminated by an illness that in corroding its entrails produces antibodies. These antibodies must not be considered in the same way as the [original] microbe. As the government controls and destroys the guerilla, the action of the antibody will disappear. . . . This is just the natural reaction of a sick body."[2]

As Cold War politics played out in South America, the Argentine junta was able to share intelligence, prisoners, and torture techniques with the neighboring right-wing dictatorships. It received significant moral, tactical, and economic support from the United States and multinational corporations.[3]

The most infamous innovation of this network of regimes was the programmatic use, against their own citizens, of "disappearance"—a vision of the total erasure of the enemy, inspired by the Nazis' program of "Night and Fog" (*Nacht und Nebel*) carried out against political prisoners in Nazi-occupied territories of Europe. In Argentina, leftists and other suspected subversives were often arrested in their homes, driven away in the dreaded favorite car of the security forces—a Ford Falcon with no license plate—and placed in a network of torture camps without any record of their arrest, usually with little chance of ever being seen again.

Some of the most famous and influential organizations in the history of human rights activism—and of social movements led by women—formed in Argentina as a result of the crime of enforced disappearance.[4] The Abuelas de Plaza de Mayo, or Grandmothers of the Disappeared, are among these groups. Like their colleagues, the Madres de Plaza de Mayo, the group was named after Buenos Aires' most important public square, where during dictatorship and beyond they conducted weekly marches, with photographs of their disappeared loved ones pinned to their clothing or plastered on signs, and white scarves tied around their heads.

The Abuelas' activism responded, specifically, to a variation on "disappearance" popular in Argentina. Targeting young activists and idealists, the security forces often kidnapped young parents with their children, as well as pregnant women.[5] The children of disappeared couples were often taken from them. Pregnant women, in the meantime, were subjected to special tortures and taken to clandestine facilities where they eventually gave birth (one torture camp even had its own "maternity ward"), sometimes supervised by doctors or nurses who used cesarean section or other artificial methods to speed up the process. Young mothers and fathers in the camps were then almost always killed; it seems that being pregnant was one of the surest indicators that a prisoner would never make it out of alive.[6] Under the "germ theory" promoted by the junta,[7] the children of these disappeared people could be "purified," turned away from subversion, if they were brought up by families affiliated with the military or the right-leaning economic elite.[8] In some cases, the children were brought to live with the very people who had tortured and murdered their parents.

The Abuelas de Plaza de Mayo largely consisted of women whose children were among the "disappeared"—*desaparecidos* in Spanish—but who suspected they might still have a missing grandchild somewhere who was growing up with no knowledge of his or her real birth family. Added to the anguish of losing their children was the sense that, with every passing day, their grandchildren (and often their only hope for a family) would become more lost to them, both physically and psychologically, as they adapted to their new homes and the identities that were being supplied to them.

In 1977, the Abuelas branched out from the Madres de Plaza de Mayo—whose story, as well as a more detailed account of repression and human rights activism in Argentina, appears here in Chapter 2—and began their own marches around the Plaza de Mayo. Through the work of both groups and their allies, disappearance in Argentina gradually attracted significant international attention. During a trip to the United States in 1982, some of the Abuelas contacted an Argentine exile, the pediatrician and geneticist Victor Penchaszadeh, about the possibility of developing a new genetic test to help them in their search for disappeared grandchildren. Instead of proving paternity, already an established procedure, the test would use genetic markers in the blood, especially human leukocyte antigens (HLAs), to provide highly reliable matches between children and their biological grandparents without requiring any information from the missing generation in between—the parents who had disappeared into torture camps and anonymous graves.[9]

While these discussions were underway, Argentina's junta, beset by economic setbacks and an embarrassing military defeat against the British in the Falkland Islands, finally lost its grip on power. In 1983, the country held democratic elections. The newly elected president, Raúl Alfonsín, permitted the exhumation of anonymous graves thought to contain thousands of Argentina's *desaparecidos*. These initial exhumations, however, were haphazard efforts, as the forensic authorities and cemetery workers who conducted them had little knowledge of the appropriate archaeological and anthropological techniques of exhumation. For the most part, they destroyed more evidence than they recovered. The Abuelas stepped in and contacted Eric Stover, then the director of the American Association for the Advancement of Science's program in Science and Human Rights,[10] who had himself briefly been detained by security forces in Argentina. Interested, but feeling out of his depth so far as forensic science was concerned, Stover contacted the American Academy of Forensic Sciences.[11] The Academy brought Stover's request to Clyde Snow, a celebrated forensic anthropologist known for identifying the remains of the fugitive Nazi "Angel of Death" Josef Mengele in Brazil, and for many other high-profile cases both contemporary and historical,[12] and to Marie-Claire King, a geneticist interested in developing the grand-paternity tests.

The Abuelas knew that scientifically sound exhumations could provide evidence for eventual trials against the torturers, murderers, rapists, and kidnappers. Even more urgent for them, however, was the possibility that the bodies of the *desaparecidos* could tell them who had given birth before being executed. At the time, it was widely believed that "pelvic scarring"—markers of motion imprinted on the bones of a woman's pelvis—was a reliable sign that a woman had given birth.[13] Through exhumations, the Abuelas could also find out whether the skeleton of a baby or fetus was buried along with its mother. When a woman known to be pregnant was found without a fetus or child in the grave with her, it was supposed that the missing child had been taken alive as "botín de guerra," war booty.[14] Their search thus reversed the usual timeline of a life: the clues found in cemeteries would take them to the cradles and bedrooms of their stolen grandchildren.

In June 1984, Stover visited Argentina along with a delegation of US experts invited by the Alfonsín government to advise on both exhumations and the identification of missing children—the search for the living and the recovery of the dead.[15] Stover's companions were Snow, King, the Chilean geneticist Cristián Orrego, the forensic pathologist Leslie Lukash, and the forensic odontologist (dentist) Lowell Levine.[16] In a story that now has a celebrated place in human rights history, Snow became deeply committed to the cause of exhuming the *desaparecidos*, spending years shuttling back and forth between his home in Oklahoma and Buenos Aires. He recruited a number of young Argentine students and trained them in his craft: Patricia Bernardi, Mercedes (Mimi) Doretti, Luis Fondebrider, Alejandro Inchaurregui, Dario Olmo, and Morris Tidball (now Tidball-Binz). These students went on to form the Equipo Argentino de Antropología Forense, or Argentine Forensic Anthropology Team: the first human rights organization devoted exclusively to forensic investigation, and (just as accurately, just as importantly) the first group of forensic experts devoted exclusively to human rights work.[17]

The collaboration between the Abuelas and forensic experts would lead to a small scientific revolution, spurring the development of methods of DNA testing that would later be used to identify missing people in many different settings, from genocides and other conflicts to natural disasters such as the 2004 Indian Ocean tsunami and Hurricane Katrina in 2005. It also created a powerful new model for human rights activism. The Argentine team was soon fielding calls from other countries seeking their expertise, and they eventually worked alongside Snow to train and form forensic teams in a number of other countries in Latin America. In the 1990s, horrific genocides unfolded in the former Yugoslavia and Rwanda; the total numbers of dead civilians and the size of the mass graves where they were buried far exceeded what the Argentine team had encountered in Latin America. Justice Richard Goldstone, a South African judge who played a high-profile role in that country's transition from Apartheid, served as the chief prosecutor of the international criminal tribunals set up to investigate human rights violations and try war criminals for both the former Yugoslavia and Rwanda. Familiar with the Argentine story, Goldstone called for forensic investigations in both regions to corroborate the testimonies of witnesses and provide evidence of genocide and other crimes on behalf of the prosecution. Snow, members of the Argentine team, their colleagues from Chile, Guatemala, and Peru, as well as other individuals mentioned later in this book, such as Bill Haglund and Clea Koff, converged at the mass graves that dotted these two troubled lands. The forensic investigation of human rights violations had become a global project.

Digging for the Disappeared is about the politics and ethics of this global project. Its central concern is what international forensic investigations of atrocity are *for*: what purposes they serve, on whose behalf, what people have come to expect of them, and what they can actually accomplish. It is a set of nested questions that, one might think, could be answered simply by reading the mission statements of the Argentine team and the various other organizations that now do similar work. Doing so, however, would give a very incomplete picture. It would fail to capture how the priorities of forensic teams have changed over time, the complexity of their decisions about where to allocate their resources and efforts in the field, and how much still remains unarticulated in the discourse about forensic work.

Further, the "why" of international forensic investigations is a question that practitioners themselves have frequently revisited. The histories of all forms of humanitarian and human rights activism are complex,[18] and they involve distinct phases in which methods and purposes changed due to internal debates, organizational competition, and geopolitical pressures, among other things.[19] Forensic teams are no strangers to any of these phenomena, and the mission statements and methods they live by today reflect layers of change made over time.

A few features stand out when analyzing the historical development of forensic science as applied to human rights causes. First is the rapid scaling of forensic human rights work, from Snow's team of students—who were working with a lot of hope, a fair bit of fear, and a shoestring budget in 1980s Argentina—to the bewildering international array of experts investigating mass graves in the former Yugoslavia and Rwanda in the 1990s.

Along with the rapid rise of international forensic investigations comes a sense (often articulated by practitioners themselves) of improvisation. The feeling that facts on the ground perpetually outpace opportunities for reflection—which is endemic to humanitarianism and human rights organizations in general (and really to any institution with a sense of urgent purpose)—has been particularly pronounced in this field. Forensic teams have tried to keep up with new conflicts, new graves, and new kinds of demands without much time to explore what historical, organizational, and even moral leaps were being made as the work pioneered in Latin America and a few other places was re-shaped into a global practice.

The Forensic Sciences Foundation defines forensic science as "the study and practice of the application of science to the purposes of the law."[20] Yet a departure from this historical, medico-legal understanding of forensics was underway almost as soon Clyde Snow and his students began exhuming the graves of *desaparecidos* in Argentina, especially when a series of immunity laws for human rights violators closed off, for decades, most of the legal uses for the forensic evidence the team was collecting. Due to both the limitations of circumstance and their own sense of broader purpose, the team began to talk about grief, history, and ritual beyond the courtroom setting.

From the time of those first human rights exhumations onward, the priorities of forensic investigations have been crafted from a complicated dance between scientific techniques that continue to evolve, a growing international consensus about the moral obligation and legal authority to exhume mass graves after atrocities, and the particular political, legal, and logistical challenges of any given post-conflict context. As individual forensic experts and the organizations they work for travel from region to region and grave to grave, they also acquire new data about what kinds of work international tribunals, families of the missing, and other concerned parties will support, where these stakeholders' priorities lie, and how they respond to limitations. There may be obstacles in the path to prosecuting human rights violators, as in Argentina, or limits on how many graves can be exhumed and individual bodies identified when resources are scarce, conditions poor, and medical infrastructure very low. There is also real and present danger: death threats, landmines, work that cannot be done because the graves are located in territory controlled by hostile forces, or because they are being watched by those who would rather not see evidence come to light.

Another major factor that shapes the involvement of international teams in mass grave exhumations is a backdrop of massive global inequality: economic, geopolitical, and otherwise. Forensic experts, like their colleagues in many humanitarian and human rights organizations, are generally aware that well-intentioned and even apparently successful assistance projects may have unintended negative consequences; they may also be interpreted in light of a long and painful history in which rich Western nations have interfered in the politics and economies of poorer nations, subsequently offering their own self-serving "cures" for the distortions introduced by imperialist ideology and thievery. As the *bodies* of historically colonized and subjugated people are lifted out of the earth and placed in the care of international scientific experts, also present in the minds of many is the legacy of colonialism's particular attentiveness to the bodies of its subjects—their exhibition, categorization, study, and regulation, and in many cases the disturbance of their final rest.[21] The mission statements of forensic teams tend to list all of the potential outcomes and priorities of their work without explaining the relationship *between* them: how one priority can pull against the other, how what forensic science *can* accomplish may differ from what is expected, or desired, from forensic teams in any given context.

It is also not so easy to answer the "why" question because there remains a great swath of undiscovered territory in forensic ethics. The conversation among forensic experts has already proceeded far beyond an exclusively medico-legal definition of forensic work, into the territories of human rights and humanitarianism, as well as transitional justice, public truth-telling, and collective memory. Yet there is still much to say about what forensic experts do for the dead bodies they exhume and identify, and for the communities of mourners around them: how forensic work responds to the dynamics of grief, the desire to care for bodies and objects, and the violations inflicted on the victims of atrocity even after their deaths.

In this book, I will apply some new tools to the ethics of international forensic investigations. I start by analyzing specific forensic investigations and the substantial ethical dialogue already taking place within the community of practitioners, but also bring in reflections from political and moral theory, anthropology and sociology, and scholarship about the politics and philosophy of human rights. The focus on human rights—looked at through multiple lenses as a legal framework, a set of concepts about the relationship between the individual and society, and especially as a discourse—is particularly important. Much of the existing humanities and social science scholarship about forensic investigation makes only passing reference to human rights. Some scholars have begun connecting issues in the practice of forensic investigation with the on-going debates that have accompanied the extraordinary rise of the human rights framework, especially the long-standing tension between universal morality and cultural difference.[22] But the question of where human rights *fit*—not only in specific investigations but also in terms of the broader "why" behind a global project of exhuming mass graves—still requires a deeper and more interdisciplinary investigation. A few of the issues I consider in this book, such as how the context of mass grave investigation provokes a unique confrontation between human rights and religious beliefs, or the relationship between human rights and the care of dead bodies, have barely been touched upon in forensic reports or scholarship.

This book combines a grounded sense of the daily life of organizations that conduct forensic human rights investigations with new, theoretically informed perspectives on those lived experiences. It is informed by my experiences as an employee at Physicians for Human Rights, observation of exhumations and visits to forensic projects or facilities in South Africa, Mexico, and Chile, semi-structured interviews with forensic experts, human rights activists, lawyers, families, and friends of missing and disappeared persons in various locations, archival research and significant reading of publications from within the field. The wide net I have cast is the product of my conviction that it is time for a historically informed set of reflections on human rights forensic investigation as a distinct, networked *field* of global activism and scientific practice, rather than a loose collection of cases.

Building a bridge between human rights scholarship and forensic practice has implications for both of the sides that are being connected. While fresh and challenging perspectives on forensic work emerge from an engagement with the many other disciplines and literatures that have begun taking human rights seriously, the realities of mass graves and scientific practice help expose places where theoretical debates have lost touch with the actual circumstances forensic experts and other human rights workers often face. In these cases, human rights scholarship has often erred too far on the side of elegant argumentation oriented toward a world that cannot exist. The people making those arguments have sometimes demanded things that human rights activism can never achieve, while failing to see major successes not easily described in their vocabularies.

This chapter offers a broad overview of forensic work in the human rights context, including major organizations in the field, disciplines and methodologies employed, and some key terms. It also highlights some of the basic ethical assumptions that both define the field and guide the daily practices of forensic teams.

International Forensic Organizations and Their Development

This book focuses on a field made up principally of independent, nonprofit organizations that mobilize forensic expertise in response to human rights violations. Some of them have also been called upon, in recent years, to apply their skills to the identification of bodies after natural disasters. Most of the exhumations discussed in these pages take place at mass graves produced as a result of violent ethnic, religious, and political conflict. These post-conflict mass graves sparked the creation of multidisciplinary human rights forensic teams and have been the focus of the most sustained dialogue on international forensic investigation—dialogues where the "why" question has been at the forefront. That dialogue, however, is changing rapidly, with forensic teams becoming involved not only at natural disaster sites, but also in cases that lie outside the "classic" ethnic, religious, and political conflicts that have defined much human rights work—cases such as the serial brutal murders of women in Mexico and Guatemala, and the unidentified economic migrants who die crossing the US-Mexico border.

The nongovernmental organizations involved in this work include the Argentine Forensic Anthropology Team, various other Latin American forensic teams, Physicians for Human Rights, the International Committee of the Red Cross, the International Commission on Missing Persons, and others—all of them described in the Appendix. I chose to focus mostly on an interrelated community of relatively long-standing organizations, which reflect the evolution of the field over time. There are other organizations that resemble these groups above in both mission and methodologies—for example, the university-based British organization Inforce (International Centre for Forensic Excellence) and the "bi-communal," UN-sponsored Greek and Turkish Cypriot team working to identify missing persons as a result of conflict there in the 1960s and 1974;[23] however, their projects and histories did not fit into the necessarily limited scope of this work. Many forensic teams, such as the various groups of European forensic scientists that exhumed graves on behalf of the International Criminal Tribunal for the former Yugoslavia and rnment–sponsored Iraq Mass Graves Team, are project-specific, ntities.[24] Finally, emerging organizations have begun to apply the nd (equally importantly) human rights/humanitarian discourse de- arlier teams in settings beyond the traditional war crimes context. The Colibri Center for Human Rights and the Reuniting Families project, both active in identifying migrant bodies at the US-Mexico border, are among them.[25]

Though there is no running count available, even the limited pool of forensic organizations discussed in this book has been involved in exhumations and other human rights investigations in scores of different countries.[26] The exhumations in Argentina and the former Yugoslavia, which receive a lot of attention in these pages, are incontestable in their importance for the field's history and the development of forensic ethics: Argentina is the origin of international forensic investigation, as well as the first appearance of significant objections to exhumations among families of the missing. The former Yugoslavia is a milestone because of the unprecedented time and resources put into forensic work there, the numbers of different experts, organizations, and family groups that converged at those graves, and deep conflicts between the priorities of the international tribunal and the needs of mourners. Because I have generally selected projects that have had a lasting influence on the dialogue about forensic ethics—where the "why" question could not be ignored—complexity and controversy run like bright threads through the various cases discussed in this book.

It is worth mentioning that there are many forensic projects in other countries, such as Guatemala and Zimbabwe, where the conditions seem to have permitted close and mutually satisfying relationships between forensic teams and mourners.[27] In Ciudad Juárez, Mexico, among the different organizations searching for answers about the crime of "femicide" and its victims, years of frustration and uneven attention from authorities led to an atmosphere so poisonous that, when I visited with Physicians for Human Rights, victims' groups were unwilling to meet at the same location. Yet, in our separate meetings with this divided community, nearly everyone expressed their support and trust of the Argentine Forensic Anthropology Team, which had begun reviewing files on the missing women.

Every organization that has applied forensic science to human rights cases has a different structure, mission, geographical reach, and history. Despite all of these differences, all of them have participated in parallel processes of institutionalization and internationalization. By institutionalization, I mean not only the process by which individual forensic experts have been incorporated into human rights organizations, but also how those organizations have come to form a wider community, disseminating their experiences through journal articles, and conferences, sharing expertise about new technologies and sometimes debating their uses, and, most importantly for this book, discussing the politics of forensic investigations and their ethical standards. Just as crucially, these experts and organizations have been active in institutionalizing the call for forensic investigations after atrocity, thus creating a language of justification for the work they do. They support programs and laws related to the search for missing persons in the countries where they work,[28] as well as relevant rights and instruments in international law, such as the right to know the fate of missing persons.[29]

An idealist might view these efforts at promoting a moral-legal framework for forensic investigation as the field's earnest effort to translate the needs and experiences of the mourners they have worked with into a meaningful response from the international community; a cynic might see them as self-serving arguments for the field's continued existence and funding.[30] Both views can be true simultaneously, and when either one is presented without the other it quickly becomes a caricature. That said, there is a choice to be made about which voice will be heard the loudest, and for reasons described later in this book, I think the cynic has no greater claim to "realism" about international forensic investigations than the idealist. Letting the idealist voice speak—not in the simplistic heroic narratives that have characterized media coverage of mass grave investigations, but rather with rigor and complexity—strikes me as both an accurate reflection of the field and a corrective to some recent scholarship.

The second process common to organizations in the field is internationalization. Most forensic teams have not exactly risen up from the grassroots: rather, they have been formed and capacitated to do their highly technical work through international collaborations. The Argentine team grew out of the contacts between the Abuelas de Plaza de Mayo and American scientists; soon after its founding, it began working beyond Argentina's borders, from El Salvador to the former Yugoslavia, as well as helping to form new forensic teams throughout Latin America. Nor has this international transmission of expertise flowed exclusively from rich to poorer countries. Bosnian experts working with the International Commission on Missing Persons assisted in the identification of victims after the September 11, 2001, attacks on the World Trade Center in New York and again in 2005 after Hurricane Katrina hit New Orleans and surrounding areas. In the latter case, DNA samples were even sent from the United States to laboratories in Bosnia and Herzegovina.[31]

As new technologies have been developed for forensic science in the human rights context, new institutions and institutional relationships have followed. DNA technology is one of the most important instigators in this process: as it becomes both more advanced and widespread, teams that traditionally specialized in the more hands-on methods of forensic anthropology and archaeology now require access to DNA laboratories. This need has translated into relationships of mutual support between different forensic teams, as in the case of the Latin American Initiative for the Identification of the Disappeared, which has successfully resulted in the construction of new DNA labs in Argentina and Guatemala.[32] But it has also led these teams, by necessity, to expand their networks through new connections to universities, law enforcement, and for-profit laboratories.[33] Each of these relationships has brought with it new questions: for example, whether the involvement of for-profit firms signals that a "post-conflict/post-disaster identification industry [is] emerging."[34] This book both charts the evolution of international forensic ethics and seeks to make new contributions to that process.

Who Forensic Experts Are and What They Do

The word "forensic" derives from the Latin root "forum": the public square of an ancient city. "Forensic" can thus technically apply to any form of speech before a gathered public, which is why "forensics" is taught in many schools as the art of debate. Forensic *science*, however, has traditionally meant the use of scientific evidence in one very particular kind of public square: the court of law. The recent wave of popular television shows and mystery novels about forensic scientists have generally reinforced this popular conception of the field as a form of high-tech homicide investigation, and there are scientists who would still reserve the term "forensics" only for legal investigations of wrongful death.[35] However, in the human rights context, much of the work of forensic teams has moved outside the court of law to focus on other issues, such as the grief and uncertainty of families, and the stability and legitimacy of transitional governments. These developments have given forensic teams a new and often thrilling sense of the contributions their work can make, but it has also led them to some soul-searching about the scope of the forensic work and the roles that are appropriate for forensic experts to play in a politically charged atmosphere.[36] There is a sense now that the traditional definition of forensic investigation does not encompass all of its new uses and purposes, particularly for human rights work—that the very idea of "forensics" has undergone a profound shift.

This book is focused specifically on the exhumation of mass graves containing the victims of human rights violations, and accompanying efforts to document those violations, identify and reassemble dead bodies, and "repatriate" them to their families or others who mourn them. In order to highlight the global nature of this work, as well as the expertise that circulates from exhumation to exhumation, I generally refer to it as "international forensic investigation" (sometimes shortened to "forensic investigation" or "forensic work"). Within the broader universe of what might be called international forensic investigation, it should be noted, are various kinds of work on behalf of the living victims of human rights violations, and drawing on forensic methods other than death investigation. Physicians for Human Rights, for example, has conducted medical investigations of torture survivors in the United States, Mexico, Turkey, Kashmir and Punjab, and many other parts of the world; it has documented the use of prohibited live ammunition against Palestinian protesters in Israel, the West Bank, and Gaza, and it is one of many human rights organizations using DNA testing and complimentary methods to reunite children kidnapped or displaced during conflict with their birth families.

Mass grave exhumations merit separate study as a unique, closely followed, and particularly difficult form of international assistance—one that is marked by contact between the living and the dead. As Irina Paperno notes, digging up remains of the dead usually comes with "a sense of collective identity, collective memory, and a promise of redemption"; in many cases, it also "articulate[s] problems of the reorganization of society" during the painful, hopeful, transformative periods following mass violence. Exhumations pose extraordinary political and ethical challenges for forensic teams, especially with regard to the relationship between an expanding sphere of international assistance, on the one hand, and the religious and cultural worldviews of mourners, on the other. Mass graves are also crucial locations for the further development of forensic ethics because of still-unanswered questions about the rights and care of dead bodies.

There is, it turns out, little agreement about the definition of a "mass grave." Some forensic experts define mass graves based purely on the number of bodies: two or three in some accounts, six in others, and in some cases more.[37] Others think a mass grave implies not only a certain number of bodies, but also specifics about how they are placed together—in contact, "indiscriminately," or clandestinely.[38] They add this criterion in part to differentiate between the "common" or "collective" graves that were considered acceptable until relatively recently in the history of the West and are still used widely in many other cultures, and the anonymous, unchosen graves inhabited by the dead victims of massacres.[39] In international law and among some forensic experts, mass graves have sometimes been defined by the specific violations that led to their creation: "extrajudicial, summary or arbitrary executions,"[40] as opposed to armed combat or natural disasters.[41] Experts *do* generally seem to agree, based on their familiarity with the landscapes of atrocity, that mass graves can and do include many things most of us would not normally think of as a grave: the "surface scatter" of dead bodies in the forests and hills of the former Yugoslavia or Rwanda,[42] the wells and latrines in which victims have been found, the houses and barns where they have been strafed with bullets or burnt to death.[43] The cases discussed in these pages, from Argentina to Kosovo to Poland, fit any and all of these definitions. What matters is the relationship between dead bodies, the political, legal, and familial institutions around them, and the forensic teams that interact with both the dead and the living. For my purposes, the combined presence of dead bodies, mourners, and forensic experts, rather than numbers of bodies or technical features of their disposal, defines the particular landscape of the mass grave.[44]

Beyond the terminology described above, the ethical and political vocabulary in this book—terms such as "stakeholders," "mourners," and "forensic care"—is discussed and defined as the terms appear. Before moving on to the ethical and political, however, I will provide a very short overview of the skills and disciplines involved in forensic investigation. The information here is far from comprehensive: basic introductions to the fundamentals of forensic science, and the particular skills most in demand in the human rights context, are available elsewhere.[45] Particular scientific issues are described in more detail as they come up throughout the book, and only at a level of detail necessary for understanding how particular forensic methodologies, or their limitations, affect the political and ethical issues that are this book's focus.

The "core" forensic disciplines, arguably, are forensic anthropology and archaeology, pathology, and odontology.[46] Forensic anthropology, a branch of physical anthropology, is focused largely on the human skeleton. Forensic anthropologists specialize in, among other things, assembling individual skeletons and analyzing their "biological profile"—age, sex, stature, and ancestry or sometimes race,[47] as well as detecting signs of physical trauma and disease. Other bodily markers of habit and experience, from the hand we wrote with to our diet, can also leave individuating signs on our bones. Forensic archaeology draws on the traditional techniques of archaeologists, as well as new technologies such as satellite photography and ground-penetrating radar, to locate graves and exhume them while preserving evidence, bodies, and objects. Archaeologists are also trained in recognizing features of the skeleton itself, and there is significant overlap between the two fields: in fact, the distinction between forensic anthropology and forensic archaeology is sometimes related less to the specific methodologies employed than to the different types of advanced training available in the education systems of particular countries.[48]

Forensic pathologists are trained in the examination of remains that still have their flesh, and in particular in performing autopsies. Pathologists are thus generally involved only with mass graves that are relatively recent, as in the former Yugoslavia, and they do more of their work in the morgue than at the gravesite (forensic pathologists can also identify signs of torture and other physical trauma on the bodies of the living). Pathologists are often the final authority on the cause of death for a particular body: bullet wound, strangulation, disease, or otherwise.[49] Forensic odontology or dentistry is the identification of bodies based on the unique structures of their teeth. Even where an individual cannot be identified by name, forensic odontology can help establish his or her age. Dental analysis is among the most reliable methods of identification in cases where accurate dental records are available for comparison: for example, where there are x-rays and records of dental work corresponding to people who have gone missing. In the poor countries and rural areas where many mass graves are located, these records do not exist and people have had little to no dental care; in these cases, forensic odontologists may still be involved in matching family members' descriptions ("he chipped his front tooth in a motorcycle accident") with bodies. Whenever identification becomes dependent on the precision of memories rather than records, however, it is less certain.

An incomplete list of other specialties involved in the forensic investigation of mass graves includes radiographers, geneticists (where DNA analysis will be used for identifications), ballistic experts, crime-scene photographers,[50] and even experts who study the types of insect life in and around a grave, or the patterns of animal scavenging, to help determine things such as the time of death or the location of remains removed from the gravesite.[51] There is no single best configuration of a forensic team; rather, the experts necessary for a particular project will depend on the type of grave or other site being investigated, the purposes of the investigation (evidence-collection, identification of individual bodies, historical testimony, training, or, often, some combination of the above), and the particular background and working methods of the organization that is helming the investigation.

The investigation of human rights violations has also required configurations of experts that depart significantly from the typical domestic homicide investigation or mass fatality unit. Collaboration with families of the missing, in particular, has made social workers, interviewers, database technicians (who develop complex models to compare information provided about missing people by their family members with the bodies and objects forensic experts are taking out of graves), international lawyers, and political mediators crucial to many large-scale mass grave investigations, even if their expertise is not in the traditional, medico-legal disciplines that once constituted forensics.[52] Case managers, who in their work for the International Commission on Missing Persons in Bosnia and Herzegovina have accompanied families in their grief, anger, and disbelief,[53] have their own crucial expertise, without which the forensic process in their country would lack the credibility and humanity it needs to move forward. I thus extend the term "forensic experts" to include these nonscientists. People involved in many other forms of labor, such as clothing-launderers, cooks, backhoe operators, and security guards—usually locals rather than traveling experts—are also required to make a forensic investigation possible and can become part of the complex politics at and around the gravesite.[54]

Forensic Ethics

The types of expertise required for forensic work, and even the basic definition of "forensics," will undoubtedly continue to evolve with changes in the technologies that can be employed and the nature of violence itself.[55] For this reason, among others, it is important to recognize the constitutive role that *ethics* play in the field of human rights forensic investigation.

Various national and international bodies, such as the International Criminal Police Organization (INTERPOL) and the International Committee of the Red Cross, have produced manuals of best practices related to the recovery and identification of victims of violent conflict and natural disasters. One of the first of these, the United Nations Manual on the Effective Prevention and Investigation of Extra-Legal, Arbitrary and Summary Executions—called the

"Minnesota Protocol"—was adopted by the United Nations in 1991. Experts such as Clyde Snow, Eric Stover, and the Chicago-based pathologist Robert Kirschner, who worked on behalf of Physicians for Human Rights until his death in 2002, were consulted during its writing.[56] The document offers model exhumation and autopsy protocols and features a straightforward acknowledgment of the factors that might affect forensic investigations in areas of conflict, such as poor conditions, lack of resources, and "the social and religious" differences that can make autopsies and other forensic practices controversial and even unwanted (as Chapters 2 and 3 explore in depth).[57] Yet, as some observers have pointed out, the Minnesota Protocol—written after the exhumation of clandestine graves in Argentina, but before the massive gravesites produced during the genocides in Rwanda and Bosnia—has more to offer those investigating individual or small-scale incidents of wrongful death than those confronting large mass graves.[58]

Subsequent reports and manuals, such as the International Committee for the Red Cross's "The Missing and Their Families" and "The Management of Dead Bodies after Disasters: A Field Manual for First Responders" have had more to say about issues such as the coordination of investigation and evidence-handling against the chaotic backdrop of humanitarian disaster and response, the dignified handling of the dead, and the psycho-social needs of families.

In general, however, these important guidelines for professionals treat ethics as a concern once the disaster response and investigation have already begun and apart from questions of politics. There is thus much left to say, in particular, about the ethics that justify forensic intervention in some cases and not others, the relationship between a universalistic scientific practice and cultural differences, the ways in which the identification of remains can empower some communities or families and not others, and other issues discussed throughout this book. Though the available guidelines do nod to constraints and imperfect circumstances, some experts still complain that when relatively well-funded institutions sit down to write things like autopsy protocols, the guidelines tend to reflect a "best-case scenario." The recommended technologies and practices, especially in the age of DNA testing, are often beyond the reach of smaller, resource-poor forensic teams in Latin America and elsewhere. For these teams, many ethical dilemmas result from having to make difficult decisions about how to go about their work when families are desperate for information, international interest in the case is limited or nonexistent, and resources are limited.[59]

Four defining ethical tenets define this diverse, but nevertheless distinctive, field of international forensic investigation: a commitment to science as a practice and privileged form of truth, political autonomy, moral universalism, and a focus on the needs of victims and mourners. In identifying these features, I am not so much concerned with the *professional* ethics of particular disciplines such as forensic archaeology or pathology—for example, codes specifying how bodies are handled, evidence collected, how to publish findings or interact with the press. Many of these "best practices" are as familiar to forensic experts in domestic crime labs as to those who work on human rights cases. Rather, the four ethical tenets I identify here encapsulate much broader, basic commitments of *international, human rights-focused* forensic teams: threads of continuity we can pull out from their mission statements, the kinds of projects they do and do not agree to pursue, and of course from the study of particular cases.

Science as a Privileged Form of Truth

In a long interview I conducted with Clyde Snow in 2013, he reflected on a career in which he served as a catalyst and longtime champion of the role of forensic science in documenting human rights violations. Suddenly, toward the end of the interview, Snow added, "I'm not a human rights activist. I'm a scientist. I'm an expert. If I have a philosophy, it's that I'm anti-homicide."[60]

Snow was not alone in asserting that his identity as a scientist—and commitment to his field of expertise—came before human rights. An organization such as Amnesty International brings people together around a shared, sometimes martyrlike commitment to human rights (to the extent that Stephen Hopgood, in his study of Amnesty International, compares it to a church congregation, referring to its core activists as "keepers of the flame"). By contrast, the primacy of scientific identity is woven into the structures by which forensic scientists are trained and interact with one another. Despite the recent debut of some interdisciplinary programs offering training in human rights issues as part of a forensic anthropology or forensic science degree,[61] most of the people who have worked on mass grave investigations were trained in the formal methods of their discipline and very little in themes such as international law or the history and philosophy of human rights.

This fragmented identity, part science and part human rights, creates paradoxes for both individuals and organizations. My former supervisor at Physicians for Human Rights, Bill Haglund, has long lived in Seattle, on the opposite side of the country from the organization's Boston headquarters. Yet for years he was employed full-time as the executive director of the group's International Forensic Program. I quickly noticed that Bill nearly always referred to the organization using the pronoun "they": "they" were sending him to do a forensic assessment in such-and-such place, "they" needed something from him for the annual report. A subtle distinction was thus made between the professional human rights activists who managed and staffed the organization, and the scientists like Haglund and Snow who have inhabited these organizations without quite identifying with them.

It is a distinction that can come to seem absurd, and not only because of the professional homes now provided for some forensic scientists within human rights organizations. Snow helped put war criminals on multiple continents in jail, identified the bodies of countless people whose lives were destroyed by murderous regimes, and worked to establish scientific human rights organizations that now operate around the world and are among the most enduring pieces of his legacy (as is the annual Clyde Snow Social Justice Award, awarded by the University of Oklahoma). If Clyde Snow was not a human rights activist, who can claim to be one?

The issue, it seems, boils down in part to how one defines the term "activist." The forensic anthropologist and author Clea Koff explains:

> I have generally felt rather out on a limb when I've put forward the question of whether there is something inherently activist about exhuming mass graves so that bodies can bear witness "for themselves" in the context of state-sponsored crimes. People have just looked back at me. I thought it might be because the prevailing stereotype of a forensic scientist in the US has been one of an apolitical and ahistorical "bearer of justice" (or possibly just a superhero) and no one wanted to problematize that. But more recently, I've started to think that they just didn't have the vocabulary to discuss it.[62]

Yet Koff—who was inspired to become a forensic anthropologist after reading about Snow in the book *Witnesses from the Grave*—feels she witnessed a meaningful difference between people who entered the field with an activist orientation and those who did not.[63] When Koff signed up to participate in exhumations in Rwanda and the former Yugoslavia, she had the sense that the very *name* of the organization coordinating the digs established an ethos: "Physicians for Human Rights. . . . I mean, that told me what we were there for."[64] As the scale of the projects grew and the United Nations eventually took over the coordinating role, she recalls, new experts arrived on the site who seemed to look at their work as a job rather than a calling. When it comes to human rights, Koff says, "the words never crossed their lips," and she was often shocked at the views they voiced about things like the backwardness or hopeless savagery of the war-torn communities around them.[65]

For scientists such as Snow and Haglund, who do *not* fit this description, the trouble with identifying as an activist, and with the human rights sector, likely lies elsewhere: in the friction between that identity and the scientific objectivity that is so central to their "expert" personae. The expert is calm, rational, and (to use Koff's term) apolitical—or at least avoids shows of political partisanship. There are, of course, rules about what objectivity and independence mean in the context of a human rights organization.[66] But those rules are somewhat different for an advocacy organization whose "forum" is the general public, lawmakers, victims, and colleagues in the human rights movement than for the traditional forensic scientist, whose audience is the jury. The fear, sometimes expressed by forensic scientists themselves, is that their truth claims—already subject to doubt as to their *scientific* legitimacy—will be even more suspect when forensic scientists are seen as crusaders for a cause.[67] In fact, forensic experts testifying in international tribunals have been grilled precisely on the level of "subjectivity" in the evidence they present.[68]

Koff's memoir, *The Bone Woman*, can be read at least partly as one young forensic anthropologist's struggles with the identity paradigm that seems so natural for Snow and Haglund: her wish to be a part of both the human rights world and the forensic science community. But science is not just bound up in the identity of the forensic expert. It is an epistemology on which rests the legitimacy of what forensic scientists do at mass graves. And since scientific authority is what gives forensic experts the perceived right to exhume the graves of other people's dead around the world, it is also a crucial component in the ethics of forensic investigation as a global project, from the broadest justifications for the existence of the field down to minute decisions made in specific investigations.

The methods of forensic science have largely been developed in a law enforcement context, where the evidence forensic experts provide has tremendous power to affect people's lives, for example by leading to their being charged with a crime and imprisoned.[69] This same context, however, has traditionally meant that the methods were approved and justified on a case-by-case basis, often for prosecutorial purposes. Unlike chemistry or biology, there are few academic departments or institutions devoted to basic research on forensic methods; for much of the field's history, there was thus little outside scrutiny of many traditional methods, such as fingerprint identification or facial reconstruction. These methods rely on "expert interpretation of observed patterns,"[70] which means that human subjectivity is part and parcel of their use. Yet there has often been little acknowledgment of uncertainty when this evidence is introduced in court. A 2009 congressionally mandated report from the National Academy of Sciences detailing these issues caused a tremendous stir in the forensic community not only in the United States but worldwide.[71] The report claimed that nuclear DNA analysis was the only forensic method that had been "rigorously shown to have the capacity to consistently, and with a high degree of certainty, demonstrate a connection between evidence and a specific individual or source,"[72] and it called for new research into the reliability of other methods.

Even where specific forensic methods are not called into question, there are reasons why the question of "subjectivity" will not go away anytime soon. Forensic evidence—both when it is used in court, and as it circulates through other public channels—is used to tell the story of a crime, its perpetrators, and its victims. There are always choices that can be made, and scholars such as Irina Paperno, Layla Renshaw, and Sarah Wagner have studied how different post-conflict communities with competing historical narratives will accord wildly different meanings to "objective" forensic evidence. Paperno describes how evidence collected during the 1943 exhumation of mass graves in the city of Vinnytsia, Ukraine, has "passed through many hands—those of the judicial authorities of the Third Reich, the US Congress, the Ukrainian émigré community, and American historians."[73] In each case, basic elements of how the story is told change—such as whether the religion, ethnicity, political beliefs, or positions of authority are the defining features of the perpetrators and victims. She writes:

> Each of the investigating agencies was striving to construct an account that would make the monstrous crime comprehensible. To this end, each tried to separate and categorize victims and perpetrators in a way that would dispel the mystery of mass murder. And though each account seemed to have achieved the immediate clarity that would serve a political goal at hand, in the end, to this day, there is no clarity.[74]

Forensic experts use a complex vocabulary to distinguish between, for example, "presumptive" and "positive" identifications—and even positive identifications are not beyond questioning. There are no absolute certainties in forensics, only different degrees of probability: every method has an error rate, and the past that is under study can never be revisited or replayed. Like other scientists, though with less research support, many forensic experts do publish both their findings and explanations of the methods and hypotheses on which these findings are based. In high-profile cases such as the identification of *desaparecidos* in Chile, forensic teams' findings have been retested when doubts surfaced and new technology became available; errors that surfaced, despite the considerable pain and embarrassment they caused, were eventually made public. All of these practices are part of good science, but they also have an ethical dimension. In part, they compensate for the most glaring asymmetries of forensic work: forensic teams possess skills and technologies that are difficult for outsiders to understand, yet the impact of their work (justice for perpetrators, bodies to grieve over, histories confirmed or denied) is felt most deeply by mourners and others whom they may barely know. In post-conflict regions especially, then, forensic experts are increasingly talking about the "public testimony" that defines forensic work as a matter not just of reporting *findings* but also of a transparent *process* that engages stakeholders from the outset.[75]

Even where forensic investigations are not focused on legal outcomes, but rather on identifying bodies or constructing a historical record, a process of open reflection about assumptions, limitations, and tradeoffs can be woven into forensic practice. This process may be especially important in the identification of individual victims, where the desire to grieve the right set of bones is so powerful, and errors so damaging. As Bill Haglund frequently reminded me when I was working at Physicians for Human Rights, a misidentified body actually implies two misidentifications: the body in front of you has been given the wrong name, and the person whose name is now erroneously attached to that body—and who may in fact still be missing—has also been misidentified.

In fact, the double nature of "identification," which is both a scientific and a social process, is the area where the relationship between the scientific standards of the forensic community and other ethical imperatives becomes most complex. As the anthropologist Sarah Wagner emphasizes, in her ethnography of the International Commission on Missing Persons' DNA identifications in postwar Bosnia and Herzegovina, no identification is complete until the relatives of the deceased have accepted it: in other words, until it has become both a scientific and a social fact. Every community of mourners has its own traditions, notions of identification, and perceptions of forensic science. A forensic expert involved in investigations of violence in Timor-Leste reports that she witnessed family members there identifying a body as their missing relative by cutting themselves and dripping the blood over the bones. Only the blood of family members, they believed, would be absorbed into the dry bones.[76] In Guatemala, forensic teams laid out objects associated with individual dead bodies, such as clothing and jewelry, in the hopes that relatives and other community members would recognize the objects and thus provide presumptive identifications for some of the bodies.[77] According to the anthropologist Victoria Sanford, in cases where a body could not be matched with identifying objects, relatives would often come forward and say, "Si no tiene dueño, entonces es mio [If it has no owner, then it's mine]."[78] Refusing to let any body go unmourned, these survivors turned an attempt at forensic identification into an affirmation of communal ties and an act of care for the dead—in part by abandoning the standards that would have made the process scientific. Though forensic teams have responded differently to these types of situations, in no instance have they completely renounced their own professional commitment to scientific method. Rather, a negotiation between two priorities that intersect and diverge at different points—scientific practice and attention to the needs of mourners—becomes part of the "public square" in which these experts operate.

Political Autonomy

All of the organizations discussed in this book see themselves as serving causes—documenting war crimes, creating an accurate historical record, and identifying bodies and returning them to mourners—rather than particular groups of people. For example, the stated purpose of the forensic teams working in Bosnia was to document attempted genocide and extrajudicial executions, not to prove the victimization of Bosnian Muslims (Bosniaks) by Bosnian Serbs. Yet these two stories intertwine and overlap, and any effort to prove the crime of genocide—defined in the 1948 Genocide Convention as "acts committed with intent to destroy, in whole or in part, a national, ethnical, racial or religious group"—demands something beyond dispassionate description of specific criminal acts committed against particular individuals.[79] The investigation of genocide requires entering into, studying, and sometimes even replicating the categories of identity that provided the logic for the crime.[80]

Political autonomy, when an organization is operating in the kinds of settings where mass graves are found, requires drawing some razor-thin lines. Forensic teams need safe access to gravesites, equipment, and resources, things that often only governments—or sometimes international institutions perceived, by local groups, as having allegiances to one side in a conflict—can provide. I have chosen to use the term "political autonomy" in a deliberate attempt to distinguish this quality from "neutrality" or even "independence."[81] Because forensic teams can rarely fund their own projects entirely or grant themselves secure access to graves and facilities, they by necessity enter consciously into a number of forms of "dependence." Neutrality, in the meantime, implies a passive or nonparticipatory stance toward political conflicts and negotiations, whereas autonomy is compatible with (and in some cases requires) action and engagement in things such as the national and international dialogue about past crimes and the rights of victims, processes of commemoration and redress. Forensic teams have found different ways of contributing to these processes depending on their own institutional rules and the context they were working in, but engagement of some sort—comfortable or not—has been the norm.

The concept of "neutrality" cannot be dismissed without mentioning an important and increasingly influential actor in the field of international forensic investigation: the International Committee of the Red Cross. The Red Cross has a long-standing commitment to political neutrality that is both central to its identity and one of the most controversial aspects of both its history and its ongoing practice.[82] The organization depends on its long-standing policies of neutrality and discretion—for example, refraining from issuing public denunciations, providing evidence for trials, or giving aid to combatants on either side—to gain access to the wounded, imprisoned, and needy who would otherwise be beyond its reach. The forensic staff at the Red Cross is involved in training other forensic experts, creating database protocols, making lists of missing people, taking testimony, helping to locate mass graves, and fostering dialogue about best practices and forensic ethics, but the organization does not participate directly in any investigation where evidence might be used for a trial.[83] We can regard this fact as, among other things, an acknowledgment of the extent to which *international* forensic investigations have challenged the traditional, medico-legal definition of forensics: where once the trial was nearly always the closing act of a forensic investigation, we now have a major forensic organization that abstains from collaboration with courts at all. Crucially, the Red Cross has spent years advocating for greater attention to missing persons issues and their impact on families, and greater coordination in the search for the missing.

The exhumation of mass graves is, in the words of the journalist Elizabeth Neuffer (who was killed while reporting from Iraq in 2003), "one of the most contentious issues for a society wishing to achieve justice in the wake of genocide."[84] For forensic teams working outside of the Red Cross's humanitarian framework, and without the same rules and traditions to guide them, political autonomy can become an even more complex dance—particularly when they are collecting evidence of war crimes. The Argentine Forensic Anthropology Team works independently of any state or political group, but was founded with the aim of exhuming victims of repression and engaging with families of the missing "from an ethical and political perspective."[85] In the early years, the team often told a particular story through its work: a story of the violence that states commit against their own people, and more specifically, of the "scorched earth," torture, and disappearance programs of right-wing Latin American governments. It is possible to tell this story factually and dispassionately, but not apolitically, unless "politics" is conceived of only in the thinnest sense of voting, running for office, civil service, and the like.[86]

The question of how to distinguish between "pure" civilians or bystanders, collaborators, and direct participants in violence has often proved difficult to answer in a satisfactory way. In the forensic context, however, there are unique challenges. International forensic teams often work in countries where their local counterparts—the forensic authorities, police, cemetery workers, and other people who may have knowledge about graves—cannot be trusted and may even be implicated in the creation of the graves in the first place. Yet, to gain access to graves, morgues, bodies, and files, forensic teams must often establish a modicum of communication and even collaboration with these institutions.

As the forensic investigation of human rights violations has become a standard part of larger "transitional justice" efforts, a new model has also emerged: the post-conflict transitional government that sponsors, through state agencies, its own investigations into the missing and disappeared. This model, currently being pursued in South Africa and Chile, requires a different sort of political autonomy: one in which the perception of objectivity and independence rests, to a great degree, on public belief in the legitimacy of the state's newly democratic institutions.

As objective as forensic investigators themselves may strive to be, the information they provide goes out into a complex post-conflict landscape, and the outcomes of forensic investigations nearly always have political force. In these cases exhumations themselves can become fuel for ongoing conflict, as well as calling into question the impartiality of international justice. There is no magic formula for maintaining scientific rigor and political autonomy while also having both a natural and professional sympathy for victims; it is, rather, a daily, self-critiquing and self-correcting practice.

Moral Universalism

According to a group of forensic experts working in Kosovo, the International Criminal Tribunal for the former Yugoslavia's decision to investigate only the war crimes committed by the Miločević regime meant that crimes against Kosovo Albanians were documented while very similar crimes against other groups, including disappearances of Kosovo Serbs, were largely ignored.[87] There are clear political hazards in treating, or even seeming to treat, Albanian victims differently from Serbs, Hutus differently from Tutsis. But the hazards go deeper than the politics of the moment. Forensic investigations play a crucial role in telling the stories of power, violence, and victimization. When exhumations contribute to a one-sided or incomplete telling of that story, they also reinforce simplistic moral fables in which an entire group or ethnicity is labeled "perpetrators" and described as bloodthirsty savages, while another group— who all come to be "victims"—come to seem like helpless, apolitical subjects in need of rescue and incapable of speaking for themselves.[88]

Forensic teams are committed to a particular version of humanism that combines the universalistic, impartial traditions of human rights and humanitarianism with a special lens that comes about through contact with the remains of the dead. In general, while the forensic investigation of human rights violations has sometimes started with teams focused on a single country, in most cases it has been bound up in the international circulation of expertise as well as the "widening circle . . . of sympathy" that has characterized not only the human rights and humanitarian movements, but also the gradual development of global democratic norms (for example, from the natural rights of property-owning white men to the Universal Declaration of Human Rights).[89]

Beyond the shared human rights/humanitarian ethic of impartiality, however, forensic investigation has its own particular humanistic narrative, one that emerges from the field's most unique feature: the material presence of dead human remains. The story forensic investigations tell, as experts collect evidence and identify victims, is about the infinite forms of variation that individuals possess at birth and accrue throughout their lives (which make them identifiable), and simultaneously about the common signs of their suffering.

Forensic science has developed tools to recognize and describe this suffering precisely because human bodies all react in similar, predictable ways to blunt trauma, bullets, and the passage of time—"consistent patterns that can be understood through careful comparison and systematic study."[90] While different standards based on ancestry may be necessary, for example, to help determine the age of a northern European woman versus a Vietnamese man, violence often speaks in more universal signs. Elaine Scarry writes:

> When the Irishman's chest is shattered, when the Armenian boy is shot through the legs and groin, when a Russian woman dies in a burning village, when an American medic is blown apart on the field, their wounds are not Irish, Armenian, Russian, or American precisely because it is the unmaking of an Irishman, the unmaking of an Armenian boy, the unmaking of a Russian woman, the unmaking of an American soldier that has just occurred, as well as in each case the unmaking of the civilization as it resides in each of those bodies.[91]

It is the unmaking of bodies, rather than the ways they are constructed as Serb or Tutsi or Kurd or "subversive," that forensic teams study. In fact, because many of the categories of race and ethnicity employed by the violent have no real biological basis,[92] some experts see good forensic science as a refutation of racism and pseudoscience, a way of turning the page on a past association between early genetic research and eugenic philosophies.[93]

Along with highlighting and sometimes critiquing the categories of race and ethnicity that are employed by the violent, forensic teams can complicate the grand political narratives that have come to dominate global, or at least "Western," discourse. Physicians for Human Rights has spent more than a decade investigating and publicizing a mass grave in Afghanistan where over two thousand Taliban prisoners are thought to have been massacred by the forces of a warlord allied with the United States.[94] The forensic team has thus placed into the category of victims a group of bodies whose common identifier in life— "Taliban"—signifies, to much of the world, "bad guys."[95]

Yet while the "widening circle of sympathy" of universal humanism is probably the most important common thread linking together all the facets of human rights and humanitarian action, it is also the most difficult to translate credibly into a daily organizational practice. In Chapter 4, I argue that there is no truly universalist vision of mass grave investigation that is also practically possible—no way to treat every grave and body as equal, even if the violence they have suffered is the same. Some graves will be too hard to reach; others will have particular significance due to their location, their story, or the evidence they contain. Recent mass graves, with living mourners around to grieve and rebury the bodies that are exhumed, will probably seem more urgent forensic projects (and easier to fund) than historical mass graves whose inhabitants may also have been victims of violence—unless those historical graves are of some particular archaeological interest, or relate to a conflict (such as the Spanish Civil War) that is the subject of resurgent attention.

Of course, the people who have lost loved ones in genocides and other episodes of ethnic, racial, and/or political violence may not agree with Scarry that the bounded social identities of the dead are "unmade" by the violence they suffered. Often, to them, the Muslim, Ogoni, or socialist man or woman died *as* a Muslim, Ogoni, or socialist, died *because* he or she was Muslim, Ogoni, or socialist, and must therefore be *buried* as a Muslim, Ogoni, or socialist. The moral universalism of forensic teams thus becomes one more value that can distance them from mourners. On the one hand, forensic experts make intimate contact with dead victims and their families, establishing what Doretti and Burrell call "a clear current of affection" between them, and often helping to support the victims' version of history.[96] On the other hand, these same forensic experts must be prepared to report facts that *contradict* the victims' version of events. They must be capable of exhuming a grave of missing Greek Cypriots and then, perhaps just days later (or even concurrently), to begin exhuming with equal care a grave of missing Turkish Cypriots. Then, having finished work in Cyprus, they must be ready to start the whole process over again on another continent, leaving behind the mourners they worked with and the bonds they formed.

The question of how any particular forensic team chooses the projects it will pursue—and of how those organizational choices form a pattern in the distribution of forensic efforts across the globe—is haunting to those who feel invested in this global project, and rightfully so.[97] The Democratic Republic of the Congo, to take one example, is home to a conflict that has killed civilians in numbers dwarfing even the genocides in the former Yugoslavia and Rwanda. Its mass graves are rendered largely inaccessible by the political and security situation there.[98] Forensic experts are also conscious that the basic, day-to-day needs of many people in the DRC, one of the world's poorest countries, are far more urgent than exhumations.

Yet, for a group of professionals scientifically and ethically committed to deconstructing racial ideologies, one large-scale pattern stands out: the effort and expense spent on the identification of relatively light-skinned bodies in countries considered part of (or on the doorstep of) the West, compared with the effort and expense put into identifying dark-skinned bodies in non-Western countries. This conversation often begins with the genocides in Rwanda and the former Yugoslavia in the 1990s, the resources spent on ongoing DNA identifications in the latter case, and the nearly complete lack of any such effort in Rwanda.[99] Only two major forensic exhumations of mass graves were conducted in Rwanda, compared with upwards of sixteen thousand bodies exhumed from hundreds of graves in Bosnia,[100] with more exhumations and ongoing identification work still underway.

There are scientific, as well as political, explanations that can be offered for this discrepancy. Rwanda is a poor country with very little in the way of medical or dental records for anthropologists to compare with the remains from mass graves.[101] As for DNA identifications, the technology is still quite expensive, and the sheer number of the dead raises the question of where investigations should start, especially knowing that there will likely not be enough funding to finish the search.[102] In Rwanda the number of dead victims of the genocide—as many as eight hundred thousand people—is enormous; by comparison, the hotly contested estimates of civilian casualties in the war in Bosnia and Herzegovina generally do not exceed forty thousand. One of the sad realities that shapes both scientific practice and post-conflict reconstruction is that the greater the scale of atrocity, the harder it is to conceive of a concrete, bounded project of repair.

In a globalizing world, forensic experts have come to realize that their own work on projects in any one country has a tendency to shape expectations in other places where they might conduct investigations in the future. In a few short decades, scientific exhumations of mass graves have gone from beyond a rarity to a standard part of the response to major conflicts, with planning for exhumations often beginning while the conflict is still unfolding.[103] In particular, due to the high-profile role played by DNA identification in the former Yugoslavia (and perhaps also to unrealistic portrayals of "DNA detectives" in popular culture), many countries and families of the missing are demanding DNA analysis while ignoring the importance of basic anthropological methods, which are also always developing and becoming more effective.[104]

One of the features that distinguished Rwanda from the former Yugoslavia, however, is that the families of victims of the Rwandan genocide appear, at least in most accounts, not to have clamored as loudly for individual identifications.[105]

Massacre sites in Rwanda often feature collective graves or public displays of commingled bones; though this practice is partially enforced through a law mandating that all remains from the genocide be displayed as a memorial and warning to future generations.[106]

Forensic experts I have interviewed seem caught between two ways of interpreting the different "expectation landscapes" encountered in Rwanda and the former Yugoslavia, relating them to the broader principles of their field, and thus drawing lessons from them for future practice. In one model, the task of forensic teams is to respond to the needs of mourners *as they express them*: if Rwandans show less interest in individual identification than Bosnians, they will get fewer identifications. In fact, some experts argue, it might even be a form of cultural imperialism to impose a DNA identification program in a place where mourners are inclined to bury their dead together in collective graves. A culturally acceptable and even "satisfying" practice of community ritual, they worry, will be undermined, leaving only the much more tenuous possibility of full scientific investigations of every grave and body in its place. Ideas about what constitutes an "identification" would also be reshaped around a particularly science-based and individualistic model associated with the industrialized West, one that may be alien to more collectivist cultures, where mourners may take more comfort in the fact that their dead are buried among their own people rather than from matching all the data points from one particular bone to the genetic markers in a DNA database.[107]

Other practitioners voice considerable skepticism about these interpretations, and in fact about any situation in which foreign experts judge that mourners expect less because of their "culture." These experts point out that the expectations of genocide survivors—people who have watched their country and their own families decimated by unexpected brutality—are likely to be based in part on the desperate circumstances in which they find themselves. They are also likely to be informed by the powerlessness these people feel before the international institutions that, in many cases, have intervened in their lives in uneven and unpredictable ways. Subsequent generations may eventually come to want information that their older relatives did not know to demand,[108] and the evidence and historical information that comes out of graves can be of interest to many stakeholders beyond families and mourners alone.[109] To experts who see the issue of expectations in these terms, the moral universalism of the forensic expert, wherever she finds herself, is a promise to practice *good science*—the kind of science that is incompatible with destroying evidence by exhuming a mass grave and allowing its contents to be commingled in a collective memorial. If she does any less than that, what she is practicing is something other than forensics.[110]

Despite their differences and even irreconcilability, these two interpretive models do belong together under the same rubric of moral universalism. They are both, at heart, attempts to make sure that there is some justificatory structure underlying forensic teams' case selection—one based not on political sympathies, but rather on an equal concern for the needs of mourners, regardless of where they are found. Both models offer compelling arguments, and raise some questions that can only be answered empirically, on a case-by-case basis.[111] They also raise normative questions, however, about how to assign moral weight to the cultural views of a given survivor population versus intuitions about the potential needs and expectations of future generations. Lingering discomfort about the distribution of forensic efforts around the globe does not resolve the issue or create conditions of global equality; however, it is, at least, a desirable sign of self-critical practice among some experts in the field.[112]

Victim/Mourner-centric

Though forensic science has always had the potential to produce important *outcomes* for victims and mourners, from putting offenders behind bars to identifying the dead, the obligations of its practitioners were largely to the courts and the law. In fact, the legitimacy of an impartial legal system has always staked itself partly on the distance it maintains from the desire for revenge, and the claims of suffering, of victims. Trials, while often closely followed and deeply desired by survivors, can be undertaken with a view to reasserting the rule of law, deterring future crimes, a perceived "duty to prosecute," and many other things beyond the needs of victims themselves.[113] In fact, in *Eichmann in Jerusalem*, Hannah Arendt famously alleges that the 1961 war crimes trial of the Nazi genocidaire Adolph Eichmann was overly concerned with recounting the many sufferings of individual Jewish Holocaust victims and the Jewish people, and not, as "Justice demands" on the specific deeds of the man standing at the docket.[114]

The field of international forensic investigation appears to be in the midst of a gradual and sometimes controversial ethical reorientation toward the needs of victims. This development, however, emerges not from some theoretical argument against views like Arendt's; nor is it entirely the result of some new sympathy that took root in forensic investigators when they began working among the bodies of genocide victims rather than the "ordinary" dead. Rather, the new importance of victims currently embraced by much of the field, and the more nuanced perspectives on them, can be traced to specific historical factors. This history starts in Argentina, with immunity laws that caused a crisis of purpose for the Argentine Forensic Anthropology Team; it then runs through some of the burgeoning field's most difficult experiences in the former Yugoslavia and beyond. Chapters 1 and 2 in this volume recount important pieces of this history and explain more about what it means, in practice, to structure forensic investigations around the needs of families of the missing and other mourners.

"Victims," "families," and "mourners," terms used throughout this book, are overlapping but not completely coextensive. It is important to take note of the types of victims not included as forensic teams have turned their attention to families of the missing and, less frequently, other mourners. The new vocabulary of "family-centric" or "humanitarian" forensic work expresses a great deal about the duties of forensic teams to *living* victims of violence—people who have lost loved ones and who have often themselves been brutalized and displaced. For a vocabulary used by people who exhume mass graves, however, it has little to say about the victims who did *not* survive—the dead bodies with whom forensic experts, often more than anyone else, make intimate, sustained, and direct contact. This book integrates, along with an account of how forensic investigations affect families and mourners, an inquiry into what forensic investigation does for the dead victims of atrocity.

These four ethical tenets help to define a field. Forensic teams are not the only organizations to see scientific method, political autonomy, moral universalism, and a focus on victims as central to their identity. Yet having scientific methods wedded so explicitly to human rights work was historically unprecedented when the Argentine team began to exhume graves in Argentina. It has since inspired and informed the use of new technologies of mapping, spatial analysis, data aggregation, and computer simulations.[115] It has also raised new dilemmas in areas such as the tension between scientific objectivity and the victim-centric moral commitments of human rights work. Forensic teams may be the only organizations in which all four tenets play such prominent, near equal, and frequently conflicting roles; moreover, it is the interactions between these principles and the particular context of mass atrocity—principles plus realities—that ultimately shape the field.

The salient fact about the realities of mass atrocity is how difficult—sometimes impossible—they can make it to fulfill every important ethical principle, especially when those principles begin to pull against each other as they are put into practice. The gaps among expectations, aspirations, and reality is at least as prominent in forensic work as in any other humanitarian effort. However, when defining a field and understanding its history, aspirations *do* matter.

It also seems significant that the most insightful and often harshest criticism of international forensic investigations I have heard have all come from practitioners themselves. Far from saints, these professionals rarely sound like missionaries either. While not all forensic experts are equally engaged in reflection on politics and ethics, a significant number of them have published articles and book chapters in which they evaluate their own work and express concerns about the future of the field.[116] During investigations, in print, and at conferences, they argue, exchange lessons learned, and (when possible) work toward agreement on shared ethical codes. Even the codes they produce are rarely described as perfect or complete, but rather as ongoing projects subject to changes in the technologies, on-the-ground circumstances, and accumulated global experience in the field.

The experts and organizations featured in this book may not always fully succeed in balancing their ethical commitments to their own or anyone else's satisfaction and may work in many contexts where important factors are out of their control. But there remains a clear difference between the principles they seek to apply and those of other organizations that work with dead bodies in a different ethical framework. The exhumations of *desaparecidos* in Argentina were not the first forensic investigations of war crimes or human rights violations, and there are now many efforts at the post-conflict identification and/or recovery of dead bodies that use methods and technologies similar to those employed by human rights organizations. There are important historical and even institutional connections between these different projects, but they remain politically and ethically distinct.

Ironically, the world's first international forensic investigations were organized by the Nazis.[117] In the early 1940s, multiple mass graves around Russia's Katyn Forest were exhumed after the massacre and clandestine burial of around twenty-two thousand Polish officers and war prisoners, at a time when Poland was suffering a double occupation by both German and Soviet forces. The Soviets were eager to pin these massacres on the Third Reich. Nazi propaganda minister Joseph Goebbels thus eagerly pursued public exhumations of the graves in Katyn Forest, accurately seeing an opportunity to sow division between the Soviets and their allies in the West as evidence of Soviet responsibility—contradicting their public denunciations of the Nazis—emerged from the graves. The "Katyn Commission" formed in 1943 by the International Red Cross, at the request of the Nazi leadership, would go on to investigate mass graves in the town of Vinnytsia, Ukraine, the site of Stalinist purges, which the Soviets also initially tried to blame on the Germans. After the war, when Soviet officials attempted to include the Katyn massacres in charges leveled against Nazi defendants at Nuremberg, US and British judges dismissed the charge from the proceedings. From very early on, then, various actors, with mixed motives, recognized the power that forensic science would have to speak to the *international* "forum" produced by the world wars and the nascent international human rights framework.

The crimes leading up to these exhumations, methods employed, and the international audience they garnered, all make them similar to contemporary human rights exhumations. Importantly, the Katyn and Vinnytsia exhumation stories illustrate how the political context around mass graves means that scientific investigations always have the potential to be both a response to conflict and a site of *ongoing* conflict. But there are also important differences between the ethical framework established when Clyde Snow and his students began searching for the *desaparecidos* in Argentina and the movement's "prehistory" at mass graves in the Soviet Union. Aside from the presence of neutral observers from the Red Cross, the "glaringly political" Katyn exhumations made little pretense of independence or objectivity.[118] They were, rather, an act of wartime public relations.[119] Of the pathologists who participated, only one was from a nation not under Nazi occupation:[120] the neutral nation of Switzerland.[121] The Nazis' reports on the Vinnytsia exhumations went to lengths to hide the presence of Jews among the victims and to highlight (by adding the term "*Jude*" immediately after the name) the Jewish background of any officers among The People's Commissariat for Internal Affairs, or NKVD, found responsible for the massacre. In this way, the Nazis shaped the identity of both perpetrators and victims to fit their "theory of communism as a 'Jewish cause.'"[122] It is also significant that the focus of these investigations was on assigning responsibility and publicizing the crimes, with little dialogue about the needs of families of the missing. Though tensions between the legal and victim-centric (or "humanitarian") priorities of forensic investigations surfaced in the 1990s, and have been part of the dialogue about the field since then, the controversy itself—and the slew of articles and reports that it has prompted—is difficult to imagine in the context of the post–World War II exhumations of

Soviet mass graves. By contrast, given the mix of moral commitments and experiences that experts from the Latin American teams, Physicians for Human Rights, and other groups brought with them to the major genocide investigations of the 1990s, the tensions that erupted there have, in retrospect, something close to an air of inevitability. In one final but rather crucial point of contrast, the Nazi leadership that organized the initial investigations of the graves in Katyn and Vinnytsia, busy elsewhere with the extermination of Jews, Roma, homosexuals, and other groups, was obviously quite unconcerned with moral universalism of any sort.

In the contemporary landscape, it is important not to exaggerate the separation between the field of human rights forensic investigations and the many institutions with which it intersects. Forensic science constitutes a relatively small world, and scientific findings, methodologies, and of course individual experts themselves circulate among various state and federal agencies, universities, branches of the military, and so on. Yet important distinctions are visible between a human rights-driven forensic investigation and other post-conflict exhumation and identification efforts: the US- military-led search for missing soldiers, for example, does not require the same sort of political autonomy pursued by human rights forensic teams. Like other military recovery efforts, it proceeds from a sense of duty to bring soldiers fallen on foreign soil back to their homeland and families, rather than from a broader human rights ethic of exposing violations, telling the stories of victims, and establishing a new historical narrative.[123] International efforts by an Orthodox Jewish organization, ZAKA, to collect Jewish remains and artifacts after natural disasters and terrorist attacks borrow tools, imagery, and rhetoric from the human rights movement, but proceed on radically different assumptions about science as an interpretive framework, the level of identification with specific political causes, and the moral value accorded to different dead bodies.[124]

One final example seems particularly crucial: the exhumations of mass graves containing victims of the Saddam Hussein regime in Iraq, whether in the Kurdish north or other places where purges took place. Unlike, for example, the postwar search for fallen soldiers in uniform, the story of the massacred and disappeared in Iraq closely parallels that of the victim populations in Rwanda, Bosnia, and other places: people targeted, with indiscriminate brutality, based on real and perceived/constructed ethnic and political identities. One of Physicians for Human Rights' earliest forensic projects, in fact, was the use of witness testimony, soil samples, and other methods to confirm

Hussein's use of chemical weapons against Kurdish people in the 1987–88 Anfal Campaign.[125] Yet Physicians for Human Rights refused to participate directly in the exhumations of Saddam Hussein-era mass graves or providing evidence for the trials in Baghdad.[126] Concerns and objections among the human rights forensic community focused on the security situation in Iraq,[127] the lack of political independence from coalition forces, the Iraqi High Tribunal's use of the death penalty, and perhaps most importantly the focus on collecting evidence of war crimes without a coherent plan to attend to other needs of families of the missing, especially through individual identification of the dead.[128] Repeated calls from independent forensic experts to bring the Iraqi exhumations more in line with the holistic, humanitarian ethic now standard elsewhere in the field,[129] including both more political autonomy and a greater focus on victims and mourners, eventually did result in a repatriation program to accompany the exhumations in Iraq.[130] Nevertheless, the exhumations were ultimately a small effort, focused on trials, in a country containing thousands of mass graves. Little has been published about them, and within the field discomfort remains about the political context and the relationship between the forensic and military efforts.

Overview: The Politics and Philosophy of Mass Graves

This book is divided, roughly, into two halves. The first half, which spans Chapters 1 and 2, focuses on the politics of mass graves. This Introduction has offered a brief account of the rise of the forensic human rights movement, identified its guiding principles, and started to show how forensic teams become political actors and influence the expectations regarding international assistance in conflict and post-conflict areas. Chapter 1 identifies the major stakeholders around mass graves and describes the influence they have had over forensic investigations—sometimes directly, by making demands about how investigations should be conducted, and sometimes indirectly, by virtue of being key players in post-conflict politics. The chapter also explores the ways in which forensic teams have reorganized their investigative priorities for a global practice. Chapter 2 is the first of two investigations into powerful objections forensic teams have faced in the field. It focuses on Argentina's Madres de Plaza de Mayo, some of whom have claimed that forensic exhumations pursue an undesirable and *de-politicizing* form of "closure"—a distraction, at best, from demands for justice. Chapter 3 explores an entirely different type of objection: religious prohibitions against exhuming graves.

Because the objections of the Madres de Plaza de Mayo largely respond to the politics of exhumation and transitional justice in Argentina, they prompt an analysis that for the most part also responds to specific political concerns about immunity laws, the collective identity of the *desaparecidos*, and the effect of exhumations on social activism (though I also examine some of the more philosophical views about grief and dead bodies that play a part in this debate). Chapter 3, in contrast, deals with a set of objections that are explicitly meant to transcend earthly politics, objections based on the claim that graves are sacred. Forensic teams cannot craft a suitable response to objections rooted in the sacred if they have no clear sense of what the sacred means: the practice of forensic work, in this case, necessitates philosophical reflection. The book turns from political-historical toward philosophical questions, then, not just as a matter of scholarly inclination; it is also responding directly to the different types of practical problems forensic experts face in the field. Chapters 3, 4, and 5, moreover, can all be seen as investigations of where human rights fit into the landscape of international forensic investigations: what happens when they appear to conflict with other, religious frameworks of understanding (Chapter 3), how to respect the limits of rights-based action in a world dotted with mass graves (Chapter 4), and what vocabularies beyond human rights might clarify the meaning of a global project of unearthing, naming, and reassembling the dead victims of atrocity (Chapter 5).

PART 1

THE POLITICS OF MASS GRAVES

Chapter 1

The Stakeholders in International Forensic Investigations

Putting Politics First

In 2000, my former supervisor at Physicians for Human Rights, the forensic anthropologist Bill Haglund, received one of many calls to testify before the International Criminal Tribunal for the former Yugoslavia. The defendant in this case was Radislav Krstić, a Bosnian Serb military commander who would ultimately be found guilty of "aiding and abetting genocide" for his participation in the Srebrenica massacre of Bosniak men and boys. After presenting forensic evidence from the graves near Srebrenica, Haglund was cross-examined by a black-robed lawyer for the defense, Tomislav Višnjić. Through a simultaneous translator, Višnjić asked Haglund how he could be sure that the graves he had examined were the result of mass murder. "On the basis of what indicators has it been established, that it was an execution, a murder in the case of all of the bodies? Could causes of death also include suicide?" he asked. Haglund, exhibiting a flair for dark humor not uncommon in his profession, could not suppress a smirk as he answered. "I have investigated many suicides," he replied. "I have never seen an individual with their hands bound behind their back shoot themselves multiple times."[1]

Višnjić's question invokes a counternarrative, one in which the victims themselves, and not his client, are somehow responsible for their own deaths. The counternarrative most likely represents not only an attempt to exonerate this particular defendant, but also taps into a culture of rumor, innuendo, backlash, and conspiracy that often springs up among communities living with atrocities in their midst.[2] The darkly absurd image Haglund offers in response, of bound prisoners somehow reaching around to shoot themselves repeatedly, exposes the defense counsel's proffered counternarrative for what it is: a lie. Haglund, using the voice of forensic science, does not simply lend credibility to the charges of war crimes; he also severs the "looped circle" of falsity and "solipsism" that become part of the culture of atrocity and that can obscure even the starkest realities of violence.[3]

These moments, in which a clear-cut scientific truth cuts through the lies of the unjust, are crucial reminders of the power of forensic science in the human rights context. They are not produced in a vacuum, however. Even Haglund's powerful testimony relied on evidence that was collected in one of the most complex, contentious, and politically charged post-conflict environments that forensic investigators have ever faced and whose full meaning in the broader story of the region is still debated today. Nearly two decades after the war, mass graves and the identification of the missing continue to exacerbate deep divisions and provoke complex negotiations in postwar Bosnia.[4]

Jennifer Burrell and Mercedes Doretti write:

> Forensic anthropology applied in the service of human rights . . . takes place at the interstices of local political agendas, NGOs' wishes, national programs, and the work of international organizations. These gray spaces add another dimension to the role of forensic anthropologists: finding a middle ground on which to carry out investigations, a search that includes negotiations of roles, positions, politics, and funding requirements.[5]

Throughout this book, I delve into examples of these sorts of negotiations, from places such as Chile, Argentina, the former Yugoslavia, Poland, and Spain. This chapter introduces some widespread common features that characterize the complex political landscape around mass graves, despite the very different contexts where they are found. The most important common threads in international forensic investigations, I suggest, are visible in three key groups that have a stake in these investigations: courts and tribunals, families and other mourners, and transitional governments.

Of course, all of these groups I call "stakeholders" are ultimately made up of *individuals*. One can recognize the ways in which certain institutions aggregate and organize individuals' moral, political, and practical claims upon forensic investigations, without making the mistake of thinking that any institution perfectly represents the interests and desires of all of its participants. Peer at any association of mourners, post-conflict government, or international tribunal for more than a minute, and you will see fissures, different voices, and competing goals.

There is little use in treating any one of these stakeholders as *analytically* more important than any of the others—though, like most forensic teams themselves, I do accord special *ethical* status to the claims of families of the missing and other mourners. Another dynamic that occurs across all of these stakeholders is the discrepancy, often quite large, between what they hope and expect from forensic investigations, on the one hand, and the results that forensic teams are able to produce, on the other. This gap emerges in part because so much of the human rights community's optimistic post-conflict vocabulary, terms such as "reconciliation" and "closure," sets hopelessly unrealistic goalposts. The achievements of forensic investigations are often folded into larger, very contentious processes, such as war crimes trials and truth commissions, or they are witnessed by only a few experts and mourners in private moments, such as when a case worker arrives in a family's living room to tell them their loved one has finally been identified. The disappointments of the work—the clashes with family members, the allegations of bias, the graves not exhumed and bodies never found, the misidentifications—are, in the meantime, often very public.

Forensic Investigations and Stakeholders, across Contexts

In nearly every place they work, forensic teams have some agency in deciding—even through omission, and even when they would prefer not to—whose voices they will listen to most closely and whose interests they will prioritize with usually quite limited resources. Decisions about priorities both impact, and are shaped by, organizational mandates and funding sources, the plan for the exhumation, the time and resources allotted to it, the type of personnel that constitute a particular team, and conditions on the ground, from bad weather to death threats to hunger-striking families of the missing.[6]

If a forensic team plans on identifying many individual dead bodies and repatriating their remains to families, for example, it must include people trained to interview the living family members and gather information about the deceased. If identifications will be made using DNA, someone must take samples from living relatives, manage a database, and inform family members with sensitivity when a body has been identified. Gathering evidence of war crimes may, by contrast, require ballistics experts, or people who can identify the tire treads of different vehicles going to and from the gravesite. The need for these particular experts may affect what organization or organizations are contacted, but these organizations bring with them their own mandates, philosophies, mixes of national backgrounds and expertise, and other factors that can reconfigure the political landscape around the investigation. Between the halls of international institutions, the offices of various nongovernmental organizations, the homes of mourners, the grave, and the morgue, a dialogue takes shape.

In the face of all these particulars, it is tempting to doubt the usefulness of talking about "international forensic investigation" in any general sense. Every new forensic investigation is so complex, so forcefully shaped by the political and cultural context in which it is carried out, that perhaps the only stories we can tell are stories of individual countries and their exhumations. This has been the approach of cultural anthropologists, and some archaeologists, who have written about the forensic investigation of human rights violations. These studies of particular exhumations or identification projects,[7] in keeping with their discipline's prevailing ethic of "observation and documentation" while disavowing any global or transhistorical generalization,[8] have eloquently described the complex role that history, cultures, technologies, and discourses (local and international) play in specific forensic investigations. In the process, they offer a needed correction to the tendency among some humanitarians to portray crucial concepts, such as "the needs of families of the missing," as simple and static, as if families were not divided among themselves and also part of larger, sometimes conflicting, interest groups.

But important continuities do exist across different contexts and forensic projects—among them the norms and codes that forensic teams bring with them to the regions they visit. Anthropologists have tended to spend less time observing how forensic teams, like the local communities around mass graves, are embedded in histories of their own. The experiences forensic experts had in the former Yugoslavia affected how they evaluated the prospects for mass grave investigations in Iraq, as well as individual and organizational decisions about whether to participate.[9] On a more personal level, a forensic anthropologist such as Clea Koff may "read" her experiences in Bosnia or Kosovo with reference to what she witnessed in Rwanda, comparing the methods of violence and types of suffering, the different needs of mourners, and the adequacy of the international response. In other words, half of the ingredients in the complex relationship between forensic teams and the communities they visit—the ones that exist not in "local culture" but in an evolving *international* culture of forensic work—are largely left out of the context-by-context approach arrived at through anthropological fieldwork. While every international tribunal, association of families of the missing, and transitional government inhabits a different place and time, there are important and by no means accidental similarities between them.

The concept of forensic "stakeholders" helps to narrow, constructively, the field of analysis; however, it is also far from perfect.[10] The term's greatest flaw is that, in a setting shot through with violence, grief, and longing, it seems detached and even businesslike.[11] It may, for that reason, seem biased toward the government offices and chambers where the officials of transitional governments and international tribunals make strategic calculations, and against the types of emotional, and sometimes religious, claims that families of the missing and other mourners tend to make. Far from minimizing or ignoring claims based on grief, care, or ideals of justice, I aim to show how those concerns are woven into even the most technical and legalistic elements of forensic practice.

Rwanda and the Former Yugoslavia: Tribunals as Stakeholders

Forensic teams investigating human rights violations have done a tremendous amount to help hold perpetrators accountable for the violence they have committed, challenge the official denial and self-granted amnesties of the powerful in courts, and thus reaffirm the return to the rule of law. They have done so in a long list of different settings, including national courts in Argentina, Peru, and Ethiopia, as well as international tribunals for Rwanda, the former Yugoslavia, and Sierra Leone. The International Criminal Court at The Hague also has a division focusing on the collection of forensic evidence.

However, criminal justice is only part of the larger project of transitioning away from authoritarian rule and often raises at least as many difficult questions as it resolves. Ruti Teitel writes:

> The debate over transitional criminal justice is marked by profound dilemmas: Whether to punish or to amnesty? Whether punishment is a backward-looking exercise in retribution or an expression of the renewal of the rule of law? To what extent is responsibility for repression appropriate to the individual, as opposed to the collective, the regime, and even the entire society?[12]

Since the post–World War II Nuremberg trials of Nazi officials, international war crimes tribunals have, as Teitel argues, changed the definition of justice in a globalizing world, narrowing the privileges associated with state sovereignty and giving victims a much larger stage on which to tell their stories and stake their claims. These tribunals have also, however, frustrated the expectations that many victims and human rights advocates have had for them. They have been expensive, slow, and have often only focused on a handful of "big fish" in a sea full of rights violators and people bearing different degrees of responsibility.[13] In this sea swim presidents and militia commanders, neighbors who turned on the people they once called friends, those who turned a blind eye to the violence, who moved into apartments emptied by the displaced, and perhaps—thinking historically—the empires and other foreign powers that often helped lay the groundwork for instability, as well as promoting racial logic and the bureaucratic techniques of control that can lay be mobilized for genocide.

Since Nuremberg, too, the accusation of "victor's justice" has plagued international trials. In the former Yugoslavia and Iraq, among other more recent conflicts, outside observers as well as defendants have cast doubt over proceedings in which only one side in a violent conflict is under investigation. As Derek Congram points out, even the temporal dimensions used to define the period of "conflict" allow for some crimes and forms of responsibility to be investigated, while others are not.[14] Furthermore, though activists and officials have often proclaimed that international tribunals would serve as a deterrent to future war criminals,[15] no hard evidence yet exists to support that claim.[16] Perhaps most importantly, while victims and mourners often care deeply about seeing perpetrators put on trial, in many cases they regard other forms of redress—such as finding out the truth about human rights violations, receiving the remains of dead loved ones, and gaining access to economic assistance—as much more urgent.[17] International efforts to try war criminals are often driven by elites both in-country and abroad, and are not necessarily focused on the needs of the victimized communities.[18]

Most forensic experts have been trained in disciplines that emphasize scientific rigor and cold, hard facts. They have often worked in domestic crime labs, on behalf of the court system in their home countries. These experts may naturally see their work in terms of its legal outcomes, and sometimes, using the precedent of domestic police forensic work, they make it sound as if contributing evidence to the prosecution of human rights violators was the original or "core" priority in international forensic investigation.[19]

The reality, however, is significantly more complex. Clyde Snow and the young students who formed the first forensic team dedicated to human rights work, the Argentine Forensic Anthropology Team, saw the justifications for their work going far beyond the quite limited trials that were possible in post-junta Argentina, before the infamous "Full Stop" and "Due Obedience" laws called a premature halt, at least for a time, to human rights prosecutions. The Argentine team faced an extremely complex landscape of stakeholders, with an influential group of activists opposing exhumations of the *desaparecidos*. Nevertheless, despite the various constraints on their work, the team sought to serve the families of the missing by identifying bodies for them to bury—if they would accept them—and conducting their exhumations with both care and scientific rigor. The young anthropologists in the group often found themselves digging up victims who were their own age and from similar social backgrounds: in some sense, as they exhumed the graves of the *desaparecidos* they were also composing a tragic history of their own generation. For all of these reasons and more, the Argentine and other Latin American forensic teams are generally credited with developing a uniquely holistic and family-centric set of priorities for forensic investigation. If one accepts the mid-1980s birth of the Argentine team as the true beginning of a coherent field of forensic science in the service of human rights, then a holistic, victim-centric, and even politically invested model of scientific activism is the field's *origin*; it was a decade later when these same Latin American anthropologists and their international colleagues discovered how different things could be when the large machinery of an international tribunal was directing their investigative priorities.

In fact, the formative controversy about the role of courts in mass grave exhumations unfolded across an ocean from where human rights forensic investigations got their start in Argentina, and under very different conditions. As the former Yugoslavia splintered in the early 1990s, then-president Slobodan Milošević mobilized Serb nationalists in an attempt to carve a united "Greater Serbia" out of ethnically heterogeneous territories in Bosnia and Herzegovina,[20] Croatia, and Kosovo through massacre, systematic rape, and expulsion. Conflict raged throughout the region, first in Croatia and Bosnia, then Kosovo, and ended only after massive civilian casualties, various (often highly controversial) forms of peacekeeping and humanitarian intervention that culminated in NATO bombing campaigns, and negotiated settlements. In July 1996, the Office of the Prosecutor of the newly formed International Criminal Tribunal for the Former Yugoslavia (ICTY) sponsored its first exhumations of mass gravesites in Bosnia, as part of the effort to hold the Serb leadership responsible for "ethnic cleansing," genocide, and other human rights violations. According to Eric Stover, while other forms of evidence (such as witness testimony) would eventually come to play a larger role than forensic evidence, exhumations played a crucial legitimizing role in the early days of the ICTY. Early footage of the forensic teams exhuming mass graves, Stover says, sent a message to a skeptical and divided public that "this is why this court exists."[21]

The ICTY invited help from a number of different national forensic authorities and nongovernmental teams, creating a confusing landscape of groups with different responsibilities and methodologies.[22] Ultimately, as it had in Rwanda just months before, Physicians for Human Rights would take on a coordinating role for the major forensic efforts in the region.[23]

All of the teams conducting exhumations in the former Yugoslavia faced significant and sometimes unprecedented difficulties in identifying the bodies of the dead. In Srebrenica, for example, Bosnian Serb forces had stripped their victims of many useful identification markers, such as their documents and jewelry, before killing them. They later used construction equipment to dig up, mix together, and rebury the bodies in an attempt to frustrate any future forensic exhumations.[24] The size and number of graves the ICTY asked forensic teams to exhume went far beyond the scope of their work in Rwanda, where only two mass graves were exhumed, yet the tribunal did not budget any money for the work.[25] In an interview, Snow recalled that, in the cases of both Rwanda and the former Yugoslavia, the lawyers working for the tribunals seemed not to understand the limitations of forensic investigation, especially under these conditions.[26]

It was also difficult for forensic teams to maintain the necessary level of expertise on the ground. For Physicians for Human Rights, recruiting forensic pathologists was particularly challenging, since experienced people in the field often work for a medical examiner's office that cannot give them leave for weeks or months on end. Travel to the investigation sites, given the distance as well as the number of necessary bureaucratic procedures and security clearances, could use up days of an expert's leave time before any work could begin.[27] The result was "constant turnover" of forensic anthropologists from the United States and other countries. Forensic anthropologists, Snow said, could often stay longer, but most of those involved in the Rwanda and former Yugoslavia investigations were beginning their careers; since they were not given any time to train together as a unit or establish shared standards, they often implemented different methodologies learned in the various universities and other settings where they had trained—leading to both errors and "chaotic" reporting of the evidence that had been uncovered.[28]

The conduct of the exhumations themselves also contributed to a highly charged and often unpleasant political climate around the graves. As Sarah Wagner describes:

> The exhumations and autopsies were carried out with the primary goal of providing evidence about a crime, such as determining the cause of death or the presence of ligatures or blindfolds, rather than the documentation of an individual identity. Thus, these workers paid close attention to the manner of death and the features of the grave and less attention to the condition of the individual skeletal remains, which might have yielded information specific to identification.[29]

Having recorded and preserved the evidence the tribunal was looking for, the forensic team—without access to adequate storage facilities—released the bodies, which were still unidentified, to local authorities possessing very few resources. Those authorities put the bodies in "an abandoned tunnel cut into a hillside in Tuzla,"[30] and later moved some to a parking lot,[31] to the outrage of families of the missing. In other words, as Morris Tidball-Binz puts it, the tribunal made it clear it was "mostly concerned with how [the victims . . .] died, not who they were":[32] nor, clearly, with how their families might feel about the treatment of the dead bodies of their loved ones. Lola Vollen, who worked in Bosnia for Physicians for Human Rights' Srebrenica Identification Project, reflects, "The ICTY's timetable for exhuming the Srebrenica graves held the unearthed remains essentially hostage to prosecutorial priorities and The Hague's logistical capacity. Survivor voices had little, if any, effect on the pace of the investigations."[33]

Similar problems continued after the war in Kosovo in 1998–99 and the NATO bombing campaign there. In the aftermath of hostilities, various countries (mostly NATO members) sent forensic teams into Kosovo to conduct exhumations at different gravesites, once again with very little coordination between them in terms of the standards, methodology, or data-collection methods being used.[34]

Evidence of genocide and other war crimes emerges from patterns forensic investigators establish at the gravesite and on the human remains they exhume. These patterns include the type of victims: "their ethnicity or their religion, whether they were men, women or children, civilians or combatants, or soldiers incapacitated by bindings or blindfolds."[35] For war crimes charges, investigators must also gather evidence of the "systematic and widespread" nature of the crimes, suggesting they were carried out as part of a plan, orders handed down through a chain of command. Sometimes, they can establish these patterns by identifying a categorical "sample" of bodies from multiple different graves—all of them Muslims, for example, or all of them tied up and shot—without having to establish individual identity, or examine all of the bodies in the grave.

In Kosovo, according to Stover and Shigekane, the various teams working on behalf of the ICTY's Office of the Prosecutor were charged with making these "categorical identifications" in order to "establish whether the victims were civilians and whether the manner in which they were killed was similar in each of the seven villages and towns named in the [Tribunal's] indictment" of Slobodan Milošević and four codefendants.[36] The investigators were working under time pressure, once again without dedicated resources for identification and repatriation of individual bodies. Some of the forensic teams collected scant if any ante-mortem identifying information from relatives, and they did not keep bone or teeth samples that would enable future identification through DNA analysis.[37] Some teams reburied the bodies they had autopsied, without creating any individual identifying markers that might have helped other forensic experts hoping to identify them. In the worst of cases, the reburial places were never recorded properly and have not been discovered since:[38] in these extreme instances, forensic teams became agents of (further) *disappearance* rather than repair. Family members and other survivors in the communities around the graves began hunger strikes and other protests against this treatment of their dead, calling for the identification of as many bodies as possible.[39]

Each of the many individuals and agencies involved in these investigations had different—but often constrained—levels of control over their circumstances, and most were trying to do what good they felt they could. Derek Congram, who worked on forensic investigations in the former Yugoslavia from 1999 onward, points out that the priority the ICTY placed on gathering evidence does not mean the tribunal was "uninterested" in identification.[40] Reports by Austrian and French teams exhuming graves in Kosovo show efforts to make at least presumptive identifications, usually based on having relatives look at the clothing on the remains.[41] By 2000, the UN-sponsored team active in the region was attempting to identify hundreds of bodies and was placing all unidentified bodies in coded individual graves.[42] It was generally hoped that, by passing identifying information along to civil society organizations formed to search for missing persons, the ICTY could contribute to ongoing repatriation efforts while maintaining its own focus on collecting evidence for prosecutions. Yet, because they added yet another layer of cross-institutional and often transnational cooperation, these efforts could be hard to coordinate well.[43] In Kosovo, the Victim Recovery and Identification Commission (VRIC), a missing persons association funded by the Organization for Security and Cooperation in Europe, existed for only a short time before folding, leaving responsibility back in the hands of the tribunal.[44]

Tensions between a family's urgent desire for information about their missing loved one and various aspects of criminal law and police work are not unique to the human rights context or to mass graves.[45] However, the international criminal tribunal introduces a new level of dissymmetry between different stakeholders. A war crimes tribunal, with its real and perceived links to human rights groups, the United Nations, NATO, and specific nation-states involved in one way or another in the region and its conflicts, seems to represent the entire "international community" in its pursuit of prosecutions. The tremendous resources and attention given to distant tribunals can exacerbate the feeling, among local populations, that trials are instruments used largely to justify the military actions of Western powers to their domestic audiences rather than to serve the cause of justice.[46] Families of the missing, unlike these highly visible and well-networked institutions, often have numerous obstacles to surmount in making themselves heard. In the case of the former Yugoslavia, many of them had fled the country, or they found themselves in a territory of contested borders whose institutions of governance, from the national down to the very local, had disintegrated. They faced a confusing proliferation of different groups offering to help them find their loved ones, including three organizations keeping separate databases of missing persons.[47]

Ultimately, though forensic evidence from mass graves in the former Yugoslavia and Rwanda (to a lesser extent) would serve as important evidence of genocide and war crimes, the complexity and unprecedented nature of the exhumations would be reflected in some proceedings. In 1999, the International Criminal Tribunal issued a sentence of life in prison to Georges Rutaganda, a leader in the Interahamwe Hutu militia movement, for his role in genocide and crimes against humanity. There was a dark spot, however, for the experts involved in the limited forensic exhumations undertaken in post-genocide Rwanda: the court's ruling that the forensic evidence collected near Rutaganda's headquarters at the Amgar Garage (on a hillside behind the building, the forensic team investigated multiple burial sites, including some bodies they had to remove from the depths of a latrine) were not satisfactory enough, in terms

of "the scientific method used by Professor Haglund," to be used in the determination of the case. Instead, the tribunal relied on witness testimony to corroborate that Tutsis who were stopped at a roadblock outside the garage had
been taken inside and killed.[48] During the trial, Rutaganda's defense team had
commissioned a report by Kathy Reichs, a highly respected forensic anthropologist, professor, and author of a best-selling series of forensic-focused murder
mysteries. The Reichs report raised multiple concerns about the Amgar garage
exhumations, from the lack of board certification among the forensic anthropologists involved, to discrepancies in reporting and conclusions made about
the age, time of death, and other aspects of the remains without recourse to
methods such as fabric analysis or forensic entomology.[49]

Reichs' report, and its impact on the Rutaganda case, raises important
questions about the application of forensic expertise in post-conflict contexts
and, equally importantly, in poor countries. Clea Koff, who was a member of
the team that conducted the investigations at the Amgar Garage, questions
whether the American Board of Forensic Anthropology is the proper creden-
tial to look for when ad hoc teams of forensic anthropologists and other experts
from around the world are being assembled by the UN and a nonprofit human
rights group—experts who, in this case, were working more or less as volunteers with only a small stipend to cover living expenses.[50] Haglund himself, in
brief comments on the report, also suggests that while some of Reichs's recommendations would be standard procedure in the United States and Canada,
where previous research on the behavior of insects around gravesites or fabric
decay can aid forensic experts as they try to estimate the time of burial and
other events, they are of questionable value in a context where no previous
research has been conducted.[51]

The Rutaganda prosecution can be seen, in retrospect, as a warning about
the complex relationship between the legal value of forensic evidence, the investigative priorities established by international tribunals, and the on-the-
ground politics of exhumations. Reichs's report would come back to cast a
shadow over evidence presented in Bosnian war crimes trials, and over Haglund himself. In the ICTY trial of Vujadin Popović, a Bosnian Serb military
commander, Haglund was asked repeatedly to answer questions about Rwanda,
his own scientific conduct and credentials, and the reliability of the evidence.[52]

In fact, the conflictive atmosphere and multiple allegations of mismanagement had already prompted the ICTY's Office of the Chief Prosecutor to con-
vene its own investigative panel, in San Antonio in 1997. The pre-investigatory

testimonies collected by the panel, from experts involved in mass grave investigations in Bosnia, were nearly evenly split between supportive and critical perspectives. Significantly, among the critics of Haglund's work was his own mentor and the most prestigious figure in the field, Clyde Snow. Snow objected to the pace of the investigations (specifically, he felt that no more than twenty bodies should be exhumed from a grave in a day), and called the work of Haglund's team "sloppy science."[53]

The San Antonio panel made a number of recommendations for future work on mass graves in the former Yugoslavia, and acknowledged "administrative and logistic . . . problems" in the management. However, it declared the science sound: "The evidence of war crimes is overwhelming at each site. A few problems of administration or temporary lapses from a scientific ideal could not jeopardize the over all [sic] quality of the evidence and its interpretation at autopsy."[54] Yet the panel had to concede the baffling effect of their interviews: "We were impressed by the variety of responses to our questions. It was as though each person had served at a site, or sites, different from all the rest. There was no clear agreement as to who was responsible for what."[55] The panel focused on the role bureaucratic complexity played in these problems—particularly "the fiscal and administrative dichotomy between the U.N. Tribunal and Physicians for Human Rights (PHR)"[56]—and avoided having its report or recommendations wade too deeply into the larger issues of priorities and politics that were at play. For example, the panel's full-throated defense of the conduct of the investigations rested on their value in proving crimes,[57] with less said about the practices that could have an impact on future efforts to identify individual bodies, such as the alleged discarding of clothing or commingling of body parts.

These experiences of post-genocide exhumations in the mid-1990s have prompted significant reflection among many of the practitioners involved, much of it playing out publicly in a string of reports and articles. In later interviews, Snow struck a more forgiving tone than in his testimony for the San Antonio panel,[58] and late in his life alluded to those years as an "experimental phase" for the growing field of international forensic investigation. "We learned the limitations and we became overextended," he said.[59] Among these limitations, it seems, were the narrow set of priorities and insufficient organizational capacities of international tribunals as sponsors of post-conflict forensic investigations.

In the aftermath of this painful, "experimental" phase, the needs of families of the missing have emerged (or *re*emerged, if we consider the Argentine experience part of the same timeline) as central to the dialogue about forensics and human rights. Courts and international tribunals are exceedingly important public forums in which forensic evidence can "speak" both to the truth about atrocities and the importance of the rule of law. They are also key avenues for justice for the surviving victims of human rights violations, but they by no means exhaust all of their claims for justice. Nor do they exhaust the purposes that forensic science can serve.

Families of the Missing and Other Mourners: Lost Bodies, Enduring Grief

Though they may have felt frustrated and ignored by the way exhumations were initially carried out in the former Yugoslavia, family members of the missing people were not exactly voiceless. From Bosnia to Croatia to Kosovo, they organized into associations to share information, provide mutual support, and articulate their demands to the organizations involved in the search for the missing, including forensic teams. Many of these groups, such as the Mothers of Srebrenica and Mothers of Vukovar, were female-led and consciously emulated the tactics of the Madres de Plaza de Mayo in Argentina. They carried placards with pictures of their missing husbands and sons, and they drew their moral authority partly from a traditional view of mothers as the affective center, or hearth-tender, of the family.[60] The creation of the International Commission on Missing Persons in 1996, at the behest of Bill Clinton, gave these family associations an important collaborator invested in working with them, building their institutional capacities, and framing their work as a crucial part of a larger "reconciliation" agenda for the region.[61]

The commission's long-standing project to identify the bodies from mass graves in the former Yugoslavia has answered calls for greater attention to the needs of families of the missing. In the process, it has also altered the landscape of international forensic work. The many years and millions of dollars that the commission has spent on identification of remains are unprecedented and dwarf the efforts in places where other large-scale genocides have taken place, such as Rwanda or Cambodia: a difference that still causes discomfort among both forensic experts and scholars of their work.[62] As Wagner describes at length, these identification efforts have also led to major advances in the application of DNA testing and analysis, developing database methods and other technologies that have since been used at the site of the World Trade Center attacks in New York and elsewhere.

Wagner's sensitive ethnography leads to another important conclusion: the necessary and well-intentioned focus on "families of the missing," depending how that term is construed, can risk oversimplifying the many different identities and ties present among communities of survivors. Religious and ethnic identities, exile and displacement, rural versus urban homes, gender, politics, and many other factors help make one group of families different from another and add heterogeneity to the experiences represented by any single family.

Family members may be more likely than anyone else to be traumatized by kidnappings and disappearances, and also to take charge of the search for a missing person's whereabouts (whether he is living or dead). They are also those most likely to face barriers to normal participation in a country's legal institutions when people have gone missing because of the irregular status that things like marriages and property ownership take on when a person is unaccounted for.[63] Scientifically, family ties are also uniquely useful in establishing positive identifications of remains through DNA testing. However, many other forms of community, from church congregations to political networks, desperately want to see the bodies of "their own" comrades, colleagues, congregants, lovers, and so on identified—and their shared history remembered—and are thus likely to join in the recovery efforts of those who have direct kinship ties to the missing. The grief of these other mourners, and their needs, must also be taken into account.

Using the word "mourners" may make it sound, to some ears, as if I operate under the assumption that missing persons are actually dead. Though often rumors that the missing or disappeared are alive—whether spread by hopeful survivors or lying perpetrators (or both)—turn out not to be true, there are indeed cases where people believed to be dead turn up in clandestine prisons, in exile, or in hiding. Families of the missing have often rightly been skeptical of the motives of anyone seeking to proclaim, without hard evidence, that their loved ones are dead. Indeed, in some situations a desire to resolve the issue of missing persons for political purposes, or for bureaucratic expediency, has led to premature declarations of death.

In order to respect the hopes of families and their demand for scientific proof, forensic experts use the phrases "missing person" and "families of the missing" in any case where an individual's body has not been located and positively identified—even when no survivors from the particular massacre have been found. Nevertheless, any person with a loved one absent from her home or her life—anyone who lives in doubt, fearing the worst—is, to my mind, in mourning. Mourning does not require certainty about whether missing persons are alive or dead. The sad truth is that the options for those without solid information—imagining the return of the beloved while fearing that he is being tortured or starved, or mourning him as dead—are equally terrible; and both are forms of mourning.[64] Though every stakeholder in forensic investigations has legitimate claims and an important role to play, no other person or institution has the same intimate connection with the victims of atrocity as their mourners. No one, except the dead, has suffered as much. Humanitarian concern, respect for the rule of law, and international sympathy all help to motivate forensic investigations. But none of them are as limitless, or as urgent, as the grief of those who have lost their husbands, wives, sisters, brothers, children, grandchildren, lovers, and friends.

Transitional Governments: Stability through Exhumations?

The nations where mass graves are located are often embroiled in wars or other violent conflicts. One need only look at the spread of conflict from Rwanda into Congo, or the continuing threats against journalists, human rights workers, and forensic investigators in Guatemala to see that declarations of peace tend to be relative rather than absolute. Supposedly "*post*-conflict" nations may still face deep divisions among their populace, refugee and other humanitarian crises, ongoing security concerns, and a host of other challenges. They must meet these challenges with very little institutional capacity, or with institutions widely distrusted by the population because of corruption and violence.[65]

Emerging democracies are often unstable, still confronting the painful and divisive legacy of the past. In many cases, human rights violators, politicians, military leaders, and sometimes businesses and foreign powers have vested interests in keeping that past silent or misunderstood; a shamed and traumatized population may also wish to get out from under the shadow of its recent history. Even in cases where mass graves are being exhumed in a relatively stable environment, such as contemporary Spain, citizens revisiting contentious histories after decades of official denial often provoke significant political and social upheaval, even if that upheaval does not reach crisis proportions.[66]

In recent years, a number of voices have emerged from within the forensic community that advocate not just striking a balance between the needs of courts and families, but also looking at how forensic investigation serves the needs of post-authoritarian or "transitional" governments.[67] For example, as Wagner explains, the International Commission on Missing Persons has increasingly framed its work in the former Yugoslavia in terms of "social reconstruction" and "transitional justice."[68] Kirsten Juhl and Odd Einar Olsen attempt to resolve some of the tensions that have emerged between evidence collection for trials and the identification of individual bodies, framing both as efforts "To (re)establish a public trust in societal institutions."[69] This trust, in turn, serves a larger goal they call "societal safety," which they define as a state's capacity to carry out its "critical social functions" and protect its citizens.[70] In this view, the broader social and political purposes of mass grave exhumations can ultimately be interpreted in terms of rebuilding a secure, democratic society. According to this narrative of cause and effect, the identification of the missing provides traumatized populations with truth and healing, in the process rebuilding their trust in authorities. In the mean time, trials help discredit and isolate the most violent members of the outgoing regime, reestablishing the rule of law and turning the page from times of conflict to an age of rebuilding.

This narrative is compelling; however, it is also based more on hope and faith than on evidence from contemporary sites of mass grave exhumations. No one has studied, across context and in a generalizable way, the relationship between international forensic investigations and a nation's stability—perhaps because isolating the particular role played by exhumations from the many other factors that impact the stability of post-conflict governments would be next to impossible. A negative version of Juhl and Olsen's thesis might be easier to support: uninvestigated mass graves of contemporary and even some older atrocities (as in Spain) tend to become sites of conflict, continuing reminders if not sources of political instability. This reasoning is among the motivators for recent exhumations of past atrocities in Cyprus and Spain,[71] as well as ongoing forensic work in places such as Argentina and the former Yugoslavia. But claiming that unexhumed mass graves are sites of ongoing tensions is not the same as proving that exhuming them creates stability and trust in institutions. Most of the cases already studied by scholars of culture and politics (the former Yugoslavia, Spain, former Soviet republics) and in my own ongoing research (Chile, Poland) suggest that exhumations *alter*, but rarely resolve, dialogue about the legitimacy, institutional capacity, and commitment to human rights of post-conflict and transitional governments.[72]

Observers and experts within the forensic community have argued for the necessity of allowing this dialogue to proceed without attempting to resolve it. Stover and Shigekane, while pushing for an international institution to guide forensic scientists in their search for the missing, nevertheless sound a caution-ary note: the new institution, they warn, "must not internationalize the search for the missing to such an extent that it undermines the capacity of local gov-ernmental and non-governmental institutions to develop culturally appropri-ate responses to what are ultimately local problems."[73] Andreas Kleiser, of the International Commission on Missing Persons, also worries that when inter-national forensic organizations are too visible for too long, they leave citizens with the impression that the new government is unable—or worse, unwilling—to answer their claims by itself.[74] His perspective is most likely informed by the rocky history of ICMP's gradual transfer of responsibilities to the Missing Persons Institute, a national organization put together from groups on opposite sides of Bosnia's ethnic dividing lines. According to Wagner, this transition has taken place in a climate in which Bosnia would not be seen as a "unified polity" or viable part of Europe unless it could sustain in-country institutions capable of treating citizens "uniformly as Bosnians."[75]

It also seems wise to be more skeptical of states than Juhl and Olsen urge us to be. While they equate "society itself" with "state authorities,"[76] in fact the needs of a divided and wounded society and the needs of a consolidating state can pull away from one another. In Chile, serious errors in the identification of *desaparecidos* exposed the worst instincts of the new democratic govern-ment—concealment, insecurity, arrogance, and insensitivity to the experiences of families and mourners. In Rwanda, the government passed a law in 2008 that all remains of genocide victims must be buried in state-funded genocide memorials meant to serve as both markers of transition and warnings to future generations—but with no option for survivors to opt out of the public purpose chosen for their dead and pursue other forms of burial or commemoration.[77]

Though nearly everyone living in a conflict zone (except, perhaps, those who feed off of ongoing violence) directly benefits from a stable state and good governance, trials for human rights violators, identification of the dead, and other forensic outcomes do not all harmonize under the common banner of nation building. Trials and identifications can be divisive as well as healing;[78] exhumations and mass commemorations can stir up nationalist fervor,[79] and "expos[e] . . . conflicting political cultures."[80] Yet they are also, unmistakably, part of that "many-layered thing" called justice.[81]

Transitional governments are extremely important stakeholders in forensic investigations because allowing independent, competent experts to exhume the evidence of atrocities is among the clearest and most material signals a government can send that it is serious about coming to terms with the past. For forensic teams, helping these governments achieve stability and credibility with the population—at least when they are sincere partners deserving of such credibility—should be a powerful motivation. The alternative to stability, a descent back into violence (or the spread of violence into neighboring countries, as has happened with Rwanda and Congo) harms everyone. But transitional governments are not, in fact, capable of bundling together all of the needs of different stakeholders into a cohesive whole, and the needs of particular state institutions will not always be the same as those of a complex society.

Other Stakeholders

Hundreds if not thousands of individuals make up the courts and tribunals, families and mourners, and transitional governments described here as major stakeholders in international forensic investigations. Yet I have also left out a number of groups, many of them undeniably important to the politics of post-conflict societies. It is worth considering these groups briefly and explaining why I have not made them a focus of this analysis of international forensic investigations.

First, there are the perpetrators of human rights violations. The people responsible for massacres and the concealment of remains in mass graves seem like natural stakeholders in what happens to this evidence. This is especially true, of course, when there is a real chance of trials and convictions. But even when perpetrators will never stand trial, exhumations may be a crucial part of a process in which the authors of organized violence—whether dictatorial regimes, paramilitary death squads, liberation armies, or another group—have their righteousness, authority, and version of history discredited before a global audience.

Perpetrators are unique "stakeholders," however, because in almost every case their stake lies in *not* having forensic investigations take place. They have sometimes gone to great lengths to tamper with graves and make investigations more difficult (as in Bosnia and more recently in Afghanistan).[82] In rare cases, forensic evidence may expose that survivors or political organizations have exaggerated the scale of violence, or minimized the extent to which their own "side" was also involved. But for the most part, perpetrators will act, if at all, primarily as obstacles to investigations. These obstacles should be taken seriously—especially cases such as Guatemala, where the armed forces have made direct threats against forensic investigators and their local partners.[83] But the perpetrators of violence and creators of mass graves have not influenced the ethical and scientific dialogue about international forensic investigation in a way that approaches the rich contributions of tribunals, families and mourners, and transitional governments.

Perhaps legal scholar David Kennedy is also right, however, that the classic human rights triad of perpetrator, victim, and bystander is too simplistic;[84] we should also ask what stake there is in forensic investigations for the many people who are neither clearly victims nor perpetrators, who were victims at one moment and perpetrators in another,[85] or who were silently complicit in a program of atrocity that they felt helpless to oppose. The popular term "bystanders" rarely does these people justice: it conjures up an image of someone standing idly by and watching atrocities unfold, and thus implies a judgment that is often (though not always) unwarranted by the complex forces that keep most individuals from resisting authoritarian regimes and other systems of oppression.[86] As Juhl and Olsen write, beyond the dead and their immediate families, "justice is . . . also about those victims who barely escaped ending up in a mass grave." They continue:

> And it is about those associated with the perpetrators by group affiliation who did not commit any crime—the innocent German, Serb or Hutu, etc. Although the legal principle may be that you are innocent until proven guilty, in group conflicts you are guilty by group affiliation until proven innocent. To avoid collective guilt in these groups, it is in their interest to have mass graves excavated, the story told and the perpetrators prosecuted.[87]

Other institutions that can influence international forensic investigations, and come to have stakes in them, include universities and media outlets. Universities play a crucial role in the formation of forensic scientists and also promote research that can advance new methods and technologies for the field. They also impact the practice of forensic work in more subtle ways. Due to increasing interest in forensic science (in part because of television shows such as *CSI*),[88] new students increasingly come to forensics from backgrounds in cultural anthropology, archaeology, or departments even "further afield" from the sciences;[89] the increasingly interdisciplinary nature of many degree programs with a forensic science component (and the growth of human rights as an established, interdisciplinary, and well-funded research field) also provides opportunities for forensic scientists to interact with scholars of human rights, refugee studies, and other related themes.

Yet universities can also be bound up in conflict and the complex politics of transitional justice in ways that complicate their contributions to human rights investigations. In Chile, for example, the medical school of the Universidad de Chile plays so important a role in promoting forensic science in the country that for many years of Chile's history the chair of the university's medico-legal science department also served concurrently as the director of Chile's nationalized system of morgues.[90] Most of the anthropologists, archaeologists, and the one forensic odontologist would make up the short-lived human rights forensic team, the Grupo de Antropología Forense (GAF), were graduates of the Universidad de Chile. Yet a climate of fear descended upon Chilean universities during the 1973–90 military dictatorship, when Pinochet replaced many university rectors with military personnel, and university students and professors featured prominently in the ranks of the *desaparecidos*. This atmosphere continued through the initial years of transition to democracy, when the GAF began exhuming graves of the disappeared and executed victims of the Pinochet regime. The group thus had little access to the peer networks, resources, and expertise at their alma mater.[91]

The role universities have played in Chile's story of human rights and forensic identification—both in terms of their presence and their absence—has required serious reexamination after major scientific questions were raised about the forensic identifications of *desaparecidos* conducted by both the Grupo de Antropología Forense and state authorities.[92] Ultimately, the process of discovering and addressing these errors has also involved an international network of universities, including forensic scientists from the University of Glasgow and Universidad de Granada who reported irregularities in the identifications, as well as university laboratories in Texas and Innsbruck where recent DNA analyses have been performed.[93]

Mass media, too, can exert significant and often ambiguous influence over forensic investigations without themselves being direct stakeholders in the work. In places such as Argentina, Chile, and Spain, early media coverage of exhumations related to human rights cases—often strategically courted by the people and organizations conducting the work—have stirred public fascination and probably helped garner acceptance of the projects.[94] In a climate of heavy media coverage, governments are less able to ignore the visibility of mass graves and their importance to a national conversation. As Renshaw, Congram and Bruno, and others have pointed out, however, the media narrative about human rights investigations has (perhaps inevitably) relied on tropes that do not necessarily do justice to the scientific or political complexity of the work. Exhumation coverage features scenes of grim, heroic forensic experts who "make the corpses tell stories,"[95] while standing above the messy politics of the place where they apply their expertise. The place itself is often portrayed in broad, stereotypical strokes as violent and uncivilized, while the forensic investigator is an emissary from a world of civilization, expertise, and expansive moral sentiments.

What about the "international community," so often invoked in discussions of global intervention? One obvious problem with analyzing this "community" as a stakeholder is the vagueness of the term, which can refer to, among other things: the economic and political relationships that bind states together, often said to have reached an unprecedented level in the age of globalization; the international networks of communication, funding, and solidarity that exist among human rights activists and humanitarians; as well as a philosophical attitude—sometimes called "cosmopolitanism"—imagining individual human beings as part of a moral community that transcends national boundaries.[96] In the war zones and post-conflict areas where mass grave investigations usually take place, the international community tends to be most visible in the roles played by international and humanitarian institutions such as the United Nations and the International Committee of the Red Cross, and by the governments of developed nations intervening through military, economic, or diplomatic means. Forensic teams may find themselves formally associated with these institutions and powers, which often serve as sources of funding, coordination, and security. Even in cases where forensic teams are more independent, however, they may be associated with the international community in the minds of local populations, who do not necessarily possess the tools to discern the difference between convoys of diplomats, journalists, humanitarian relief workers, and forensic teams, among others.[97]

Foreign governments have a particularly complex stake in post-conflict forensic investigations. Mass graves can be powerful reminders of the human cost of these governments' earlier failures to act. On July 11, 1995, NATO botched a long-awaited air strike against the Bosnian Serb forces surrounding Srebrenica. Over the next few days, in this territory the United Nations had declared a "safe area,"[98] Dutch peacekeepers on the ground gradually left the largely Muslim population of the Srebrenica enclave in the hands of the Serb soldiers, who separated the men and older boys from the women and children, destroyed their identity documents and other personal effects, and led them on forced marches to various sites where more than eight thousand of them were executed and buried in mass graves.[99] When forensic teams later began unearthing these graves, they found dead bodies wearing the standard-issue shoes delivered by humanitarian organizations—shoes the refugee populations came to call "*mtvare*," or "dead man's shoes."[100] These donated shoes served as a vivid reminder that the men and boys in these graves were killed after the "international community" had designated this population as in need of aid and protection. The story their graves tell is not one of invisible or unknown victims, but rather of people abandoned to a cruel fate more or less in full view of their protectors.[101]

By funding and supporting the ongoing exhumations and identification programs in Bosnia, though, the Dutch, American, and other governments have also found a way to atone for these failings. Wagner writes, "If inaction characterized the international community's response to the events of July 1995, then documenting the story of the enclave and its fall, its mass graves, and its missing has become a principle means of redressing the failure to act."[102] In contrast to official apologies, the exhumations and identifications "offer these international actors a means by which to measure their investment . . . bodies exhumed, blood samples collected, successful DNA matches."[103]

Paying attention to both the interests and impact of various international institutions is crucial to understanding most mass grave investigations. Yet "international community" is a term that seeks and usually fails to ascribe one voice to individuals in tribunal offices in The Hague and Arusha, in the White House and on Downing Street, at local Amnesty International chapters in schools and living rooms around the world, and, not at all insignificantly, gathering at mass graves as members of forensic teams. In each of these institutional and geographical settings, there are different reasons to support, oppose, or remain indifferent to forensic investigations.

Forensic teams and individual forensic experts also have their own stakes in their activities around mass graves. Many practitioners clearly have deep personal commitments to human rights, as well as respect and sympathy for the dead and their mourners. Sometimes a historical outlook on their profession informs their sense that anthropologists and other experts in human biology have an obligation to pursue justice wherever great crimes have been rationalized through pseudoscientific ideas about race and ethnicity.[104] As in any professional pursuit, including all forms of humanitarianism, there are also less altruistic motivations for practitioners to get involved—though the fact that these motivations are not altruistic does not necessarily mean they are a predictor of unethical behavior in the field. Along with media exposure, participation in an international forensic investigation can confer impressive international experience and a paycheck while an expert is on "vacation" from her regular job; it also provides the opportunity to write up findings and impressions for publication, the thrill of work in a combat zone, and the chance to see oneself as a hero.[105] My own tendency toward "critical generosity" is undoubtedly shaped by the fact that I have had more contact with full-time employees of organizations such as Physicians for Human Rights and various Latin American forensic teams, and with thoughtful experts such as Clyde Snow and Clea Koff who have actively sought opportunities for public reflection, than with the short-term "hired guns" sometimes brought in on missions in crisis zones.[106]

On an organizational level, too, moral and political commitments always mix together with other vested interests. Whether it is Physicians for Human Rights, the International Commission on Missing Persons, one of the Latin American teams, or another group, these are organizations with administrative and field staff to pay and offices and equipment to maintain, as well as other programs that are perhaps even more poorly funded than their forensic units. It is most likely impossible to separate the very real moral imperative these organizations feel to offer their expertise to people and nations in need, as well as to contribute to the ongoing development of the field, from the stake they naturally acquire in keeping themselves relevant and funded. These factors must be kept in mind when looking at the specific decisions forensic teams make in a particular time and place. But at the level of theories or broad characterizations, it is simply too simplistic to champion an ideal of "pure" motivation in the abstract while criticizing all of the other needs and interests that arise in any organizational culture.

Of course, motivation is only part of the equation. More sophisticated analyses, often informed by postmodern critiques of both science and humanitarianism, point out that, regardless of their own best intentions, forensic scientists participate in a broader culture of "knowledge production"—a culture into which ideology is inescapably woven. Among the features of this culture are an overconfidence in the potential of the scientific method to *reveal* facts rather than *construct* desired narratives, and a starry-eyed belief in human rights and international law—one that tends to justify the intervention of rich, powerful countries in the affairs of others while bypassing a deep understanding of colonialism (historical or present-day) or an internal critique of injustice within the rich, aid-giving societies.

These perspectives should be taken seriously by anyone examining the work of scientists or human rights activists—and perhaps even *more* seriously when one is looking at the intersection of those two worlds. Forensic evidence is neither fully neutral nor purely objective. It enters a landscape of contested narratives and is interpreted differently depending on those narratives; it thus provides uneven and unpredictable political and moral capital depending on how stakeholders deploy it. These observations were necessary and original when scholars such as Paperno and Wagner, drawing on rich evidence from the contests around forensic evidence in the former Soviet Union and Bosnia, began making them. Since then, however, the same basic critique has begun to appear with ever less contextual information at hand and a seemingly willful ignorance of new developments, such as the field's own reckoning with the sub-jectivity of its methods in the aftermath of the National Academy of Sciences report. The repetition of these same well-trodden theoretical perspectives threatens to render stale what is still a new field of inquiry—humanistic schol-arship about forensic investigation—while closing off opportunities for pro-ductive dialogue between nonscientist scholars and forensic practitioners.[107]

Too much recent scholarship about human rights and humanitarianism seems to turn a willful blind eye to the fact that individuals involved in these fields, with forensic experts being no exception, are often deeply and vocally self-critical. When academics present "new," jargon-laden critiques of humani-tarian practice that are already well known and much discussed in the field, they rob these professionals of their heterogeneous voices and ignore their agency (the very sins that, ironically, these critics have in the past accurately accused humanitarians of doing to refugees and other aid recipients). For those willing to listen, there is much to learn from forensic experts themselves about their accomplishments, failures, and most importantly the many things that can look like both accomplishments *and* failures, depending on the moment and the angle of one's approach.

Writing History, Grave by Grave

A stakeholder-focused approach to the analysis of forensic investigations sheds a practical light on the specific actors and interests that lie behind some of the conceptual vocabularies used in the study of post-conflict politics and human rights activism. This section and the next look at historical or collective memory, as well as capacity building, as important discourses used to describe and justify the actions of forensic teams. By identifying the stakeholders that promote, and are sometimes the subjects of, this discourse, the two sections attempt to clarify the interests and purposes behind efforts undertaken in the name of collective memory and capacity building.

The information produced by scientific investigations of mass graves can shed a crucial light on historical disputes between warring parties or oppressors and their victims. Forensic teams have contributed evidence to many truth commissions and fact-finding bodies. The mission statement of Physicians for Human Rights' International Forensic Program lists, as one of its primary aims, "to establish a historic record grounded in science and resistant to revisionism."[108] The forensic anthropologist Clea Koff goes one step further: to her, the effort "to tell the whole story and get the facts on record" is not just one mission among many, but rather constitutes the "human rights perspective" on mass grave investigations.[109] "Human rights," in keeping with Koff's many references to translating or speaking on behalf of the dead, becomes a particular way of writing history: fighting the lies of the violent with the truth of the victims.

This definition of a human rights perspective on forensic work envisions a very particular political context. It applies best where a government or dominant group has committed the majority of the violence and has subsequently attempted to cover up its crimes with a distorted version of history. In these cases, as in Haglund's testimony at The Hague, scientific evidence of human rights violations can be the most important challenge to the revisionist narrative (or "official story," as in the title of Luis Puenzo's famous film about disappearance in Argentina).[110] Koff's idea of a single human rights perspective becomes more complicated, however, in situations where the violators never denied their wrongdoings, but rather saw them as justified (as is the case with the September 11, 2001, attacks on the United States)—or, even more commonly, where the story forensic investigators seek to piece together is one of widespread and multilateral violence. In a divided society each faction will see every grave that is exhumed and every body identified through the lens of its own view of history. Each of these "historical communities" may feel it has a story of victimization—a human rights story—to tell.

If exhumation comes to be seen as a form of historical research or testimony, there are a series of practical decisions to be made about what *form* of history is being pursued. Derek Congram and Dawnie Wolfe Steadman, forensic anthropologists who have been involved in the exhumation of victims from Spain's 1936–39 Civil War and the ensuing years of Francisco Franco's dictatorship, write, "If a Spanish organization envisions the recovery of historical memory as a matter of documenting the scale of the atrocities against the Republicans, then the logical objective would be to excavate as many large mass graves as possible, even if there is little chance the victims could be identified."[111] If, however, the goal were to identify specific individuals—and thus allow their families to receive reparations payments from the Spanish government—forensic teams would probably be best off exhuming smaller graves where some documentation exists about the victims who might be buried there. In other words, the people requesting exhumations of Spanish victims have faced a conceptual question of whether history is best told through numbers, or through the representative stories of particular individuals—a tension that has always been present in the design of memorials and other markers of atrocity.[112] Congram and Steadman add, "Neither approach is morally, ethically or professionally incorrect but will certainly deliver different outcomes."[113] These outcomes, they might have added, differ not so much morally, ethically, or professionally, as they do in terms of the *political meanings* they will lend to forensic investigations.

The ongoing Spanish Civil War exhumations can help clarify the real stakeholders who shape and employ the rhetoric of historical memory or a "duty to history." In recent years, various "historical memory associations" have sprung up around Spain.[114] Some of the members of these groups are direct descendants of people killed by Franco's forces, while others are historians or concerned citizens.[115] These associations have been the loudest voices demanding exhumations.

The Spanish case, like Argentina, has featured conflicts between families and among the broader community of mourners: most famously, the controversy over whether to exhume the suspected grave of the poet Federico García Lorca. To many historians and members of the general public, Garcia Lorca's grave has special historical significance. The poet and dramatist is known worldwide, and the killing of an artist and known homosexual contributes to an understanding of Francoist repression as a cultural "purge" rather than simply (as the official narrative long portrayed it) as acts of war. Amid the wave of new exhumations, historical memory activists, a trade union, as well as the families of some individuals who may have been buried alongside García Lorca eagerly pushed for exhumations at his suspected gravesite, identified three decades earlier by a man who claimed to have helped dig the grave.[116] Members of García Lorca's own family, however, initially opposed the exhumation, citing concern over the future "YouTube" spectacle of his bones being lifted out of the grave.[117]

García Lorca's own niece, who is the head of the García Lorca Foundation, argued passionately against constructing a history of Franco's repression that elevated Lorca above other victims. In a letter to the *New Yorker*, Laura García-Lorca outlined an alternative, fiercely democratic vision of history: "We would choose to leave Lorca where he is, in the company of all victims, whether named or unnamed, whether remembered silently by their relatives or forgotten because they have none. We feel that the best way to remember all victims of the terrible crimes committed by Franco's troops is to preserve and protect this burial ground, where Lorca is one victim among many."

The controversy over García Lorca's grave proved largely needless, at least in the short term: exhumations at the alleged gravesite were called to a halt in late 2009 because archaeologists found no bodies or body parts in the area where García Lorca was thought to be buried. It appears that the layer of hard rock beneath the surface soil in that area would have made it impossible to dig a grave there in the first place.[118] There are, nevertheless, lessons to draw from the history of this nongrave, among them that there are nearly as many "historical approaches" to mass graves as there are mourners and other stakeholders, each with their own opinions on the means by which history should be written and the political vision that should inform it.

When communities of mourners begin to form organizations, their interests often undergo a transformation in both language and content. For example, the fact that a historian helped to found the most prominent Spanish group advocating exhumations undoubtedly had some influence over that group's decision to frame its demands in terms of Spain's need for "historical memory." Yet other Spanish historians have also been influential in disputing the very idea of historical memory and competing organizations define the concept quite differently.[119] According to Layla Renshaw, the most prominent Spanish historical memory association, the Asociación para la Recuperación de la Memoria Histórica, has developed an "external discourse" that advocates exhumation in the name of "personal history, identity, 'closure,' and the fulfillment of familial duty."[120] The organization "seek[s] to avoid charges of political axe-grinding"—charges they presumably would face if they spoke more often of the "collective identities" of the dead "as socialists, atheists, or trade union members."[121] Precisely because of this somewhat depoliticized discourse, however, a competing, Communist Party-affiliated group, the Foro por la Memoria, has accused the Asociación of being "'neoliberals of memory' who, through their focus on the individual, engage in the 'privatisation' of suffering."[122]

These ideological differences between family associations in Spain resemble disputes that split apart the Madres de Plaza de Mayo in Argentina. The conflicts are fueled by demographic differences between mourners and competing traditions of activism that existed long before any exhumation, but they are also revived and sometimes reconfigured through the forensic process. Writing history may, indeed, be an important part of human rights work in the post-conflict context; forensic science has an undeniably important part to play in this work. Over time, however, it becomes difficult to sustain the idea that this work is as simple as a triumph of the "collective memory" of the victims over the revisionism of the perpetrators. The construction of history, even among those who have been victimized, is a contest between different stakeholders over whose history counts and how to remember it.

Capacity Building

Some experts rightly worry about forensic science becoming one more facet of an aid "industry" already associated with elite cadres of aid workers parachuting into conflict areas for short-term work, applying a set of highly technical methods in contexts where they may be poorly understood or culturally inappropriate, and leaving behind a sense of dependency. In response, forensic organizations have joined many others in humanitarian fields in embracing the language of "capacity building."[123] The capacity-building ethic stresses that among the most crucial tasks of international experts is to build and improve local institutions.[124] For forensic teams, this largely means teaching local health professionals, investigators, and sometimes even mourners to do the type of investigative and identification work that international teams have undertaken over the past few decades.[125]

All of the forensic organizations mentioned thus far, including Physicians for Human Rights, the Argentine Forensic Anthropology Team, and the International Commission on Missing Persons, along with newer organizations such as Inforce, are increasingly acting as consultants and trainers. During the time I worked at Physicians for Human Rights, major conflicts were raging in Iraq, Darfur, and Congo—places that were too unstable and/or dangerous to permit any large-scale mass grave investigations (as well as, in the case of Darfur and Congo, having few sources of funding for this sort of project). The organization was, instead, performing "assessments" in Iraq and Mexico: identifying probable grave locations, explaining to the potential sponsors of forensic investigations what kinds of specialists, equipment, time, and money they might require, surveying the landscape of family and religious organizations, and seeing what level of forensic expertise—and what forensic facilities and equipment, if any—each country could offer.[126] Like the Argentine team and Inforce, Physicians for Human Rights was also developing a curriculum for use in training local forensic and other health professionals in the science, politics, and ethics of mass grave investigation.[127]

In planning for the future, it seems, these organizations are thinking less of the iconic scenes of the 1980s and 1990s, documented in Giles Peress's photos from Bosnia and in Koff's memoir, in which foreign forensic experts bend down over the bodies of massacre victims in distant lands.[128] The scenes of their daily work are now as likely to take place in the classroom and the laboratory as at the gravesite, and when it is the gravesite, local partners are nearly always working alongside the international experts.

The capacity-building approach answers concerns about the scope of international involvement with a plan for limited engagement. The teams who adopt it aspire to leave well-trained and well-supported forensic experts on the ground in every place they visit. In some cases, the approach can also help establish new nongovernmental organizations working on a national or regional level, such as the forensic teams that Clyde Snow and the Argentine team trained in various Latin American countries throughout the 1980s, 1990s, and into the 2000s.[129] These regional organizations combine new levels of expertise with sensitivity to the particular context in which they work. They can also generate atypical flows of humanitarian knowledge from one relatively poor country to another: the Peruvian Forensic Anthropology Team's trainings for prosecutors, judges, human rights workers, and investigators in the Philippines, Nepal, and Congo is one example.[130]

South Africa's Missing Persons Task Team, which works under the state's National Prosecuting Authority, is currently working to identify disappeared and executed victims of Apartheid-era violence. The Argentine team trained the group, and an Argentine anthropologist, Claudia Bisso, resides in South Africa and works with the Missing Persons Task Team on a long-term basis.[131] I visited the team in March 2012, as they searched for the remains of Charles Sandile Ngqobe. Ngqobe was a member of the Umkhonto we Sizwe (or "MK"), the armed wing of the African National Congress. He was shot in 1986 by South African security forces. The forensic team, exhuming what they suspected was Ngqobe's grave at a small cemetery in Soweto township, was accompanied by a group of ex-MK guerillas who wanted to aid in the search for a fallen comrade. These former liberation soldiers, who often accompany the team at the gravesite and in meetings with families of the missing, arrived for the exhumation attired in clean fatigues, berets, and black boots. Far from mere observers, they did much of the manual labor at the gravesite and, as one member of the team explained, provided a sense of security for a group of all-female, mixed-race investigators exhuming a politically charged grave in a country with high rates of rape, robbery, and other violence.

While, on the one hand, the team was relying on Bisso, their Argentine colleague, to make some of the tough calls at the gravesite and watch over the work of younger investigators, the symbiotic and quite affectionate relationship between the team and the former guerillas seemed like a benefit that only a trusted, local institution could achieve—strengthened by the history the team's director, Madeleine Fullard, has with both the anti-Apartheid cause and as a researcher for South Africa's Truth and Reconciliation Commission. In many ways, it was an ideal vision of capacity building: the expertise and quality control that circulate through international networks mixing together with the local knowledge, trust, and sustainability that comes with in-country leadership. Clyde Snow argued that the most successful international forensic teams are "indigenous to their own countries," "properly trained," and "independently working with families."[132]

The capacity-building approach can also address a number of practical concerns about the relationship between forensic teams and less "expert" people involved in exhumation. In countries dotted with mass graves, international forensic teams are almost never able to conduct exhumations on a scale or in a timeframe that will satisfy all stakeholders. In Argentina and Colombia, forensic teams have had to investigate graves of *desaparecidos* that were already dug up by local authorities with no forensic training or inappropriate training.[133] These authorities destroyed evidence and clues to identity and sometimes even reburied the bodies in new, anonymous graves[134]—in effect, "re-disappearing" them. Forensic teams can use a capacity-building approach to engage with the authorities that have made these missteps, training them for better work in the future, including on cases not related to human rights violations.

In Iraq and elsewhere, communities of mourners have sometimes taken it upon themselves to dig the bodies out of mass graves. It is no surprise they would do so: the future of their countries is often uncertain, and the interest of foreign states and international institutions fickle. In the meantime, the need to have answers, to follow important religious precepts regarding burial, and to restore dignity to their dead has been deferred for too long. These local-run exhumations have caused dismay among forensic experts, who are understandably concerned about the destructive effects that poor exhumation practices can have on both evidence and identifications.[135]

Though the media occasionally portrays these amateur exhumations as a sort of mob scene, John Hunter and Barrie Simpson report that in Iraq, at least, many of the community-led exhumations have been highly organized affairs, led by educated leaders who did their best to keep records and create protocols.[136] Nevertheless, forensic experts have legitimate ethical concerns about the extent to which they should assist "unscientific" exhumations that fall short of their own standards and may even destroy crucial evidence.[137] There is humanitarian spirit in the idea of allowing mourners to take charge in ending a situation that may seem intolerable, even blasphemous, to them. Yet reliable scientific methods are crucial to the professionalism of forensic experts and often to their sense of what is owed to future generations.

A capacity-building approach allows these experts to work with families and other informal groups through trainings and other interventions, without having to take sole responsibility for the outcomes, scientific and otherwise, of every exhumation. Forensic teams in a capacity-building role have more leeway to intervene in exhumations conducted under compromised circumstances, without "impos[ing] an alternative strategy . . . guaranteed to lose the sympathy of the very people whose support is essential."[138]

By casting themselves as trainers and institution-builders, organizations such as Physicians for Human Rights and the Argentine team can reach out on a broad international basis even as they scale back the time, cost, and staff burnout involved in undertaking massive exhumation projects like the ones in the former Yugoslavia.[139] They can also buy themselves crucial political wiggle-room. In the Introduction, I described how Physicians for Human Rights and some of their colleague organizations distanced themselves from forensic work in Iraq after the fall of the Hussein regime because of security concerns and objections to the way coalition forces approached the issues of missing persons, international justice, and reconstruction. The capacity-building approach can allow human rights groups to have some impact on forensic investigations in places where they are not willing to establish a presence of their own: Inforce, for example, has led a sequence of workshops to train Iraqis in forensic investigation, but it has held these trainings off-site in the United Kingdom, Bosnia, and South Africa.[140]

Questions about Capacity: A View from Chile

The capacity-building approach also has its limits. In some places the level of forensic expertise and facilities on the ground is close to nothing, whether because of endemic poverty or the destruction violent conflict wreaks on a nation's infrastructure.[141] In Afghanistan and Darfur, among other regions, the capacity of local institutions to participate in rigorous and impartial investigations is close to nonexistent. When and if the graves in these places are investigated in earnest, international experts are likely to be at the forefront of the process.

Even in countries with highly developed governmental and scientific institutions, it can be difficult to discern the level of oversight necessary. When are local experts truly "capacitated"? When should the international experts leave?

The Latin American experience with in-country forensic teams, starting with the Argentine team, has largely been hailed as a success story. Argentina's neighbor Chile, however, is a more problematic example of the diffusion of forensic knowledge. In some ways, creating a human rights forensic team in Chile should have been easier than in poorer Latin American countries such as Peru and Guatemala. Compared to these countries, Chile possessed significant existing forensic infrastructure, a robust and institutionalized human rights sector, and, by the early 1990s, a relatively (though far from perfectly) safe atmosphere in which investigations could be conducted. Unlike Bosnia, moreover, Chile did not have multiple ethnic groups separately pursuing identification of "their" dead. The country's surprisingly bumpy road toward an identification process that could serve all of its stakeholders is worth a closer look, especially given the famed success of the "Latin American model."

In 1988, Chile's right-wing dictator Augusto Pinochet was defeated by a plebiscite, paving the way for democratic elections and the 1990 inauguration of Pinochet's first democratic successor, Patricio Aylwin. A group of young anthropologists and archaeologists saw the democratic transition as a chance to begin independent, rigorous forensic investigations.

For some of the group's members, this work was a personal calling. When I met with one of the founders, anthropologist Isabel Reveco, in late 2012, she had recently attended a memorial service for Jenny Barra Rosales, a childhood friend and leftist activist who disappeared in 1977.[142] Barra was the first female *desaparecida* to be identified by Chile's state forensic service, which sent samples of the fragments of her remains that were found in abandoned mine to a DNA laboratory in Innsbruck, Austria.[143] Reveco told me that throughout her years of exhuming and analyzing the remains of *desaparecidos*, she had always hoped she might find her friend. Her career in scientific human rights work was in some ways a substitute for the political activism she avoided when she was younger—in other words, for being more like Jenny.[144] Other members of the group had seen family members detained,[145] or been detained and tortured themselves.[146]

The Chileans arranged for Clyde Snow and the Argentine team, who had already begun some work in the north of Chile, to offer them trainings.[147] In 1989, the Grupo Chileno de Antropología Forense (Chilean Forensic Anthropology Group), or GAF, was formed, largely subscribing to the Argentine team's family-centric and multidisciplinary model.[148] However, the team's history was in other ways very different from that of the Argentines. Though the GAF took on important projects, its existence was precarious and short-lived. Lacking funding and equipment, and losing members who needed to seek a more stable income, the two remaining permanent members—Reveco and the archaeologist Iván Cáceres—had a falling out in 1994, and the group disbanded. A new Identification Unit of the state's Instituto Médico Legal (since renamed the Servicio Médico Legal), soon took over official responsibility for the work, employing Reveco as an anthropologist.[149]

In early interviews, Snow talked up the credentials of the Chilean team, whom he said came to human rights work with more scientific background than their counterparts in Argentina.[150] The Chilean identification efforts, like those in other countries, were hailed by human rights activists internationally and a subject of considerable fascination at home. They inspired a documentary, *Fernando ha vuelto* (Fernando is back), about the identification of a *desaparecido* named Fernando Olivares.[151]

The remains Chilean experts identified as belonging to Fernando Olivares had been exhumed from Patio 29, a quiet section of Santiago's vast General Cemetery. Patio 29 was among the first mass graves created to solve the body disposal "problem" after Pinochet's September 11, 1973, coup, whose initial burst of violence resulted in bodies littering the streets and alleyways of Santiago, floating down the Mapocho River, and piling up in the freezers and hallways of the capital's morgue. Less than a week after the coup, the authotities began conducting secret burials at Patio 29.[152]

The site was uniquely important in the popular imagination. The first mass burial site known to the public (rumors quickly made their way from cemetery workers to families of the *desaparecidos* and human rights groups), it sat in the heart of the capital, "secret" evidence of the regime's brutality in plain view of the public. During Pinochet's long rule, Patio 29 became a natural focal point in the search for Chile's *desaparecidos*; after the dictatorship, it remained a crucial site where the country's new leaders could demonstrate their commitment to examining past repression.[153]

Despite the site's accessibility, when Patio 29 was finally exhumed, it would prove uniquely challenging for investigators. Patio 29 was normally used for temporary burial of indigent or unidentified Chileans whose deaths had no relation to political violence; these were removed from the site every five years, and these nontechnical operations conducted by manual labor at the cemetery may have caused older remains to commingle with the bodies of Pinochet's victims. Of those victims, some were taken directly to Patio 29 for burial, while others lingered at the state morgue—another place where the bodies of political victims and the indigent may have intermixed in the chaos—where they were registered and partially autopsied.[154] These corpses were brought over from the morgue and buried at the same site, often two or three to a single coffin—a practice Pinochet would later jokingly call "great savings."[155] Finally, in 1979, in an operation cruelly labeled "television re-trieval" ("retiro de televisores"), Patio 29 was among the sites that security agents of the regime clandestinely exhumed, removing many of the remains to throw into the sea or hide in more remote graves.[156] An additional challenge at Patio 29, according to Cáceres, is that many of the unidentified bodies buried there shared common features, most of them being young men of relatively similar background and ancestry.[157]

In the early 1990s, the GAF did its most closely followed work at Patio 29, where it exhumed 107 coffins containing 126 bodies. At first the GAF, and then (after the group disbanded) the state's Identification Unit, began announcing identifications and returning these remains to families in emotional ceremonies, which were followed by reburial at private plots or at the General Cemetery's own collective memorial for the *desaparecidos*.[158] (See Figure 1.)

In 2006, however, family members of the Patio 29 *desaparecidos* were called to the central offices of the state's medico-legal services for an unwelcome an-nouncement: independent experts had found that forty-eight of the ninety-six identifications from Patio 29 were mistaken, and another thirty-seven remained in question.[159] Rumors and reports of questionable findings had, in fact, plagued the Chilean identification process from at least 1994, when scientists in Glasgow began examining plaster casts made from the crania that had been used in the Patio 29 identifications (a Chilean judge forbid the removal of actual remains

Figure 1. Part of a memorial to the *desaparecidos* in the General Cemetery in Santiago, Chile. Photograph by the author.

from the country) and conducting mitochondrial DNA tests on samples sent from Chile.[160] Fernando Olivares, whose body was the subject of *Fernando ha vuelto*, was among those who turned out to be misidentified. The body reburied in a family mausoleum was not, in fact, Fernando. In a moving show of solidarity and communal memory, his brother, Miguel, has continued leaving flowers at the same tomb, out of respect for the now unknown victim resting inside.[161]

The Patio 29 misidentifications have raised a number of difficult questions, starting with how the number of misidentifications could possibly be so high.[162] Some of the anthropological identification methods initially used in Chile are no longer considered as reliable as they once were. Principle among these is craniofacial superimposition, in which a photograph of a living individual's face is superimposed over photographic or video images of a skull.[163] Various points are then measured to see whether the person's facial appearance matches the unique underlying skeletal structure, given estimates for the amount of soft tissue generally present in different areas of the human face.[164]

When I spoke with Clyde Snow, who has worked on teams that used superimposition in making identifications,[165] he emphasized the importance of combining superimposition with other methods to obtain a reliable identification. Superimposition, he and other experts say, is more suited to *excluding* potential individuals whose facial structures do not seem to match a particular skull than to making identifications.[166] Depending whose account one believes, the early identifications in Chile may have relied too heavily on superimposition, and may have compared fewer points of correspondence between face and skull than are recommended.[167] The anthropologists were conducting this work without recourse to a significant body of research on facial and other physical variation specific to Chile's population,[168] and declaring identifications 100 percent positive when the techniques being used could not possibly yield that kind of certainty.[169]

Bound up with the scientific question of how errors made their way into laboratory results is a complex and closely related political story. While the disbanding of the GAF and the creation of a state-run identification process resolved a few practical problems (such as salary, office space, and storage for remains), the working conditions of the Identification Unit were still far from optimal in terms of funding and equipment.[170] Perhaps more damaging, according to Reveco, numerous requests for further training from the Argentines were refused (aside from a visit from one member of the team, Luis Fondebrider, in 1998).[171] Especially under the 1994–2000 presidency of Eduardo Frei Ruiz-Tagle, the Chilean state appears to have been interested in "finishing up" the reconciliation process and putting human rights issues behind it.[172] Opinions differ greatly, even among those involved in the work of the GAF and the Identification Unit, as to the effect of these pressures on the daily work of the understaffed and underequipped Identification Unit, but few of my Chilean informants doubted that the combination of pressure for results and little real support had an impact on the scientific conduct of the identifications.[173]

Even under the two Socialist Party presidents who succeeded Frei, both considered much more friendly to the cause of human rights, the medico-legal service continued to cover up reports from experts—Chilean and foreign— warning of possible misidentifications and voicing reservations about the methods and qualifications of the Identification Unit.[174] Some of these findings were passed along to Chile's Agrupación de Familiares de Detenidos Desaparecidos, the major association for families of Chile's *desaparecidos*.[175] In covering up the reports they had received—and failing even to halt the return of remains to families given the mounting evidence of errors—the medico-legal service lost the opportunity to address the crisis in a timely manner.[176] Instead, it wound up reviving a dictatorship-era sense that the institutions of the state had, in Pamela Pereira's apt phrase, been "instrumentalized for the hiding of information."[177]

The dynamic between the forensic team and the transitional government is not the only one that has come under scrutiny. Questions remain, too, about how the group interacted with Chile's highly organized families of the missing and internalized their needs. One of the stories now repeated about both the GAF and the Identification Unit is that they were "buenos chicos"—good kids—who allowed their commitment to the cause, and their urgent desire to provide information to families, to outpace their inadequate scientific capability. In other words, returning to the basic tenets of forensic ethics I outlined in the Introduction, one version of what happened in Chile is that the victim- and mourner-centric perspective of the anthropologists trying to identify the *desaparecidos*, as well as their political commitments, overtly or subtly undermined the privileged role scientific method must play in constructing forensic facts.

The story of the "buenos chicos" who got in over their heads may contain an element of truth. However, it assigns blame to specific individuals while ignoring the climate of neglect, paternalism, and lack of transparency in which they worked. It also exposes a double bind that existed from the start when it came to identifying Chile's *desparecidos*. Exhuming mass graves in the 1990s in Chile was potentially dangerous, far from remunerative, and, given the conditions of Patio 29 and other gravesites, was bound to be extraordinarily difficult. The work was thus unlikely to attract anyone *not* motivated by a deep personal commitment to human rights or (less abstractly) Pinochet's victims and their families. It was for the most part incompatible with the simultaneous pursuit of a more traditional career.[178] As former GAF member Elias Padilla remarks, "Perhaps the one criticism [of the GAF] is that we were very young, that we didn't have much experience. But everyone older who had more experience didn't want to join the group."[179] So the team was, of necessity, comprised of the sort of deeply committed, somewhat unseasoned investigator who is now often blamed—sometimes with indignation, sometimes with rueful tolerance—for the misidentifications.

To the Argentine team's mentor, Clyde Snow, the identification efforts in Chile went wrong—and departed from the model they had chosen to follow—the moment the state medico-legal authorities became involved.[180] Yet with few sustainable sources of funding and little meaningful support from the state, it is unclear what other long-term options the GAF had.[181]

Beyond the financial realities, there is a deeper cultural and historical background to the acceptance of state control over the identification process in Chile. While its neighbor Argentina had a long history of instability and violence before its "Dirty War,"[182] Chile was long considered a uniquely stable and democratic outpost in Latin America, with a robust middle class.[183] Because of this history, Chileans share what human rights lawyer Pamela Pereira calls a "culture of institutionalism."[184] Even under Pinochet, Pereira points out, the day-to-day functions of state institutions were preserved,[185] and Pinochet himself worked hard to retain the appearance, if not the substance, of legality.[186] A surprising number of Chileans I spoke with, including longtime activists and victims of state repression, felt it was preferable for Chile's newly democratic institutions to work their way through the errors and mistrust to create a credible program for identifying the *desaparecidos*. These Chileans saw the state as being under the obligation to right its own wrongs, not only in the highly public politics of trials and truth commissions, but also in the more quotidian tasks of restoring the legitimacy of the state medico-legal system and attaching names to the dead victims of state violence.

Starting in 2006, in the wake of the Patio 29 scandal, President Michelle Bachelet ordered a restructuring of the state's medico-legal service. Efforts to identify the *desaparecidos* would now include DNA analysis conducted in laboratories abroad, with oversight from an international panel of experts. The panel included the Chilean geneticist Cristián Orrego, who had called for a halt to the identification process in 2003, warning that further errors would only exacerbate the situation.[187] Also on the panel were Luis Fondebrider of the Argentine team, Thomas Parsons of the International Commission for Missing Persons, Morris Tidball-Binz of the International Committee of the Red Cross (and formerly the Argentine team), Clyde Snow, and other well-known figures in the field.[188]

The new identification efforts have had important successes, both scientific and political.[189] Breaking with a tradition of closed-door appointments made by political parties within Chile's ruling coalition, Bachelet solicited applications from the general public for the new director of the medico-legal services. The result was the hiring of Patricio Bustos, a respected surgeon and health administrator who had suffered torture, imprisonment, and exile during the Pinochet years for his leftist militancy.[190] Both Bustos and Marisol Intriago, who directs the special unit that works on the identification of *desapareci-dos*,[191] speak with great knowledge and feeling about their vision of identification work in Chile as a participatory, democratic process with many stages; it is a process they see as challenging Pinochet's legacy, which was to recast Chile's historically active relationship between citizen and state with a logic of markets and individual consumption.[192] Since 2007, Servicio Médico Legal has positively identified 148 *desaparecidos* using DNA technology and following international standards of quality assurance[193]—including 58 out of the 124 sets of remains associated with Patio 29.

Yet the controversy over identifications in Chile has rippled through the landscape of stakeholders in undeniably damaging ways. For families of the *desaparecidos*, it turned the already painful process of accepting and reburying remains into yet another source of grief and uncertainty—this time inflicted not by the perpetrators who disappeared their loved ones, but rather by the democratic institutions charged with assistance.[194] The controversy has divided the community of forensic experts in Chile,[195] with a very public exchange of charges and countercharges—mostly about scientific methods that are poorly understood by the general public—serving to further distance forensic experts from the stakeholders they are supposed to serve.

There is an important international story here too. The trainings from Clyde Snow and the Argentines, which conferred legitimacy on the emerging Grupo Chileno de Antropología Forense in the late 1980s, were not sustained enough to guarantee the scientific credentials of the new team. The project of identifying Chile's *desaparecidos* ultimately had to take steps backward in order to move forward again—for families who must once again suffer through the digging up of bodies, but also for Chilean forensic investigators who now, once again, have had to turn to foreign experts for oversight and legitimacy. In effect, Chile has been through two separate waves of post-conflict forensic capacity building: once with the construction of an independent human rights team, and once to capacitate the Chilean state itself. Capacity building may present a powerful, sustainable model for the development of a global forensic human rights infrastructure, but cases such as Chile illustrate that there is no simple transfer of expertise from one context to another, and that even capacity-building efforts are far from risk-free.

Conclusion: An Emerging Consensus, an Unfinished Conversation

International forensic investigations are balancing acts in a complex landscape of stakeholders; courts and tribunals, transitional governments, and families and other mourners, especially, can exert significant influence over how an investigation is conducted. Most forensic teams have undertaken different types of investigations at different points in their history: Physicians for Human Rights and the Argentine Forensic Anthropology Team, for example, have provided evidence to courts and tribunals. They have also, however, helped to shape a field-wide focus on families of the missing that emphasizes the identification of individual bodies and their return to families and other mourners. More recently, both groups have focused major efforts on training and capacity building for the people who will be dealing with mass graves over the long term in post-conflict nations. Forensic teams rarely pursue one overarching ideal, such as historical memory or the transition to democracy. Rather, they shape their methodologies and approaches through a mixture of their own core values and case-by-case responses to the voices of different stakeholders.

It is precisely this combination of core values with adaptation to context that makes juggling priorities in the field so difficult. For example, the community-led exhumations in Iraq might be of comfort and value to families of the missing, even as they destroy evidence that could potentially be useful to courts. How much assistance should experts offer, if they value both legal accountability and mourners' desires to rebury their dead? Moreover, if a forensic team is committed to aiding efforts at transitional justice and societal rebuilding, how do its members decide which activity has a greater claim on their limited time and resources: evidence-collection for courts, or the identification of individual bodies? Despite the enormous scholarly literature devoted to transitional justice, the concrete benefits of different courses of action, and the conflicts between them, are still far from well understood.[196]

Forensic experts are quite vocal about how far their field has to go in terms of establishing ethical standards for conducting human rights investigations.[197] For those experts accustomed to the strict procedures of crime labs and domestic courts, the negotiations and tradeoffs involved in human rights work, particularly in a post-conflict landscape, can appear as a chaotic frontier.

Yet there is also an argument for seeing the glass as half full rather than half empty. After a bit more than twenty-five years of collective experience, the field of international forensics has moved toward consensus that all of the stakeholders and concerns described in this chapter are legitimate elements of the search for the missing that cannot be ignored. For example, in a set of recommendations for forensic assistance in Iraq after Saddam Hussein's removal, the prominent experts Eric Stover, Bill Haglund, and Margaret Samuels outlined a "comprehensive strategy" for a "central coordinating body" dealing with missing persons. Within a single paragraph, they invoked "the humanitarian needs of the families of the missing," "the legal needs of criminal trials," and a "larger strategy to rebuild Iraq's health care system" that would include training in identification of the dead and psychosocial support for families of the missing. They also warned their colleagues not to "undermine the capacity of local institutions" by overinternationalizing the search for the missing.[198] Their list amounted to a rich, though incredibly demanding, vision of how forensic science can be applied in the aftermath of atrocity. If we consider forensic human rights work as not just an extension of the domestic crime lab, but as a completely new field—a very young field at that[199]—we may better recognize how much progress has been made. Forensic teams have adapted to unexpected challenges in the field, carefully describing the different priorities involved in their work, and coming together, even across lines of institutional competition, to share their knowledge. The basic structure of an ethical consensus (in terms of what questions are being asked, and with what stakeholders in mind) is known, even if its details are not fully worked out. The following two chapters examine some contexts where the devil is very much in these details.

Chapter 2

The Politics of Grief

"[I]f you are fighting for life, you leave the dead where they are."
—*Hebe de Bonafini, President, Asociación Madres de Plaza de Mayo*

"It's a contradiction to speak of genocide and not identify cadavers."
—*Graciela Fernández Mejide, Asamblea Permanente por los Derechos Humanos*

Challenges to Exhumation

It is easy to imagine how ardently families and mourners must wish for the bodies of their loved ones to be taken out of the pits and clandestine graves where their murderers left them. One can understand, too, the mixture of nearly unbearable pain and sense of necessity with which they seek to have the story of what their loved ones suffered told with scientific precision, so that the world will know both the crimes of perpetrators and the agony of victims and survivors. Last but not least, there is the physical satisfaction of having the body returned to them so that it can be honored and laid to rest according to the articles of their faith or the practices they find most appropriate. Experts who travel the world exhuming mass graves generally do so in a spirit of humanitarianism, with the understanding that grief, uncertainty, and the official denial of atrocity inflict ongoing torment on the loved ones of the missing and the disappeared. Like aid workers arriving at a famine with sacks of rice, forensic teams come equipped with tools to alleviate suffering, and in the abstract it can be hard to understand how anyone in pain would refuse their help.

Yet this is precisely what people have done, in different places and for different reasons, since forensic investigations first became part of the response atrocity. These varieties of refusal signify an important challenge to the logic of human rights forensic investigations and to anyone's faith that digging up bodies is always a form of "help." Their history starts right along with the first major program of human rights-focused exhumations, in Argentina.

A central, and now infamous, feature of the 1976–83 military junta's rule in Argentina was the "disappearance" of somewhere between ten and thirty thousand of its citizens: leftist militants, university students and professors, journalists, psychiatrists, Jews, social workers, unionists, rural activists, and many others who did not fit into the ruling junta's semifascist conception of a purer, "reorganized" Argentina.[1] These people were taken from their homes and workplaces and then tortured and imprisoned in clandestine camps that had been set up in factories and beneath shopping malls. They were raped, drugged, and in most cases murdered. Their bodies were sometimes dumped into the sea from airplanes, sometimes buried in graves registered as "N.N."— "ningún nombre" or "no name." The N.N. label had long been used to refer to bodies of the indigent or unidentifiable that wound up in Argentine cemeteries,[2] but it was now repurposed by the security forces for one final act of "disappearance," erasing the connection between the *desaparecidos'* names and their bodies.

In 1985, just over two years after Argentina's return to democracy, a judge investigating N.N. graves in the Parque Cemetery, in the coastal city of Mar del Plata, asked Clyde Snow and his students (who would soon form the Argentine Forensic Anthropology Team) to exhume plots where it was believed that three *desaparecidos* might be found.[3] Their names were Liliana Pereyra, Ana María Torti, and Néstor Fonseca. The mother of twenty-one-year-old Liliana Pereyra, Jorgelina "Coche" de Pereyra, had discovered baby clothing in her daughter's abandoned rented room and received reports that Liliana, five months pregnant at the time of her disappearance, had given birth in captivity.[4] Knowing that she might have a living grandchild somewhere, Coche de Pereyra joined the Abuelas de Plaza de Mayo, Argentina's Grandmothers of the Disappeared, and began to search for the missing child.

While the cemetery's records of N.N. burials made it relatively easy to guess where Néstor Fonseca might be buried, both Liliana and Ana María Torti were close in height, weight, and the other descriptors available for the bodies buried in the other two graves.[5] In other words, the team had little certainty in advance of the exhumations regarding which grave might contain each of the two women. This potential difficulty loomed large: while Coche de Pereyra hesitated little before throwing her support behind the Parque Cemetery exhumations,[6] Torti's sister vacillated about whether she wanted her sibling's body exhumed.[7] Though at one point she appeared to give grudging consent to the team's work, she soon contacted members of the Madres de Plaza de Mayo—the Mothers of the Disappeared, Argentina's world-famous association of families of the missing—and seems to have given them the impression that exhumations were going forward without the family's consent.[8]

Among the Madres who heard Torti's complaint was Hebe de Bonafini, an early member of the group who counts two sons and a daughter-in-law among the *desaparecidos*. De Bonafini would eventually come to lead a large faction of the Madres, now called the Asociación Madres de Plaza de Mayo. This faction has been the fiercest opponent, within the human rights community, of forensic exhumations in Argentina.[9] Though de Bonafini is from humble origins and never received more than an elementary school education,[10] she has been the intellectual architect of many of the Madres' strategies and much of their rhetoric,[11] and she remains a powerful and extremely divisive figure both among the Madres themselves and in Argentine public life in general.

Snow and his students, fresh from their first few successful exhumations of N.N. graves around Buenos Aires, agreed to the judge's request that they visit Mar del Plata. In fact, when the governmental sponsors of Snow's work, the Secretariat for Human Rights (headed by the Argentine philosopher Eduardo Rabossi), denied the students funding for their travel and lodging, they paid their own way.[12] Here, as one of the secretariat's representatives, María Julia Bihurriet, recounts, is the scene that greeted the team of investigators early on the second morning of their work at the Parque Cemetery:

> As we entered . . . we could see a large group of people standing around the partially open grave. There must have been about fifteen of them, mostly women. We stopped first at a small shed. We heard shouts. But we couldn't make out what they were saying. . . . A policeman came up and told us the people at the grave were members of the Madres. They wouldn't let anyone near the graves that we had dug. He said that when he and his men approached, they hurled stones at them, so they backed off.
>
> Well, I decided if they were Madres, I could talk to them. The policeman warned me not to go, but I did anyway. When I got about thirty meters away, I recognized Hebe de Bonafini. But before I could say anything, they began shouting insults. . . . Then the policeman grabbed me and pulled me back.[13]

Bihurriet's testimony reveals not only how unexpected the Madres' objections were for the newly minted forensic team, but also that—contrary to the reaction she encountered at the gravesite—Bihurriet perceived a natural affinity between the forensic team and the Madres as human rights activists: "I decided if they were Madres, I could talk to them."

The shock of what happened instead, this nearly violent rejection of exhumations by some Madres, is of tremendous importance for understanding the politics of disappearance and transitional justice in Argentina, as well as of forensic exhumations on the international stage. At the Parque Cemetery, the members of the Argentine team gained an early understanding of the extent to which other considerations, beyond a shared commitment to human rights, could distance forensic teams from the families and mourners they sought to help. They also began to see the extent to which communities of mourners could become divided internally. These divisions are of paramount importance because family members are widely recognized as having the greatest moral authority and deepest connection to mass graves, even if they do not have the same resources or international recognition as war crimes tribunals or international human rights networks.

Tense encounters with families of the missing are recounted, nearly always with a sense of shock and even bafflement, in various histories and memoirs of forensic investigations. Examples include Joyce and Stover's *Witnesses from the Grave*, which details the formation of the Argentine team and early exhumations in Argentina, and Clea Koff's *The Bone Woman*, based on the author's experiences as a forensic anthropologist in Rwanda and the former Yugoslavia. More recently, families and mourners' objections to the exhumation of their dead have become a focus for emerging scholarship about international forensic investigations.[14] Documents about ethics and best practices from within the field itself have mentioned these controversies around gravesites,[15] though according to Derek Congram and Ariana Fernández, "the subject of mixed support for mass grave exhumations by primary stakeholders (mainly families of the victims) has been largely, shamefully, avoided in forensic anthropology literature." Attention to these objections to exhumation is crucial, in part for the simple fact that scenes like the one in the Parque Cemetery keep repeating themselves—albeit with some very important variations—at other mass gravesites throughout the world, from the former Yugoslavia to Poland to Spain.

This chapter focuses on the reasons why some family members, mostly Madres, have opposed exhuming Argentina's *desaparecidos*. However, unlike other scholarship on the subject, it also treats the arguments *in favor* of exhumation as equally worthy of analysis. Objections to exhumation are, just like the justifications forensic teams offer for their work, *arguments*. They rest on specific assumptions about the world, ideas about the dead, political readings of history, forms of rhetoric, and so on. Like other arguments, they can be understood better when these underlying assumptions are examined and even critically interrogated. This chapter and the next one analyze two different sets of objections to human rights forensic investigations—first political, then religious (though in each case, arguably, those two categories begin to shade into one another).

In fact, there are important similarities between these seemingly disparate sources of anti-exhumation sentiment. First, in each case the challenge comes from people who assert a relationship with mass graves and the bodies within them that forensic experts do not have: an authority rooted in intimate, local ties. The groups objecting to exhumations speak either as grieving family members of the victims, or as people who share in their religion and culture. Second, and unlike other major stakeholders, these groups seek not merely to influence the *conduct* of forensic exhumations, but rather to bring those exhumations to a halt. In each case, the uncompromising stance has its roots in a philosophical view that is largely—though perhaps not entirely—incompatible with the work forensic teams do. The moral universalism that is a central feature of forensic ethics runs into counterclaims based on the particularity of political, religious, and cultural contexts. The responses forensic teams craft to these challenges must traverse a minefield of highly sensitive issues about respect for local culture, secular versus sacred values, and the imposition of "Western" science and technology—or political hegemony—on other belief systems and political projects.

Perhaps not surprisingly, given all the issues at stake, forensic teams have responded to both forms of objection with an abundance of caution. No human rights organization wants to be seen as deaf to the cries of mourning relatives or as violators of the sacred beliefs of local communities. Part of the moral universalism of forensic teams, in fact, means not only according the same respect to all individuals, but also trying to take the beliefs and claims of different *groups* equally seriously—a task that is particularly difficult when groups who make authoritative claims about mass graves also disagree with one another.

Forensic teams have sought accommodations and negotiations with groups that object to their work, sometimes with satisfying results. But they have also seemed reluctant to subject the arguments against exhumation to scrutiny. It is difficult to question beliefs about the relationship between exhumation and justice, or mass graves and the sacred, without appearing to contest the authority of the survivors and believers who make them. As a result, objections that should be the beginning of a dialogue have sometimes translated, too quickly, into either/or decisions: for example, either ignore family objections, or abandon forensic exhumations.

Mothers and Graves

As people throughout Argentina disappeared from their homes, often in the secret police's dreaded Ford Falcons, their family members began lonely and usually futile searches through official and unofficial channels for information about the missing persons' whereabouts. As their loneliness and frustration mounted, these family members gradually began to network with one another. The associations they formed first served to support the search for individuals, but ultimately also took on the broader—and quite dangerous—task of documenting and denouncing the junta's human rights violations.[16]

The most famous of these organizations are the Madres de Plaza de Mayo and the Abuelas de Plaza de Mayo, the Mothers and Grandmothers of the Disappeared—groups formed mostly by middle-aged women. Men and young people were more likely than their wives or mothers to be detained themselves. They were also more likely, in that era at least, to be their family's breadwinner and thus unable to spend days searching, marching, meeting with priests and bureaucrats, and filing habeas corpus petitions.[17] The Madres and Abuelas helped bring torture and disappearance to the world's attention.[18] Having played a vital role in discrediting the dictatorship, they also remained active during the long democratic transition. In fact, all of the groups described in this chapter are still operating in Argentina, though their members are aging and some major figures, such as Renée Epelbaum (a founding member of the Asociación Madres de Plaza de Mayo and, later, of the Madres de Plaza de Mayo-Línea Fundadora), have died.

The Madres and Abuelas have long been a source of fascination for feminist scholars, human rights advocates, and other social activists.[19] Many of the women who joined these organizations were originally housewives, often from the middle and working classes and relatively uneducated. They started their search for their husbands and children in the face of denials and threats from the authorities. From the public, they faced terrible indifference spiked with fear. Nevertheless, these women ultimately crafted a new form of social movement, one that combined fierce courage with an ongoing, careful attention to language and creative organizing methods. The Madres also created a now well-known iconography of resistance, tying white handkerchiefs—originally cloth diapers the Madres had brought from their homes[20]—around their heads and carrying placards with photographs of their disappeared loved ones. Their organizing methods have relied heavily on ritual, repetition, symbolism, and visibility, starting with their weekly march around Buenos Aires' central Plaza de Mayo, where painted silhouettes of absent human figures often marked their path. (See Figure 2.) Crucially, for many Madres, the process of becoming a member of an organization, defining a strategy, and achieving organizational discipline has not only helped give voice to their demands but has also *altered* those demands in important ways.

Beyond Argentina, the information-sharing and solidarity networks established between these grassroots activists, international human rights organizations such as Amnesty International, and concerned governments are considered to have helped shape the contemporary global human rights movement.[21] The importance and influence of the Madres and Abuelas should

Figure 2. Silhouette of a *desaparecido* painted on the ground at the Plaza de Mayo, Buenos Aires, Argentina, where for decades the Madres and Abuelas de Plaza de Mayo held their weekly marches. Photograph by the author.

not be underestimated. In keeping with the wide influence of their activism, their different views on forensic investigation have also traveled far beyond Argentina's borders.

In the case of the Parque Cemetery, a strict legal interpretation of the judge's orders would have permitted the Argentine team to overlook the family's objections. Nevertheless, after exhuming a body they eventually successfully identified as Liliana Pereyra's, they abandoned their work on the grave that they had come to believe belonged to Ana María Torti.[22] This responsiveness to the different views of families is the hallmark of an approach to exhumation that the Argentine team was just beginning to articulate and that would eventually become their most recognizable signature.

Amnesty, Reconciliation, and Exhumation

There are a number of historical precedents, as well as political and philosophical claims, that weave together in the anti-exhumation position taken by the women who, after the Madres split into two groups in 1986, remained under Hebe de Bonafini's leadership in the Asociación Madres de Plaza de Mayo. It is equally important to understand, however, what these objections are *not* about. The Asociación Madres have made no complaint about the ways in which the Argentine Forensic Anthropology Team treats the bodies they exhume from N.N. graves (an objection families in the former Yugoslavia leveled against some of the forensic teams operating there). They do not worry, as families of the *desaparecidos* in Chile rightly did, that the identifications made by the team might lack scientific credibility—though *all* of the Madres have rightly been skeptical of earlier "identifications" made by poorly trained and politically compromised Argentine medico-legal personnel.[23] Nor do these Madres claim, as some of the religious leaders and communities described in the next chapter do, that graves are sacred or that exhumation itself is a form of violation. Their criticism is thus not of forensic exhumation *as such* or of the Argentine team, but rather of the role they think exhumations play in Argentina's post-dictatorship landscape.

The Asociación Madres consistently interpret exhumations as one piece of a broader transitional justice or "reconciliation" project in Argentina. They—along with their colleagues in the other groups—largely see that project as having been flawed and disappointing (though that disappointment has eased significantly since 2003 because of a wave of new human rights prosecutions under presidents Néstor Kirchner and Cristina Fernández de Kirchner). Their refusal to accept exhumations is thus an element of a broader strategy for protesting the unsatisfactory efforts of Argentina's government to address human rights violations.

In 1982, suffering from economic woes, corruption scandals, and a humiliating military defeat in the war against England for the Falkland Islands, the Argentine military junta began phasing out its program of repression and restoring democratic rule. The election of the respected human rights activist Raúl Alfonsín to the presidency was widely greeted with enthusiasm. Announcing the formation of the National Commission on the Disappearance of Persons (known by its acronym, CONADEP) just days after his election, Alfonsín signaled to victims and others in the human rights community that he would be making a clear break from the past.[24]

As in so many other cases of transitional justice around the world, however, breaking with the past turned out to be not only a moral project but also a significant practical challenge. Under Alfonsín, five of the nine generals who led Argentina's military dictatorship received convictions for human rights violations; however, high levels of foreign debt, hyperinflation,[25] and open revolts by Argentina's coup-prone military all threatened the stability of his government.[26] Under these conditions, in Mauricio Cohen Salama's view:

> Alfonsín chose a middle path, whose instruments he created step by step, and which wound up leaving everyone unsatisfied. In his public speeches, Alfonsín presented himself as an uncompromising defender of human rights, and was recognized as such globally; in its deeds, however, his government tried to limit judicial procedures [against perpetrators of human rights violations] in order to prevent conflict with the armed forces, which it felt too weak to oppose. . . . Alfonsín's politics . . . oscillated between rhetoric about founding the new state on absolute ethical principles, and negotiations with those who had formerly held power to achieve gradual changes.[27]

The most infamous of the constraints Alfonsín put on the judiciary were two laws passed in late 1986 and early 1987, now referred to as the "Leyes de Impunidad," or amnesty laws.[28] The first law, called the "Punto Final," or full stop law, allowed plaintiffs sixty days to file suit, after which no new charges could be filed for crimes during the period of Argentina's "Dirty War"[29]—with the notable exception of cases of disappeared children, who were not considered murdered or disappeared (crimes covered by the amnesty) but rather kidnapped. The second law, announced after a tense standoff with a ficers who were pushing for a blanket amnesty against all prosecution called the "Obediencia Debida," or due obedience law. Unlike its predecessor, it focused not on a specific time limitation but on the chain of command, limiting responsibility for human rights violations to the chiefs of security forces—a tiny pool of the torturers and murderers.[31]

Argentina's amnesty laws were both annulled in 2003, under the presidency of Néstor Kirchner. Kirchner and his wife Cristina, who have consecutively held the presidency in Argentina since 2003, have actively pursued an agenda of prosecutions for dictatorship-era human rights violations (Néstor Kirchner died in 2010, three years after Cristina Fernandez de Kirchner succeeded him as president). All of the Madres have supported them in these efforts, though the new climate of trials and public acknowledgment seems not to have fully assuaged tensions between the two groups of Madres or altered their differing positions on exhumations.[32] As Hebe de Bonafini and a small group of Madres protested the exhumations in the Parque Cemetery in 1985, divisions within the larger group were already beginning to appear. Some Madres were highly critical of the National Commission on the Disappearance of Persons for its limitations, which included a lack of subpoena power, a short mandate, and civilian rather than congressional oversight.[33] Others saw it as a necessary first step, constrained by circumstances but valuable, particularly for its highly public acknowledgment of the crimes committed and the names of victims. To all of the Madres, however, real justice for the *desaparecidos* and their families—if possible at all—seemed like a faint hope. The Punto Final and Obediencia Debida laws, announced shortly after the incident at the Parque Cemetery, seemed to all but extinguish that hope. The laws most likely significantly hardened the antipathy of some Madres (particularly those who were concurrently forming into the group's larger faction, the Asociación Madres Plaza de Mayo) toward exhumations and any other program that could be seen as part of the transition agenda helmed by Alfonsín.

The Madres—first the entire organization, and after the breakup the Asociación Madres faction—stated their positions on exhumations and these other programs in a sort of double-language. They mixed particulars, such as the amnesty laws they found so unacceptable, with a powerful metaphorical language about death, disappearance, and grief, prompting Temma Kaplan to observe that their "use of symbolism . . . [was] their greatest weapon."[34] This double-language, repeated in countless interviews, newsletters, and protests, offers multiple rationales for the Asociación Madres' oppositions to exhumations of the *desaparecidos*, principally, and also to other state-sponsored attempts to address the violence of the past.

Aparición con Vida: Beyond Metaphor

The slogan "aparición con vida" translates literally to "appearance with life," but is more clearly rendered in English as "let them appear alive." "Them" refers to Argentina's *desaparecidos*. On its face, in other words, the phrase is a demand that the *desaparecidos* reappear not as corpses being lifted out of mass graves, but as living individuals. "Aparición con vida" is by far the most recognizable slogan of the Asociación Madres' anti-exhumation position. It is also, however, the most resistant to a simple interpretation.[35] The slogan is, in fact, *crafted* to be confusing, for these Madres rightly saw that the more it confounded and even frustrated outside observers, the longer it would keep them and their radical stance on reconciliation efforts in the public eye.

"Aparición con vida" has a number of metaphorical and even quasi-religious meanings; however, it is still very much a piece of political rhetoric, oriented toward the specifics of the Argentine transition and its accompanying public dialogue. Significantly, the Madres first used the slogan not at one of their public protests against the dictatorship, but rather among their peers in the human rights community. From that point on, it has served partly as a way of setting them apart from their own allies. According to Cohen Salama, a group of Madres spent the night crafting the slogan in Oslo, in 1980, where they had traveled to celebrate the awarding of the Nobel Peace Prize to the Argentine human rights leader Adolfo Pérez Esquivel. The women were outraged because Emilio Mignone, another celebrated human rights figure in Argentina, had apparently signaled in his remarks for the occasion that he considered the *desaparecidos* (among whom he could count his own daughter) to be dead—a declaration the Madres found unacceptable, since so much about the fate of the *desaparecidos* had yet to be clarified.[36]

From the start the Madres' demand that all of the *desaparecidos* be returned alive could not be taken entirely literally; even before the coup, Argentina had entered a period of sustained political violence and at least *some* of the *desaparecidos* had surely been killed. Nevertheless, "aparición con vida" did make some literal sense during the years of the dictatorship itself. Throughout that era, though bodies were washing up on beaches and appearing in strikingly inflated numbers at morgues and cemeteries, many *desaparecidos* were indeed still alive in the regime's torture centers. Even during the early period of the Alfonsín presidency, some clandestine prisons remained in operation and "aparición con vida" plausibly referred to living people who might be liberated—though tragically, in the few cases that are known, these prisoners disappeared even as democratic rule was being reconstructed around the walls of their prisons.[37]

However, the post-breakup Asociación Madres have continued to use the slogan past the point when the consolidation of democracy, the dismantling of dictatorship-era prisons, and the exhumation of graves of the *desapareci-dos* throughout Argentina made it more or less impossible to believe that their loved ones would be returned to them alive.[38] The question, then, is what purpose "aparición con vida" has served after the logic behind its literal meaning, always attenuated, faded.

A partial answer is that the slogan came to encapsulate not just a concrete demand that the *desaparecidos* be returned alive, but rather a whole cluster of positions the Asociación Madres took toward efforts to address the legacy of the "Dirty War." The group has another, more explicit though less rhetorically compelling slogan it uses to summarize these positions: "No exhumations, no posthumous homage, and no economic reparation."[39] In fact, however, the "aparición con vida" slogan summarizes, but also transcends, this three-part objection to post-dictatorship transition efforts.

To some forensic experts and many in the popular press, the seemingly illogical demand of "aparición con vida" could best be understood through the concept of trauma, which for decades now has been migrating from psychoanalysis into studies of post-conflict societies.[40] As various popular accounts put it, the Asociación Madres had gone mad with grief, were "ignoring" the evidence emerging from the N.N. graves,[41] and staking their activism on an impossible hope.[42]

There is, indeed, an affective dimension to the slogan that should not be ignored. The impossible demand of "aparición con vida" signals, quite powerfully, that some experiences can never be resolved. Grief over a disappeared loved one is without end, and true "reconciliation" may never be possible with people who committed unthinkable acts of torture.[43] Far from crazy or unrealistic in this sense, "aparición con vida" reminds us of the scope of grief, the permanence of some injustices, and the limits of forgiveness.

There are problems, however, with seeing "aparición con vida" as the symptom or expression of collective trauma. The first is the way in which this view echoes the junta's long-standing attempt to paint the Madres as a bunch of "locas," or crazy women, who could not accept that their children had fled to other countries or died in guerrilla battles against the forces of order.[44] The second is that labeling the Madres irrational and traumatized leaves only two options open: to dismiss "aparición con vida" as unanswerable, not a legitimate part of the discourse about Argentina's exhumations and other transitional justice programs, or alternatively to cast the Madres as the keepers of some sort of higher spiritual truth, as some scholars have done.[45]

One of the most valuable accomplishments of recent scholarship on the Madres, particularly by Kaplan and Zoë Crossland, is to situate the slogan more firmly in its specific context and thus analyze it as a political strategy rather than a pure metaphor. The Asociación Madres see exhumation, reparations, and all of the other official programs aimed at families of the *desaparecidos* as tools of false closure—a consolation prize offered to the "losers" of the dictatorship era, who must be kept quiet in the service of a progress from which they, and the political ideals of their dead children, are largely excluded. They counter these attempts to "resolve" the issue of disappearance with the impossible demand that their loved ones be returned alive;[46] they thus condemn the exhumation and reparations programs to a preordained failure. In answer to the common reaction that the Madres are crazy with grief, moreover, Kaplan and Crossland argue that "aparición con vida" actually employs a targeted *appearance* of irrationality. As Kaplan explains, "Appearing crazy and uncompromising became a way to get the attention of their fellow citizens."[47]

The Punto Final and Obediencia Debida laws undoubtedly hardened many Madres' views on exhumation and Alfonsín's democratic transition. However, the roots of "aparición con vida" reach back further than either of these laws, to official attempts by the military junta to deal with the issue of disappearance during its rule. In September 1979, the junta issued a "presumption of death by disappearance" law. The law declared that anyone who had gone missing between November 6, 1974, and Sept. 6, 1979, would officially be considered dead. It was the first of two efforts by the generals to issue blanket declarations of this sort about the *desaparecidos*.[48] Monetary reparations were offered to the surviving family members of each *desaparecido*, but underneath the veneer of concern and generosity, the laws were barely concealed attempts to close the book on disappearances as swiftly as possible. Gravediggers and other unqualified personnel conducted the first exhumations of N.N. graves, destroying or leaving behind more evidence than they collected. Their "identifications" relied on poor sources, such as the information provided to cemetery staff by the murderers who had come to dump bodies there. Family members were not asked to provide the kinds of antemortem descriptions that are often necessary for a positive identification.[49] Some of the bodies that were turned over to families in this era, when reexamined, turned out not even to be of the right sex.[50]

These errors cannot be attributed to incompetence alone. Rather, the personnel in charge of exhumations had often been complicit in covering up the crimes in the first place and in the production of unmarked graves.[51] Perhaps worst of all, the paperwork that accompanied the declarations of death—which the authorities asked family members to sign before they could retrieve the bodies of their loved ones—usually listed the *desaparecido* as having been killed in armed combat against security forces.[52] Each signed declaration was thus an affirmation of the dictatorship's narrative of a civil war against subversives, akin to the simulated shootouts that were staged on the streets of Argentina's cities and the bogus articles published by acquiescent media outlets. The model for the junta's program of identifications and reparations, in other words, could be summarized as a simple trade: a body (*any* body), plus some money, in exchange for silence.[53]

Through its unscientific "identifications" and bureaucratic declaration of death, the junta thus polluted any future attempt to use the tools of science and law to establish the true fate of the *desaparecidos*. To the Asociación Madres, *any* declaration of death will be forever tainted by the words of the junta: "dead" is just one of the descriptors, along with "terrorist," "subversive," and "immoral," that the murdering regime used to promote its own self-serving image of their children. That image must be combated comprehensively or not at all. Anyone who declares or even implies that the *desaparecidos* are dead—whether it is the junta, Alfonsín's government, or allies in the human rights sector—has placed himself in the enemy's camp.

The same logic eventually led the Asociación Madres to oppose not only exhumation but also all memorials for individual *desaparecidos* or the collective victims of the dictatorship. It is no longer just the exhumed bodies of the *desaparecidos* that threaten to render them politically "dead," but also any plaque, wall, or monument remembering them in a format long used for bygone historical figures.[54] This is the landscape that Snow and his students stepped into when they arrived at the Parque Cemetery, and it is because of a complex political, legal, and *forensic* history—not merely a wish that the *desaparecidos* remain "liminal" or haunting—that exhuming N.N. graves was like opening Pandora's box.

If "aparición con vida" is meant to turn the conversation away from exhumations, reparations, and memorials, toward what other destination does it [poin]t? Because the Asociación Madres are unwilling to participate in exhumations or memorials, the only avenue of redress they leave open to those who wish to make amends is the avenue of justice. Justice, as this group of Madres has long defined it, would be a full accounting of all the mechanisms of repression and people involved in it, followed by prosecutions. It is, as the Asociación Madres have repeatedly declared, a model in which the names and fates of the *murderers* are of paramount importance, and the bodies of the *desaparecidos*—anything about them, in fact, aside from their status as innocent victims or martyrs to a cause—are largely irrelevant. As Beatriz de Rubinstein, president of the Mar del Plata branch of the Asociación Madres, puts it: "Exhumations have nothing to do with justice."[55]

The "aparición con vida" slogan and its associated strategies have been singularly divisive, alienating Madres who did not agree with its logic, forensic investigators and other members of the human rights community, and many among the general public. It would be imprecise, however, to view this divisiveness as an unfortunate by-product of a principled stance: rather, it is *part of what the stance seeks to achieve*. The Madres' activism, both before the split in 1986 and afterward, brought them international attention and made them a model for other groups in Latin America and far beyond—a trend both factions have actively supported. The Asociación Madres clearly saw how much they stood to gain from the spread of their type of activism both at home and abroad: influence, legacy, and solidarity, among other things. But they must also have seen that they had something to lose. As their own organization split apart and groups like the Abuelas, an offshoot of the Madres that was much quicker to establish an international network, garnered attention and praise, the Asociación Madres may have become aware of the fragility of their own place in an increasingly complex, expanding human rights landscape. "Aparición con vida," the refusal to participate in any form of exhumation or commemoration, thus became the unique identifier that marked them as the original mothers' group, the most ideologically pure, the ones uniquely focused on life and transformation—which these Madres cast as starkly incompatible with grieving over deaths.

Testimonies like this one, from Graciela de Jeger, show how "aparición con vida" became a tool for carving out a distinct identity, demarcating a boundary between the positions accepted by the wider sphere of the Madres' supporters and those of the group itself: "Aparición con vida is the most controversial of our slogans because a lot of people support us, but say aparición con vida, no. You're mad . . . "[56] The slogan serves the dual purpose of differentiating the

Asociación Madres from other groups while promoting unity within the group, whose members reaffirm that only within their limited sphere can they find others who understand and support such a counterintuitive position.

In fact, the slogan helped the Asociación Madres differentiate themselves not only from their colleagues within the Argentine human rights community, but also from mothers' groups abroad who were swiftly adopting their model. A member of the group, speaking to the scholar Marguerite Bouvard, portrays her group's denial of death as the central feature distinguishing them from their foreign colleagues. She also creates a heroic historical narrative for the role "aparición con vida" has played in setting Argentina apart from other transitional justice contexts:

> Also we have something different from other organizations. . . . The Chilean women accepted the death of their children immediately, without anybody telling them what happened. [The children] were taken away, killed, and the mothers then wore black handkerchiefs and black clothing. The Brazilian women, who also had children taken away and killed, also wore black handkerchief[s] and black clothing, and because they wore [this] clothing the affair ended rapidly because they accepted death. But we wear white handkerchiefs first because we don't accept death and second because we fight for life, even if our children are not here. Therefore there is a great difference.[57]

The woman claims that by acknowledging the deaths of their children, foreign mothers' groups allowed murderous regimes to close the books on injustice. This reading of history could certainly be subjected to critical scrutiny.[58] Yet while the factual accuracy of the declaration depends on unoffered evidence, it nevertheless speaks eloquently to the role "aparición con vida" came to play in articulating an entire distinct *philosophy* for the Asociación Madres. According to Hebe de Bonafini:

> In Guatemala they lose all their time looking for cemeteries and places like that. I said, "You are losing a tremendous amount of time when you could fight for the lives of others. Why do you want the dead bodies? . . . You have to bury them in some other place anyway. And in the meantime they [the perpetrators] kill other people. So if you are fighting for life, you leave the dead where they are."[59]

The Asociación Madres envision themselves as focused, uniquely, on life and on political struggle, while other groups both at home and abroad persist in taking a self-defeating and almost macabre interest in the material remnants of the past—particularly in the graves and the bones of their dead children. There is no way, de Bonafini and her followers seem to say, to look backward with grief while also making demands of the future.

Activist Identities and Individual Grief

The Asociación Madres distance themselves from the bodies of the *desaparecidos*, and thus from an entire set of traditional associations between mothers, bodies, and grieving. As Hebe de Bonafini says, "The tremendous affection we have for our children is not expressed properly by looking for a pile of bones. Our children are something else, they have become something else, they are in all of those who continue their political struggle."[60] Though I have titled this chapter "The Politics of Grief," the Asociación Madres see mourning over individual dead bodies as fundamentally *apolitical*—a private, rather than public or collective, endeavor. To them, politics is not grief; politics is transformation. For this reason, members of the group often repeat that their disappeared children gave birth to them, and not the other way around.[61]

The Asociación Madres' rejection of the *desaparecidos'* material remains is thus related to their emphasis on radical self-transformation. It is also related to their search for a new group of "children" to carry on their fight. Understanding these aspects of their activism clarifies how the oppositions of memory versus closure, and grief versus politics—versions of the old activist slogan "Don't mourn—organize!" updated for the transitional justice context[62]—have remained so potent in discussions of dictatorship, disappearance, and exhumation in Argentina and beyond.

Books and articles about both groups of Madres are full of personal accounts in which a lonely, marginalized, and terrified woman, searching for her missing child, gradually discovers both purpose and community in her political activism. The question that has divided the Madres, however, is whether the life of activism and community can go on after the personal search has ended. According to Beatriz de Rubinstein, "The exhumations were another part of the government's strategy. It's very difficult for a mother who has received the remains of her child to go on fighting . . . "[63] Achieving certainty about a loved one's fate and mourning over a body are, in this formulation, not merely apolitical but actually *depoliticizing*: they turn *Madres*, members of an activist organization, back into merely *madres*, mothers in the conventional sense.

Though they may exist, I have found no record of a case where a woman left her life of activism, or retired from the Madres, due to having the remains of her child identified. The original idea of solidarity embraced by the Madres and Abuelas was the sense that their search had become a collective one. By joining together and creating permanent institutions dedicated to the search for the missing, they posited that each mother's desperation and each identified *desaparecido* mattered as much as another. Yet the Asociación Madres, each with her own history of loss and her own family members to mourn, see not a fusion but a fundamental tension between the particularity of grief and the unity of their struggle. Refusing exhumations, for them, becomes something of a rite of passage, a way of reaffirming one's identity within the collective by sacrificing one's "individualist" grief. Each of the Asociación Madres must move on "from looking for our own son to looking for all the children"[64]—one cannot, in their philosophical framework, do both at the same time.

One of the principle ways in which the Asociación Madres have been "looking for all the children" is by anointing a younger generation of activists as their successors. In the past, they developed close connections with a group called the Front for Human Rights, and more recently they created their own "Universidad de las Madres," or Madres University, which holds workshops and other events for young people. Members of the group have called the young people that surround them "the reincarnation of our children" and consistently describe the relationship as one of mother and child;[65] yet close observers (even sympathetic ones) allege that the power dynamic is very much the reverse. Bouvard writes that these young people have "capitalized on the women's affection" and replaced the Madres' former, improvised political model with an orthodox Latin American leftism: "Subsequently, their newspapers gushed with images of rifle-toting, revolutionary fighters from Cuba and articles in praise of Fidel Castro."[66]

Whether through outside influences or the development of their own political sensibilities, the Asociación Madres have evolved from human rights activists focused on disappearance and accountability into full-blown representatives of the Latin American left. In recent decades, Hebe de Bonafini has issued a series of inflammatory statements on everything from the war in Yugoslavia to the September 11, 2001, attacks on the Twin Towers in New York—statements in which the United States invariably appears as the "the worst enemy of humanity."[67] These remarks inevitably spark a media circus (which may, of course, be their goal). Yet while commentators either applaud or bemoan the political evolution of de Bonafini and her organization, they have rarely examined the relationship between their broader political worldview and the claims the Asociación Madres have long made about exhuming and identifying the *desaparecidos.*

The forensic identification and reburial of individual bodies, in the Asociación Madres' view, is "an individualistic struggle" that supplies only the names and bodies of isolated victims.[68] It does not support a narrative of political genocide conducted against a class of activists, which is the story the Asociación Madres want to tell.[69] Nor does it bring individual families together through a language of solidarity. Bouvard, embracing this perspective, writes that the Asociación Madres had a "policy of not putting their individual desires to give their children a resting place before the needs of the thirty thousand [*desaparecidos*]."[70]

These Madres were certainly correct that the amnesty laws drastically limited the potential for forensic evidence to contribute to charges of genocide and other crimes against humanity. However, Néstor Kirchner's eventual repeal of these laws, and the subsequent use of the Argentine team's work in numerous human rights prosecutions, have served as a powerful reminder that well-preserved and well-documented forensic evidence can easily outlive bad laws.

At the time they were issued, the amnesty laws caused a crisis of purpose for the newly formed Argentine team, dashing their hopes of putting human rights violators in jail. Instead, the young investigators focused on accompanying families through the process of identification and reburial,[71] as well as constructing a scientific counterhistory to the lies of the regime.[72] This reorientation of the Argentine teams' purposes has ultimately played a major role in defining and expanding the role that forensic investigations can play in the human rights context; nevertheless, the Asociación Madres rightly perceived it as partly an acknowledgment of limitation. Forensic exhumations turned toward family grief when other avenues of public action had been foreclosed.

This history does not support the claim, however, that exhumation without prosecutions *only* impacts individuals or isolated families. In fact, one of the projects Clyde Snow undertook while helping to form the Argentine team was a statistical study of all the unidentified bodies buried in Argentine cemeteries between 1976 and 1984, during and just after the junta's rule. A statistical study, of course, is distinct from an exhumation, and thus not the direct target of the Asociación Madres' objections. However, Snow's study was used in part to identify the cemeteries where *desaparecidos* had been buried, providing support for future exhumations in those cemeteries and relying on the skills of the same experts.[73] The study found that N.N. burials, though a long-standing way of dealing with bodies of the indigent, had spiked two- or three-fold at a number of cemeteries—cemeteries, as it turned out, that were located near military detention centers. The numbers also reflected a large increase in the percentage of unidentified bodies who were women, and a huge new population of unidentified bodies between eighteen and thirty-five years of age. In the cemeteries near detention centers, the number of N.N.'s who had died of gunshot wounds rose from about 5.5 to 50 percent during the period 1976–78.[74]

Snow and Bihurriet's study offered a data-driven and largely incontestable collective portrait of the *desaparecidos*, one that could aid exhumations—and thus help individual mourners rebury their dead—but that also had a tremendous amount to say about who the *desaparecidos* were, as a group, how and where they were killed. While all of the Madres remember, with outrage, the junta's attempts to pair the return of remains with fabricated stories of gunbattles between subversives and the police, the study gave some of the earliest and most conclusive proof against this narrative: if a war against subversives was taking place in the open, on the streets of Argentina, why were so many of the dead clustered around detention centers? Far from a continuation of the whitewashing conducted by police and medico-legal authorities during the dictatorship, the study also served as an indictment of officials who accepted and buried, in N.N. graves, execution victims who were far from unknown or unidentifiable. Last but not least, by showing in which particular detention centers the most people had disappeared, the data opened a path toward naming individual commanders and torturers responsible, the principle concern of the Asociación Madres.

The collective portrait assembled by Snow, Bihurriet, and the Argentine team can be compared with the Asociación Madres' own attempts to ascribe a collective identity and single political project to the *desaparecidos*. Many of the *desaparecidos* were, indeed, militants during a particularly turbulent time in Argentina's history. Some surviving family members, many of whom did not know about their children's clandestine activities, have preferred to ignore or minimize this reality in favor of a simpler narrative of innocents swallowed up in a repression without logic.[75] However, it is also true that the junta actively promoted a set of tenuous associations between things like psychiatry, Judaism, social work, and the university, on the one hand, and socialism or Marxism, on the other. In one particularly infamous case, called "The Night of the Pencils," a group of high school students who organized to demand subsidized bus fares for rides to school were disappeared, tortured, some of them raped, and (aside from three who were ultimately released) executed as if they were the worst of Marxist subversives.[76] This pattern of paranoia and vicious brutality cannot rightly be called "excesses" of the regime because it was a central and repeated facet of their repression.

The Asociación Madres are not alone in worrying about what it would mean for transitional justice processes, from truth commissions to forensic exhumations, to have exclusive authority over the history of violence in a place like Argentina. Truth commissions, such as Argentina's National Commission on the Disappeared, generally catalog human rights violations suffered by individuals without much detail about the political beliefs common among victims or the languages of solidarity and transformation they employed.[77] Nor do they focus on the international interests that have often propped up and collaborated with authoritarian regimes: for example, the way US-trained economists and multinational corporations took advantage of Argentina's repression to implement free-market, corporate-friendly reforms there without democratic opposition.[78]

But the alternative the Asociación Madres propose is at least as narrow as the truth commission's emphasis on names of victims and specific violations; more importantly, it is often simply inaccurate as a portrait of the country's *desaparecidos*. Placing the *desaparecidos* under the banner of Che Guevara, Fidel Castro, and (far more strangely) Saddam Hussein,[79] the group lends support to the junta's own story of an existential struggle with Marxist forces over the fate of Argentina (this story is often referred to by critics as the "theory of the two demons")[80]—rather than the reality of a paranoid, extralegal purge. The Asociación Madres thus wind up mimicking and even amplifying the claims of the military regime itself: that the *desaparecidos* formed a secret brotherhood of subversion, that they were "all alike."

The Other Mothers

The various groups of Madres, and especially the Asociación Madres, saw much at stake in how they chose to participate (or not) in Argentina's various programs to address its violent past—exhumations in particular. The decision about whether to collaborate with exhumations came to imply, at least for some Madres, a set of positions on a panoply of other issues: the collective identity of the *desaparecidos*, the level of sincerity with which the new government was addressing the abuses of the dictatorship, and the obligation of survivors to commit their lives to a particular brand of activism. Along with the intertwined arguments the Asociación Madres have used to justify their objections to exhumation, it is thus also crucial to describe why some Madres (and Abuelas) chose a different path.

The Madres de Plaza de Mayo-Línea Fundadora broke away from the larger Asociación Madres in January 1986. Among the twelve women who started the Línea Fundadora, as the organization's name implies, were many who had helped to create the original Madres group and develop their model of activism. Like their former colleagues in the Asociación Madres, the Línea Fundadora's members have participated in activism on a wide range of issues that extend beyond Argentina's "Dirty War," including programs for low-income children, advocacy of indigenous causes, and politics in Cuba, Honduras, and elsewhere.

The two groups of Madres generally acknowledge that their cause is the same. Though their positions on exhumations, memorials, and reparations differ radically, both groups have agreed (along with the Argentine team) that an exhumation should take place only if the family members of the *desaparecido(s)* believed to be in the grave approve of it.[81] The organizations avoid overt hostilities, though some mutual discomfort clearly remains.[82]

Yet the public truce between the two groups does not erase their philosophical differences; if the Asociación Madres believe their own statements, to them every exhumation or memorial the Línea Fundadora and Abuelas sponsor is a way of helping to close the book, forget the *desaparecidos*, and even of "murdering them once more."[83] If one pays careful attention to the words of the women in the Línea Fundadora, though the style is generally less bombastic, one finds a diametrically opposed view: to reject exhumations is to close off concrete, if imperfect, possibilities for justice and accountability. "Aparición con vida" and the positions associated with it, in this view, are *obstacles* to the very causes of justice and punishment that all of the Madres claim as a goal. Adopting the platform of "aparición con vida," the Asociación Madres also turn their backs on equally important, though harder to articulate, values connected to collective mourning and the care of the dead.

Not all of the divisions between the groups of Madres are so deeply philosophical. There are undercurrents of class conflict between some Asociación Madres and the largely middle- or upper-middle-class leaders of the Línea Fundadora and Abuelas.[84] Some observers have also raised the question of anti-Semitism, pointing out that many of the Madres who left to form the Línea Fundadora "were either Jewish or married to Jewish men."[85] These background differences of class and religion are undoubtedly important and may add significant fuel to the tension between the Madres; however, they do little to explain the divergent views the two organizations (three, if we factor in the Abuelas) have about the meaning and utility of exhumations.

De Bonafini's own complex and captivating history—which can be painted in broad strokes as either the blossoming of a revolutionary leader or the tragic deformation of an activist turned ideologue—threatens to obscure the broader story of the Madres as a fragmented institution. The Madres of the Línea Fundadora have often cited de Bonafini's undemocratic leadership, and their desire for freedom to articulate their own positions through a more "horizontal" structure,[86] as a major reason for their departure from the larger group.[87] It would thus seem a disservice to interpret their views only through lenses of class and anti-Semitism. Furthermore, the fact remains that the many Madres who remain under de Bonafini's leadership have embraced the program of "aparición con vida."[88] They reject any active search for their children's remains, a decision that even for the most committed members of the group must at times be painful. Given the stakes, it seems unlikely that all of these Madres are fueled only by resentment, or by unquestioning obedience to their charismatic leader. Rather, the intellectual and philosophical differences between the groups of Madres are real.

While a few scholars have written about the Línea Fundadora, in general the group has received far less attention than their colleagues. In part, this is because their organization maintains a generally lower profile. First, its less hierarchical structure and less explicit political affiliations mean that it has no lightning-rod figurehead along the lines of de Bonafini. Though the current size of the two groups hovers around the same number of sixty active members,[89] the Asociación Madres have far more financial resources (including, in the Kirchner years, funds from Argentina's government—something the Línea Fundadora has not sought). The Asociación Madres thus enjoy greater infrastructure and a more public presence, including a radio show and the Universidad de las Madres.[90]

The lack of attention to the Línea Fundadora in the scholarship about Argentine human rights activism, however, also follows a noticeable intellectual trajectory. Because the Asociación Madres are so controversial and seemingly "irrational," the assumption seems to be that the Línea Fundadora's stances are straightforward and rational; they can thus simply be reported without further comment. I disagree. The fact that the Línea Fundadora's positions are more intelligible or less controversial than those of the Asociación Madres does not mean they are any less philosophically rich. Nor does it necessarily mean that they are less politically charged. There is room to doubt the widely accepted notion that the Asociación Madres' "aparición con vida" program is more radical, more challenging to amnesty laws or the reconciliation agenda, than the pro-exhumation stance of the Línea Fundadora.

To explore these doubts is also to counter the soft contempt that is often embedded in the scholarly treatment of the Línea Fundadora. For example, when Bouvard says that the Asociación Madres are putting "their individual desires" aside to tend to the needs "of the thirty thousand" *desaparecidos*,[91] by implication she is saying that mourners who favor exhumation—the Línea Fundadora, Abuelas, and many other family members—are being selfish, that the desire for a body to bury is somehow egoistic. This is the same accusation of individualism and "privatized" grief that radical leftist groups in Spain have also deployed in their rhetoric against more "reformist" colleagues.[92]

Ewa Domanska, in a somewhat different vein, writes that "maintaining the liminal condition of the disappeared was important to those who were more interested in 'crime, guilt, and punishment' (trials and punishing those guilty) than 'mourning, forgiveness, and forgetting' (soothing memories and building a new reality together)."[93] She thus repeats, without critical reflection, the Asociación Madres' own rhetoric, as does Jenny Edkins. "If they [the Madres] had accepted their children's remains," Edkins writes, "Their children would have disappeared a second time. The children would have been returned to parents, returned to the home, the private sphere, but their political life, and the political voice of the Madres, would have ended."[94]

Linking the work of the Línea Fundadora with "forgiving," "forgetting," or "soothing" of any kind, as Domanska does, requires a strange blindness to both the political goals of the group and the outcomes of the forensic investigations it has supported. Edkins goes a step further, obliquely accusing the steadfast human rights activists in the Línea Fundadora of disappearing their children "a second time" just before presenting the Asociación Madres' ideological activism as "the only way" to politicize their children's deaths.[95] Failing to explore the positions of the Línea Fundadora in any depth, these descriptions do not give the ethical and political dimensions of exhuming the *desaparecidos* the consideration they are due—do not delve into exhumation's many meanings, both overt and subtle, as has been done so many times with the more overtly mystical rhetoric of "aparición con vida."

The Línea Fundadora justifies its decision to support exhumations largely in terms of holding perpetrators accountable. Ironically, this goal is thus the centerpiece of two programs that are opposed in every other way: the Asociación Madres' *refusal* of exhumations and the Línea Fundadora's *participation* in them. The difference seems to lie both in the conditions each group would place on exhumations and the extent to which they are willing to accept—and thus navigate strategically through—the limits of the law. Hebe de Mascia, of the Asociación Madres (no relation to Hebe de Bonafini), told Bouvard that her group might "accept their [children's] death"—and thus, presumably, their children's bodies—"when they tell us who the murderers were, why and how our children were killed."[96] De Mascia leaves it unspecified who "they" refers to, but presumably the onus is on the democratic government to go beyond the work of the National Commission on the Disappearance of Persons in its account of the abuses of the previous regime.

The Asociación Madres thus call *first* for a full accounting, *after* which exhumations may proceed. But the question remains how exactly the unnamed institutions to which de Mascia refers will be able to compile the full history of repression she demands, when the perpetrators are uncooperative or dead, the victims' bodies in unmarked graves, and many of the junta's records of its practices lost or destroyed. Especially in the absence of these records, exhumation is among the essential tools for answering the basic facts about how the *desaparecidos* were killed, as well as who killed them. The Línea Fundadora activists thus see little sense in demanding a full accounting of repression as a precondition for exhumations; rather, they want exhumations to provide the evidence that will make a full accounting possible.

The Línea Fundadora has been willing to work within and sometimes around the limitations of Argentine law. For example, in a 1993 letter, Renée Epelbaum explained that while a 1985 federal court decision against the junta called forced disappearance a crime against humanity, the decision could not be applied retroactively to crimes before 1985. Without evidence of other violations, then, nearly all of the disappearances the junta carried out during their rule could only be considered illegitimate arrests, a charge that carries a maximum five-to-six-year sentence. A longer conviction required proof of torture or murder. Those proofs, for the most part, were buried with the bodies in N.N. graves. "For this reason," Epelbaum wrote, "the Línea Fundadora accepts the exhumation of cadavers as long as it is ordered by a judge in the course of investigation and carried out by forensic experts, such as the group of anthropologists Clyde Snow trained in our country, who are pursuing their difficult and painful work with complete dedication."[97]

Epelbaum's words also speak to another difference between the Madres of the Línea Fundadora and their former colleagues. At least until the Kirschner presidencies, the Asociación Madres tended to argue that, until every perpetrator had been tried and every detail of repression brought to light, Argentina's democracy was a tainted one.[98] The Línea Fundadora's positions on exhumation and reparations, in the meantime, are largely based on distinguishing them from the reconciliation and reparations programs that have come before, even when the mechanisms share surface similarities. In the same spirit, Epelbaum's letter singles out Snow's protégés in the Argentine Forensic Anthropology Team in order to highlight the differences between them and the compromised, underequipped authorities responsible for earlier exhumations.[99]

The Asociación Madres continue to talk about exhumations as a way of declaring the *desaparecidos* dead, in an apparent reference to the junta's Presumption of Death Law, which tied reparations payments to the return of remains and an official declaration of death. The reparations program under Alfonsín, however, required no declaration of death. In fact, it stipulated that financial payments from the government would end if the *desaparecido* should reappear. In other words, far from declaring the *desaparecidos* dead, the Alfonsín-era reparations law formalized the unresolved nature of disappearance,[100] going so far as to leave the *desaparecidos* inscribed in voting registers.[101]

Reparations payments also expose the distinct visions of motherhood that the two organizations have developed. While the Asociación Madres devote themselves to creating a new generation of young people to emulate the *desaparecidos*—or, perhaps, the group's particular vision of what they stood for—the Línea Fundadora has argued for reparations payments based on the needs of the *desaparecidos'* biological children. Kaplan points out that the majority of *desaparecidos* "were working-class people, largely in their twenties and thirties, and many of them were parents of young children. Often the abducted provided the sole support for their families."[102] Though the Madres of the Línea Fundadora may themselves be from more privileged backgrounds, their arguments for reparations have focused largely on the economic needs of these working-class families: "We believe that the many children of the *desaparecidos* have the right not to experience hunger, to have decent clothing, the school supplies they need, and chances for recreation, like all other children."[103] Providing for these children, they argue, is something concrete that the state can do—and in no way implies that the injustices committed in the past can ever be fully repaired.

The ongoing search for all of these biological children of the *desaparecidos* is, in fact, central to both the Línea Fundadora and the Abuelas de Plaza de Mayo's missions—and may be an underlying reason why these two groups, who still define family more biologically than ideologically, are perceived as more "conservative" than their peers.[104] Locating and identifying kidnapped living children is inevitably linked to exhumations of their disappeared parents because, for so many grandmothers and other family members, the first question exhumation can help answer is whether there is a living child for whom to search.

The Asociación Madres repeatedly criticize exhumations for being focused on death and cadavers. Those who pursue exhumations, in Argentina or elsewhere, are called "mothers of the dead."[105] But this leaves out a crucial part of the narrative of exhumation in Argentina. For Coche de Pereyra, the most important finding of the Argentine team's efforts to exhume and identify Liliana Pereyra's body at the Parque Cemetery—where some Madres protested against the investigation—was that no fetal bones were buried with Liliana, who was pregnant at the time she disappeared. Soon after the exhumation at the Parque Cemetery, the Argentine team investigated the case of a couple, Roberto and Amelia Lanuscou. Authorities claimed the couple was killed, along with their three small children, in a shoot-out with security forces. The forensic team was able to show, based on the remains, that the couple and the two older children (Barbara and Roberto, four and six years old) had indeed been murdered, execution-style, and buried together. At least as importantly, however, "in the baby coffin that belonged to six-month-old Matilde, the forensic team found bones that upon close inspection proved to be those of a man's foot. They also recovered baby clothes and a pacifier that had no traces of a decomposing body or bones."[106] By way of explanation, a forensic doctor the state had assigned to the case told the baby's grandmother, Amelia Herrera de Miranda, that Matilde "was so tender that she dissolved like water."[107] Rejecting the cynical fable, Amelia Miranda joined the Abuelas de Plaza de Mayo to search for her missing granddaughter, though she died without finding her.[108] It is hard to see how the Línea Fundadora's and Abuelas' support for exhumations, so connected to the search for these grandchildren, is focused singularly on death.[109]

Nor is it at all clear, especially once the connection between exhumations and the search for living children has been made, that the pro-exhumation groups really are more reformist and less radical—*in their actual effects on*

Argentine society—than the Asociación Madres. The search for disappeared children has been a transformative process. It has helped to expose the ideology of the dictatorship, which in its attempt to cleanse the country of subversive elements treated the *desaparecidos* as a pseudoracial, monolithic category. Like colonialists in North America and Australia who stole indigenous children from their families, the military in Argentina (with the support of figures in the Catholic Church, it is widely believed) proposed that they could "rescue" the children of so-called subversives by placing them with "good" families, in the process treating subversion as something transmitted through kinship lines.[110] Since the UN's Genocide Convention considers "forcibly transferring" the children of one national group to another a form of genocide,[111] this kidnapping program and the racialized thinking behind it are perhaps the best evidence that repression in Argentina was a form of genocide—a term the Asociación Madres themselves have long insisted should be used.

Some of the children who have been reunited with their birth families through the Abuelas' work have joined activist organizations, envisioning themselves not as spiritual "reincarnations" of the *desaparecidos*, but rather as children of a decimated generation. These children are dedicated to *both* "individual historical reconstruction" and their parents' "spirit of struggle,"[112] rather than seeing the one as somehow opposed to the other.

Néstor Kirchner's election to the presidency, following a period of economic crisis and a rapid succession of presidents, led to the annulment of the Punto Final and Obediencia Debida laws. Before then, however, the search for missing children opened one of the few cracks in the cloak of impunity surrounding perpetrators. While providing cover for torturers and murderers, the amnesty laws did not cover kidnapping or child trafficking; thus evidence of disappeared living children led to a number of high-profile convictions. In 1998, Jorge Videla and Emilio Massera, two members of the military junta who had been pardoned by Alfonsín's successor, Carlos Saúl Menem,[113] were rearrested on charges of kidnapping thirty-four babies.[114] In July 2012, in recognition that as many as four hundred babies had been taken, new convictions were issued for Videla and the final junta president, Reynaldo Bignone (Massera died in 2010).[115]

Graciela de Jeger, dismissing the efforts of forensic experts in Argentina, says, "We already know that thousands of *desaparecidos* were secretly murdered and buried. The exhumations don't tell us anything we don't already know."[116] Whereas it is typical of the Asociación Madres to minimize the *juridical* power to exhumations (as when Beatriz de Rubinstein remarked that they have "nothing to do with justice"), de Jeger also denies their capacity to create new knowledge. This claim can be contrasted with a passage from Margaret Keck and Kathryn Sikkink's *Activists Beyond Borders*, about the Argentine Forensic Anthropology Team's exhumation of Laura Carlotto. Laura was the daughter of Estela Barnes de Carlotto, the current president of the Abuelas de Plaza de Mayo:

> Clyde Snow . . . knew that Laura had given birth because there were distinctive marks in the bones of the pelvis.[117] He was also able to tell Estela that her daughter had been assassinated at a distance of about thirty centimeters, which directly contradicted the military's story of a shootout at a roadblock. Given the direction of the bullets, it appeared that Laura had been shot in the back of the head at close range. Snow also told Estela that while it was clear her daughter had taken care of her teeth and they were in good shape, in the period before her death they had deteriorated, which suggested that she had been detained and could not take care of them. Combined with the testimony of witnesses who had seen Laura in secret prisons, Snow's information was sufficient for Estela to include the case of her daughter's murder in the request for the United States to extradite ex-general Carlos Guillermo Suárez Mason, who had been in charge of the region where Laura was held.[118]

Notable in this passage is not only how much information could be collected from the exhumation of one *desaparecida*, but also how many different dimensions and uses that information had. The exhumation impacted Carlotto's ongoing activism because it seemed to confirm for her that a grandchild of hers—a child stolen from her murdered daughter—was out there somewhere, living a lie. (In 2014, the eighty-three-year-old Carlotto was reunited with her thirty-six-year-old grandson Guido Carlotto, a musician who had grown up under a different name but with enough suspicions to request a DNA test. "I didn't want to die without hugging him," Carlotto told the press).[119] Far from complicit in attempts to limit the prosecution of torturers, the exhumation also provided evidence used in a successful extradition request that ultimately helped put Suárez Mason in prison, where he died in 2005. The evidence of Laura's body contradicted the lies told by the regime, not just in the very broad strokes offered by de Jeger ("thousands of *desaparecidos* were secretly murdered and buried") but rather with great precision ("thirty centimeters," "back of the head"). Last but not least, the exhumation provided information that both confirmed and deepened Carlotto's knowledge of her daughter's habits, character, and story—for example, the care she had taken of her teeth, and the evidence of her long detention marked by the cessation of this care. In other words, far from reducing Laura to "bare life" (as Edkins would have us believe),[120] the exhumation helped to reconstruct the person being mourned for her mourners.

This last task performed in exhumation—the task of reconstruction—exposes a truly radical difference between the two groups of Madres that usually goes unmentioned: the importance each group accords to the act of *caring* for the bodies of dead *desaparecidos*.

Caring to Exhume, Exhuming to Care

Part of the "hardness" and radicalism associated with Hebe de Bonafini and the Asociación Madres is related to their uncompromising political stances. It also stems, however, from their willingness to do the opposite of what most mourners, from Sophocles' tragic heroine Antigone to the Mothers of Srebrenica, have done in post-conflict settings: to insist that the most basic right they have is the right to bury the bodies of their loved ones. The political force and public attention the Asociación Madres have gained by refusing exhumations are now well understood, but no one seems willing to focus sustained attention on what they have given up.

Exhumations can provide information about the *desaparecidos*—information that is both evidentiary (Laura was shot from thirty centimeters away) and part of a personal history (Laura took good care of her teeth, but she had no toothbrush in the camps). In Argentina, the exhumation of a dead body can also lead directly to the search for living offspring. But the bodies in unmarked graves and the mutilated, decayed bodies that have washed up on Argentine and neighboring Uruguayan beaches are not only pieces of evidence. They are also victims of ongoing violence, violence characterized not just by the absence of any respect or care for the corpse, but also *the deliberate attempt to deprive that corpse of the possibility of being cared for*. N.N. graves and mutilated bodies hearken back to practices such as leaving one's enemies outside the city walls to be eaten by scavengers (the fate that awaited Antigone's brother, Polyneices, until Sophocles's tragic heroine intervened) or the posthumous violence long carried out against criminals and slaves.[121] The idea is not just to dishonor the body, but also to make sure that it is physically destroyed or placed beyond the reach of anyone who cared about the person in life. When it becomes impossible to show respect or care for the dead body, both the victim herself and her loved ones enter a state of permanent suffering, which cannot be eased or reversed except through the most extraordinary measures.[122]

These "extraordinary measures" are the often-overlooked ethical heart of international forensic investigation. As described further in Chapter 5, forensic teams are able, in some though not all circumstances, to bring the bodies of the dead out of mass graves and back into a world touched by care. Though many of their practices emerge from the long relationship between criminal justice and forensic science, when these teams enter the context of mass atrocity the meanings of their work evolve; they respond to new scales and types of violence with new forms of care and repair.

The most persistent efforts, over the past decades, to bring the idea of care—care of *bodies*, especially—into ethical theory and political scholarship have come from feminist scholars. For these thinkers, the most basic ethical relationship that exists is the relationship between interdependent bodies, particularly those of mother and child.[123] It thus seems strange that scholars such as Bouvard and Kaplan, both avowed feminists, leave the question of caring for the dead *desaparecidos* more or less unmentioned. Each of them describes the many political uses to which both groups of Madres have put the concept of motherhood. Like the Asociación Madres themselves, however, they seem to see the continued existence of bodies of the *desaparecidos*—and the possibility of bringing them back into some kind of direct relationship with their loved ones—as something private and personal, beyond the scope of an analysis of the Madres and their positions on exhumation.

When the question of care is on the table, however, it becomes possible to see some problems with the moral authority the Asociación Madres claim for themselves as the sole group keeping the memory of their children alive, or supervising their rebirth—both of which ultimately add up to claims of ownership over all of the *desaparecidos*. The Asociación Madres have a fine-tuned and admirable sense of the perils of stability-oriented compromise and reconciliation as a national project. The "aparición con vida" program, however, leaves no room for an acknowledgment of the full dimensions of violence visited upon their loved ones. If the Línea Fundadora had a figure as moralizing as Hebe de Bonafini, she might point out that the Asociación Madres have abandoned their dead to the graves their murderers dug for them—graves which were designed from the start as an *extension* of the camps and basements where these people were tortured, raped, and killed. Reclaiming corpses is not only about mourning and closure, she might say: it is also about refusing to let their murderers be the ones to determine the final resting place of the *desaparecidos* and the care that they receive.

Zoë Crossland calls "aparición con vida" a strategy of "exaggerat[ing] the separation between the physical remains of the dead and their lived histories in order to contribute to the disembodiment of the disappeared."[124] While the Argentine Forensic Anthropology Team and their allies have emphasized "the names and stories of the people they excavated," she writes, the Asociación Madres "seized the concept of bodies as evidence, rather than people, and used this strategy to keep the disappeared in the public eye."[125] Crossland rightly points out the irony here: forensic experts, who generally operate in the rigorously impersonal framework of criminal justice proceedings,[126] have in Argentina insisted that each *desaparecido* be viewed as an individual story, while some of these *desaparecidos'* own family members demand that their stories and bodies be subsumed to a larger project of "transforming justice."[127] The Argentine team and the Línea Fundadora treat the bodies of *desaparecidos* as "people," while the Asociación Madres have chosen to treat them—like the pamphlets, headscarves, radio station, and other tools of their activism—as pieces of a complex media strategy. The Asociación Madres have enlisted the bodies of the *desaparecidos* in their cause while insulating themselves from their material presence (at a psychological cost, of course, which is made clear by support the group sought from psychoanalysts as they consolidated their opposition to exhumations).[128]

The Línea Fundadora and the Abuelas have, in the meantime, worked to take "ownership"—if only temporarily—of their loved ones in the most tangible way possible, by accepting and reburying their bones. Not every family member will wish to do what Berta Schubaroff, a member of the Abuelas, did after the Argentine team identified the bones of her son: "I became very moved. . . . I began to kiss him, kiss all of his bones, touch him, and caress him. But the feeling was mixed with pain, because now that I had found him, I knew that he was dead . . ."[129] It is true, as the Asociación Madres allege, that this moment transformed Schubaroff from the mother of a *desaparecido* into a mother of the dead. But to Hebe de Bonafini's question, "Why do you want the dead bodies?" Schubaroff provides a powerful, but simple, answer: to touch them, to love them. To the extent her encounter with her son's bones involved some form of closure, it is a closure that has nothing to do with *forgetting*. Neither she, nor any other mother, seems more likely to forget her son or the violence he suffered because his body has been found and been touched—just the opposite.[130]

The claim that "the political voice of the Madres . . . end[s]" when the bodies of the *desaparecidos* are unearthed rests on the assumption that caring for
and reburying the dead is necessarily an individualistic, apolitical act.[131] In fact,
the Línea Fundadora performs and reinforces its solidarity through exhumation and reburial. As Matilde Mellibovsky, a member of the Línea Fundadora,
explains, the group "accompanies each family at the moment of the exhumation and recovery of the remains of their loved ones."[132] In the early days, when
the Argentine authorities were carrying out their own suspect "identifications,"
some family members accepted bodies that they knew might not really be their
children. They believed that whoever's child was now in their custody, he or she
deserved a decent burial[133]—deserved to receive the same care these families
were waiting to bestow upon their own dead. Political and social ties did, in
this case, trump biological kinship, but in a way that did not require the rejection of material remains.

Among the bodies the Argentine team has exhumed and identified are three
of the earliest members of the Madres de Plaza de Mayo: Azucena Villaflor de
Vicente (who was the group's leader before Hebe de Bonafini); María Eugenia
Ponce de Bianco; and Esther Ballestrino de Careaga. After a naval captain, Alfredo Astiz, infiltrated the organization, the three were imprisoned, tortured,
thrown into the sea, and then—after their bodies washed up together on the
beach—buried in an anonymous grave.[134] "Together they were taken away, together they struggled, together they were killed and together the sea returned
them,"[135] says a note on the Línea Fundadora's website. The group clearly considers the exhumation and reburial of these bodies an act of solidarity and historical memory of their own struggles. Further down on the same web page, with
no intimation of a conflict between mourning and activism, or between care
and remembrance, these women have written: "No forgetting, no forgiveness."[136]

Families and Forensic Teams in International Perspective

The key events described in this chapter—exhumations by the Argentina Forensic Anthropology Team, as well as the internal divisions within the Madres
de Plaza de Mayo—took place as these organizations were beginning separate
but parallel processes of internationalization. In the mid-1990s, members of
the Argentine team were involved in Physicians for Human Rights' investigations into Saddam Hussein's genocidal "Anfal campaign" against Kurds and
other minorities in Iraq,[137] and then in exhumations on behalf of the International Criminal Tribunal for the Former Yugoslavia.[138] The Argentines and

Clyde Snow also worked closer to home to train and establish forensic teams in Chile and Guatemala, which were dedicated to bringing scientific expertise to the investigation of human rights violations in their respective countries.[139] Amnesty laws and other political constraints limited all of these teams' hopes of contributing evidence to prosecutions of human rights violators. Because of these limitations—and also, surely, because the Argentines developed their working methods in such a complex landscape of Madres and Abuelas with contradictory views of exhumation—the Argentine team and other Latin American organizations are associated with a family-centric model of foren-sic investigation. This model features close working relationships with family groups (when possible), a high value placed on identifications and reburials, and often close ties with the larger human rights community. The Latin Ameri-can organizations have more recently formed a federation, the Asociación Latinoamericana de Antropología Forense (Latin American Forensic Anthro-pology Association), which conducts trainings throughout the region and holds an annual conference.

In the meantime, the various groups of Madres and Abuelas have also shared their model of activism with women in similar situations abroad. In 1981, before the Madres split apart, the organization helped form the Latin American Federation of Families of the Detained-Disappeared (FEDEFAM), which includes groups from fourteen countries in Latin America. The Línea Fundadora and Abuelas have maintained ties with this federation, which has a formal relationship with the United Nations and promotes the development of international norms against forced disappearance.[140] The Abuelas have also assisted a group in El Salvador that uses DNA testing to identify children taken from their parents during the Salvadoran civil war.

Bouvard chronicles the formation of support groups for the Madres through-out Europe, as well as the spread of various mothers' groups who have borrowed and adapted the Madres' iconography, using headscarves and other symbols in their campaigns to address radiation poisoning from the Chernobyl meltdown, drug trafficking and Mafia crimes, the fate of street children, and other causes. In 1994, the Asociación Madres began organizing international conferences for these groups,[141] which focus more on building solidarity between the mothers' organizations, and less on collaboration with international institutions, than the Latin American Federation of Families of the Detained-Disappeared. When war broke out in the former Yugoslavia, the Madres' European support groups began sending food and medical supplies to the Mothers of Sarajevo.

The Argentine team and the Madres/Abuelas were thus not only different facets of a multidimensional human rights movement in Argentina, they were also the pioneering examples of two new *categories* of human rights organization, their peers and heirs destined to meet again and again based on the interest both constituents have in the search for missing people and the investigation of mass graves.

These two institutional archetypes, the international forensic team and the mothers' association, had their first major interactions of the 1990s in the former Yugoslavia. The search for the missing throughout the former Yugoslavia gave rise to a number of family associations, among them the Mothers of Srebrenica in Bosnia and Mothers of Vukovar in Croatia. There are important differences in the exhumation politics in the former Yugoslavia and Argentina, beginning with the conduct of the investigations themselves and extending through the institutions involved in the search for the missing, technologies available, political context, and of course the cultural practices of memory, grief, exhumation, and reburial in each case.[142] The mothers' groups in the Balkans borrowed tactics and inspiration from the Madres de Plaza de Mayo,[143] but their demands were often different. For example, while the Madres protested amnesty laws blocking the prosecution of human rights violators, the Mothers of Srebrenica criticized the international tribunal's focus on prosecutions, demanding individual identifications and reburials for all victims. Their criticism of the exhumation process, in other words, was almost the inverse of "aparición con vida," with its call for prosecutions but no individual identifications.

Elsewhere, however, the echoes of Argentina are hard to miss. In 1996, Physicians for Human Rights assembled a team to exhume a mass grave in Ovčara, in northeastern Croatia. In the grave they would find prisoners of war, wounded combatants, and patients taken from the Vukovar hospital by members of the Yugoslav National Army (JNA) and Serb paramilitary groups to nearby agricultural lands, where they were murdered. As Clea Koff recounts, the women in the Mothers of Vukovar organization—like many of their counterparts throughout the former Yugoslavia—had heard rumors that their husbands and sons were all in prisoner-of-war camps. From that point on, most of the women's efforts had gone into finding their relatives alive somewhere. When the forensic team arrived, the mother's group embraced a strategy much like "aparición con vida," protesting the exhumations because, as Koff writes, "They didn't want to be survivors of the dead, but seekers of the living."[144]

Koff's shock at this resistance from families of the missing recalls Bihurriet's surprise at her rebuff from the Madres in the Parque Cemetery: "I had always kept in mind the idea that if I worked in this field, I might be in contact with families, and they would be glad that people like me were there," Koff recalls, dismayed.[145]

The Vukovar mothers' objections were framed in less transcendent tones than those of the Asociación Madres. They had no objection to individual mourning or "closure," but rather wanted a full explanation as to why the bodies in the graves were believed to belong to their missing men.[146] Nevertheless, as in Argentina, the initial reaction to these women was to consider them traumatized and irrational. One forensic expert working in the region contrasted the "calm and professional" mothers with the "hysterical ones, always crying and wailing that everybody is guilty—I'm guilty, the President's guilty, the U.N.'s guilty. Some mothers expected a miracle to happen, something God-sent, which would magically return the child [alive]."[147]

It is an unfortunate dynamic: the most challenging claims made around mass graves are considered irrational, and thus subjected to little analysis or critical reflection. This pattern appears with regard to political claims, such as "aparición con vida," as well as to religious ones. Forensic experts can be contemptuous, as in the example above, or on the contrary deeply respectful. Both reactions, if they do not treat these objections as *arguments*, translate into the same form of disengagement. The Mothers of Srebrenica's demands for individual identification have influenced an ongoing and rich dialogue about the tensions between tribunals and mourners, evidence collection and identification; they have also prompted significant changes in the institutional landscape of international forensic investigation (especially the formation of the International Commission on Missing Persons and the International Committee for the Red Cross' campaign on "The Missing"). No one in the field, however, seems to have engaged as fully with the more strident objections of the Asociación Madres de Plaza de Mayo or Mothers of Vukovar.

Another aspect of exhumation politics in Argentina that has resurfaced elsewhere is the tension, real or perceived, between individual grief and collective solidarity—or, in the words of one Spanish activist, "particular deaths" versus "social deaths."[148] As described in Chapter 1, the major historical memory group in Spain, the Asociación por la Recuperación de la Memoria Histórica, has strategically downplayed the political affiliations of the civil war dead, casting the exhumation of graves as a search for "husbands, sons, or fathers."[149]

Another group, Foro por la Memoria—which like the Asociación Madres is closely affiliated with leftist causes—has advocated a more political retelling of Spanish history.

Though their leftist politics, sharp rhetoric, and insistence on reading history through the lens of ideological struggle are similar to those of the Asociación Madres, there is a crucial difference between Foro por la Memoria and the Asociación Madres: Foro por la Memoria does not oppose exhumations. Rather, the group demands *more* from exhumations. Foro members have called for a "multidisciplinary team" of "lawyers, historians, psychologists, archaeologists, anthropologists, documentarians, archivists" and others,[150] who would use forensic evidence to "give answers to families, but also social and political responses" to the legacy of Francoist violence.[151] This position shows that a socialist or collectivist perspective on history need not imply, as the Asociación Madres argue it must, a stance against exhumations. Complete disengagement from the forensic process, in fact, may have foreclosed similar opportunities for the Asociación Madres to argue for how the information emerging from the graves of the *desaparecidos* supports their broader narrative of political genocide and a revolutionary legacy.

The claims family members, religious groups, and others make about mass graves may in some cases be inconsistent, ill informed, or even reactionary, but they are rarely wholly "irrational." Rather, their purported irrationality too often becomes an excuse not to think hard about them or try to craft an answer. Whatever the fate of a mass grave, the decision to exhume or not to exhume always has political, social, and moral consequences. It affects the opportunities to prosecute human rights violators and base historical arguments on physical evidence. It organizes space in a post-conflict nation: whether it is a home to unmarked graves, untouchable sacred spaces, collective reburial plots, or memorials. It reflects the value placed on caring for violated bodies. Last but not least, it tends to raise questions about who speaks for mourners and the dead, and even who is anointed the successors or "children" of the missing and disappeared.

Conclusion: Forking Paths

Exhumation politics in Argentina were the starting point for ongoing, sometimes quite difficult dynamics between forensic teams and family associations on an international stage. They also offer an often-overlooked critical perspective on popular narratives about transitional justice. When Domanska portrays the Asociación Madres as concerned with "crime, guilt, and punishment" and the Línea Fundadora with "mourning, forgiveness, and forgetting," she is placing her analysis within a framework familiar to those who study post-conflict and post-atrocity politics. The crucial idea is that transitional justice is, by nature, a process full of terrible tradeoffs between conflicting values.[152]

Even in scholarship that is quite sympathetic to forensic exhumations, it is repeated that the Asociación Madres' efforts to create a mystical, unresolved category out of the *desaparecidos* "plays a vital role in maintaining the memory of the abuses of the military, and in preventing the creation of a new national identity based on leaving the years of the 'dirty war' behind in the past."[153] This interpretation is never supported with concrete evidence of what the Asociación Madres' anti-exhumation position, or their refusal of reparations and memorials, has actually done to keep memory alive in Argentina. Nor does it explain how the exhumations conducted by the Argentine team are complicit in resolving or closing off a traumatic past. In fact, if one looks at the role exhumations have played in prosecutions, the attention they receive in the press, and the painful public dialogue about the search for disappeared children (which does not always require exhumations, but is connected with those efforts), there is significant reason to believe that the forensic process actually promotes the causes of memory, public dialogue, and legal accountability.

Rather than glorifying one approach or the other, however, it is more urgent to question the very idea of an inevitable tradeoff between politicized memory and individual closure. The stark binaries of transitional justice studies have taken on a life of their own. The idea that post-conflict populations face a choice between open, bleeding wounds and a comfortable but thoughtless "oblivion" now serves,[154] much like the "theory of the two demons," as a way of appearing shrewd and dispassionate while disregarding the full spectrum of possibilities available in political life, even in times of fear and violence.

When it comes to exhuming the *desaparecidos*, Cohen Salama makes a trenchant point: "From a logical point of view, there is no need to 'subordinate' one kind of information to another."[155] The identification and reburial of individual bodies is not in some sort of existential contest with information about the program of repression that killed them, or about the beliefs for which they died. According to Jay Aronson, some of the families of victims of Apartheid-era violence in South Africa, by demanding exhumations, military funerals, and other official recognition from the post-Apartheid government, have arrived at a "an overtly political understanding of closure";[156] closure, for them, is not achieved in the home but rather through public arrangements negotiated with the post-Apartheid state. These families rejected—or simply ignored—the psychoanalytic definition of closure as bounded within "the private, emotional sphere."[157] Like the Línea Fundadora and the Abuelas, they have exposed the false choice behind the old slogan "Don't mourn—organize!" Because of grief they came together and got organized, and one of the goals of their organizing is a satisfactory (and thus necessarily public) mourning process.[158]

Nathan Englander's 2007 novel *The Ministry of Special Cases* tells the story of an Argentine couple, Kaddish and Lillian Poznan, and their teenage son, Pato, who is disappeared soon after the 1976 military coup. As their search proceeds, Kaddish and Lillian, each pursuing different avenues, begin to grow apart. Their methods of searching—sitting in government offices, bribing priests for information, interviewing a former torture camp operative—lead to different truths about Pato's disappearance.

The growing divisions between Kaddish and Lillian can be compared to—though not made equivalent with—the two groups of Madres. Lillian's position resembles that of the Asociación Madres, who reject any statement, policy, or monument that acknowledges the likelihood their children are dead. Kaddish, at the other extreme, seeks out a body to mourn in the most intimate, most physical way he can. The most tragic aspect of *The Ministry of Special Cases*— far worse, in its own way, than the disappearance of Pato, a character we barely begin to know before he is rushed off-stage—is the forking paths of Kaddish and Lillian, who find themselves, almost helplessly, giving structure and permanence to the violence that has been done to their family. They cannot live simultaneously with the desire that someone, somewhere, be called to account for Pato as if he were a living boy and with the need to mourn his probable death, so they become stuck in the divergent narratives that the crime of disappearance imposes on them. Kaddish and Lillian's inability to create a shared and multifaceted model of closure constitutes a triumph for the dictatorship that lives long past its own demise. It ensures ongoing suffering for a couple whose last remaining comfort, the shared grief of parents, has now been taken from them. Failing to find a way to love, fight for, and mourn Pato together, Kaddish and Lillian manage to keep alive only the crimes that have been committed against them.

There is an argument embedded in the way Englander avoids allowing his reader to sympathize exclusively with Kaddish or Lillian. To have a loved one disappeared and then to go on living requires reinventing the self. Nowhere in

Englander's novel do we find a narrator or judge telling us why one strategy of making meaning out of senselessness is more poetic, or more radical, than the other. The task is not to elevate one model of grief above another, but to work among the varieties of grief and locate a path wide enough for everyone.

PART 2

THE PHILOSOPHY OF MASS GRAVES

Chapter 3

Forensics of the Sacred

Human Rights Investigations, Religious Prohibitions

The forensic anthropologist Bill Haglund earned an international reputation exhuming mass graves in Rwanda and the former Yugoslavia in the wake of the genocides there in the mid-1990s. In 2001, he traveled to the small town of Jedwabne, Poland, on a mission for Physicians for Human Rights, where Haglund was director of the International Forensic Program. Much of Jedwabne's Jewish community had been wiped out in a 1941 massacre. First, a group of about forty of the town's Jewish men were forced to march through town, holding a statue of Lenin (as a demonstration of their supposed Soviet sympathies), to a barn where they were killed. Later in the day, the remaining Jedwabne Jews—likely somewhere between 250 and 300 men, women, and children—were locked in a barn and burnt alive. The charred remains were then buried in two mass graves.

For a long time afterward, the story in Poland was that Nazi occupiers were responsible for this heinous crime. A memorial in the town bore the inscription "The site of torment of Jewish people. The Gestapo and the Nazi police burnt alive 1,600 Jews on 10 July 1941."[1] However, in a widely publicized and controversial 2001 book, *Neighbors*, the Polish-American historian Jan Gross alleged that responsibility for the massacre lay largely with the town's own Polish people.

The book continues to be the subject of fierce debates about Polish versus German culpability in the genocide of Polish Jews, as well as the validity of Gross's own historical methodology.[2] It has also become part of a difficult and divisive national conversation about World War II and the Holocaust in

Poland, discourse that is complicated by the complex victim/perpetrator roles the country played: as oppressor of its own native Jewish population (a role that predated World War II, notably in the pogroms of the nineteenth and early twentieth centuries), host to death camps built under Nazi occupation, and as the victim of terrible crimes by both the Nazis and the Soviets.[3] Gross, who has published subsequent books emphasizing Polish participation in anti-Semitic violence and looting (*Golden Harvest* and *Fear*), continues to pursue this tense terrain of dialogue;[4] more recently, the Polish filmmaker Władysław Pasikowski has joined him with a 2012 film, *Aftermath*, that is loosely based on Gross's narrative of the events in Jedwabne.

The *Neighbors* controversy had many concrete results. Polish President Aleksander Kwásniewski issued an official apology for the Jedwabne massacre. A new memorial was built in the town, though the mayor did not attend its dedication.[5] The Polish Institute of National Remembrance (IPN), the agency charged with the investigation of World War II-era war crimes in the country, also began preliminary forensic exhumations at the two mass graves believed to contain the remains of the massacred Jews.[6] Haglund was asked to observe the work of the Polish anthropologists at the site.

The evidence produced by the investigations, which relied on witness testimony as well as analysis of the graves, supported some details of Gross's account, such as Polish participation in the murders, but they also showed that German soldiers were present in the village at the time.[7] Furious debate continues over whether what happened in Jedwabne was a "spontaneous anti-Jewish pogrom" carried out largely by the town's Poles, or whether "the Germans staged the massacre and some Poles assisted them."[8]

This chapter is not about these debates over Holocaust history, already the subject of a large body of scholarship. Rather, it explores one of the major reasons our knowledge about what really happened in Jedwabne is likely to remain forever murky. The five-day exhumation in Jedwabne was brought to a halt by objections from Orthodox Jews, who claimed that the disturbance of the graves and bodies was against Jewish law.[9] Young Polish Jews, many arriving from Warsaw, recited psalms at the gravesite,[10] while a series of rabbis from Warsaw, Israel, and London came to oversee the digging and minimize any potential desecration.[11] Haglund's report on his visit states, in a carefully clinical tone, "In accordance with the Old Testament book of Samuel once bones were buried they were to be left undisturbed. Disturbance of the mortal remains of an individual also disturbed the soul."[12]

Ultimately, the Polish authorities reached a compromise with the religious representatives: only the top layer of the grave would be exhumed, with small fragmentary remains removed for examination and photography. Larger bones would be left in place. Objects associated with the remains were taken into custody.[13] In a scene of some historical irony, as Haglund remembers it, the exhumation ended with some of the non-Jewish Polish investigators weeping in frustration as they watched one of the rabbis lowering the charred teeth and bone fragments of Jewish victims—which had been painstakingly screened out from among other debris—back into the graves.[14] (See Figure 3.)

Figure 3. A rabbi returns burned fragments of Jews killed in Jedwabne, Poland, to the mass grave they were buried in before Polish anthropologists exhumed them. Photograph by William Haglund.

A mass grave exhumation without the removal and investigation of dead bodies is severely limited in the number of conclusions it can draw about the manner of death and number of victims, as well as the certainty with which it can make those conclusions. The Polish Institute of National Remembrance's report estimates that thirty to forty bodies were in one grave and around three hundred in another,[15] but as the Polish-American historian Marek Jan Chodakiewicz observes, this estimate was based on looking at the top layer of one grave and making calculations about its size and the number of "human beings per 100 kilograms of ashes." "Only a complete exhumation of every single bone," he continues, "would have revealed the exact number of victims."[16] The number of victims has become, predictably, one of the major sticking points in the bitter clash between Gross and his critics.[17]

Despite the inconclusive and, to many, unsatisfying nature of the forensic investigation, the Polish Institute of National Remembrance and Physicians for Human Rights abandoned plans for future forensic work in Jedwabne. Religious opposition, coming from the very Jewish community that these institutions had seen as principle stakeholders in the exhumations, was politically unworkable.[18] The aborted Jedwabne exhumation is thus a powerful example of the challenge that forensic teams and other human rights organizations face in balancing their own core commitments with sensitivity to the voices of other stakeholders. Haglund and the Polish anthropologists (as well as Gross and many of his critics) are all guided by the idea that an accurate history of atrocity is one way of restoring justice to both the living and the dead. However, many forensic experts are also wary of imposing particular scientific solutions on local communities that do not actually want them.

With some variations, the clash between investigation and preservation—between the desire to uncover hidden truths and the desire to respect sacred spaces—has become a persistent feature of post-Holocaust politics in Poland. For example, a memorial to the Holocaust dead on the grounds of the former death camp Belzec was the site of more controversy and an attempted lawsuit over "a 12–foot-wide pathway 30 feet below ground, envisioned by the memorial's Polish designers as an interstice running hundreds of feet through the camp like a crack in the earth." Though the American Jewish Committee supported the project and a rabbi supervised it, opponents alleged the "trench" would inevitably disturb the Jewish dead.[19]

Yet Poland is only one context in which mass grave exhumations have had to contend with claims about the sacredness of bodies and graves. In fact, forensic teams have encountered religious prohibitions against exhumation in many different locations, with varied religious doctrines being invoked.

This chapter surveys some religious objections to post-conflict exhumations and begins a process of both investigation and comparison. Religious objections to forensic work have received far less attention than the more ideological battles in Argentina and Spain. In those places, religious identity sometimes plays a role in attitudes toward the search for the missing,[20] but it is largely subordinated to the question of how exhumation renarrates the past and what role politics play in that narrative. There are important similarities, however, in how these challenges to exhumation can be understood. The Madres de Plaza de Mayos' slogan of "aparición con vida," which both summarized and reaffirmed their objection to exhuming the *desaparecidos*, had an important prehistory and served multiple purposes, rhetorical and organizational as much as philosophical. Religious prohibitions against exhuming mass graves also have distinct backstories and multiple potential purposes—not all of which are fundamentally religious in their character. Exploring both the universality and the particularities of sacred graves offers insight into what they can teach us about human rights.

Sacred Graves

Religious prohibitions need not always bring forensic investigations to a complete halt, as they did in Jedwabne. In some cases, forensic experts could find justification simply to ignore the objections of religious people. The historian Chodakiewicz seems to wish this had been the case in Jedwabne, remarking in frustration that "despite the constitutional division between church and state," the Polish authorities bowed to the objections of Orthodox Jews.[21] In fact, the separation between church and state in many democracies has not solved the complicated status of the dead body. As Alison Dundes Renteln writes, medico-legal authorities often must seek consent from next-of-kin to conduct an autopsy; where there are religious objections, they must prove "sufficiently compelling interest to outweigh the right to religious freedom,"[22] such as the need to conduct a criminal investigation or concerns about public health. Moreover, even if *state authorities* have the right to disregard religious beliefs for investigations into criminal actions, by calling upon nongovernmental organizations such as Physicians for Human Rights, they introduce a different set of constraints. Ignoring objections from the communities around mass graves is incompatible with the victim- and mourner-centric ethic embraced by most international forensic teams—regardless of the constitutional justifications or support they would have from the state.

With mediation between forensic teams and religious leaders, some exhumations have moved forward despite initial objections. Recalling an investigation in Indonesia, Haglund says, "All we needed was for the imam to come and say a prayer at the site before we began. . . . Usually in any country, the needs of justice supersede religious objections."[23] In reality, the issue may not so much be one of justice "superseding" religious objections, but rather of allowing religious figures the chance to craft an explanation as to why exhumations are compatible with the sacredness of the dead. In indigenous Guatemalan villages confronting the aftermath of 1980s "scorched earth" campaigns, anthropologist Victoria Sanford witnessed this sort of reinterpretation:

> After lighting the candles, burning copal incense, and adorning the area with red gladiolas and pine needles, the Maya priest would speak with God to explain why the exhumation should take place and ask permission from God to disturb the bones. Then the priest would call upon the spirits to explain to them that God had given permission for the exhumation to take place. . . . Instead of using their powers against those who disturb the bones, the priest asked the spirits to use their powers to bless and protect the forensic team and all who worked at the exhumation.[24]

In the case of Orthodox Jewish beliefs and the Jedwabne mass graves, as in many other areas of Jewish practice, there is a rich tradition of debate over the interpretation of scripture. Jacob Baker, a rabbi born in Jedwabne who emigrated to the United States in 1937 as the climate for Jews in Poland worsened,[25] spoke in favor of relocating the remains of the town's murdered Jews to a Jewish burial ground, perhaps in Israel.[26] After Haglund's return from Poland, Physicians for Human Rights asked Boston University's Hillel rabbi, Joseph Polak, to investigate Jewish views on exhumation and reburial. The result, a lengthy and erudite discussion in a Jewish scholarly journal, *Tradition*, describes more than one potential interpretation of Jewish law. In one interpretation, dead souls watch over their resting places and are pained by any disturbance. In another interpretation, for which Rabbi Polak argues passionately, numerous aspects of the undignified and sacrilegious burial of Jews in Jedwabne's mass graves make it "not only appropriate but also *obligatory*" that the bodies be exhumed and reburied.[27] Among these factors is the lack of space between bodies and their location beyond the confines of a nearby Jewish cemetery. If it is feasible,

Polak argues, Jewish bodies interred in the vicinity of a cemetery but outside of its boundaries should be moved. He cites Talmudic commentary: "If a grave is found in an unusual place (outside a cemetery) . . . the *met* [corpse] may be reinterred in a Jewish cemetery."[28]

Rabbi Polak's argument is broadly similar to the one made by some survivor communities in Guatemala: "Peace will not come to Guatemala . . . as long as the remains of our massacred relatives continue to be buried in clandestine cemeteries and we cannot give them Christian burials."[29] In the best of circumstances, then, the forensic investigation of mass graves is not just compatible with a claim that dead bodies are sacred; rather, one of the possible nonscientific outcomes of forensic investigation is allowing mourners to offer the dead sacred treatment—in effect, to undo blasphemy and resacralize them.

Nevertheless, Jedwabne is far from an aberration. "From Poland to Bosnia to Congo," G. Jeffrey MacDonald writes in the *Christian Science Monitor*, "survivors of varied religious backgrounds have at times made a common plea: Our loved ones suffered enough in life. Let them at least have peace in death."

MacDonald is correct that forensic teams have been asked, in all of these cases, not to dig up bodies. However, the plea may not be as "common" as it looks at first glance. There are important ways in which objections to mass grave investigations, framed in religious language, vary across context.

The first variation is the sincerity with which the claim is made. Like human rights, the sacred is a powerful rhetorical tool and can be used as a smokescreen for other goals. The example of Congo, mentioned in MacDonald's article, is instructive. In 1997–98, the United Nations contracted with the Argentine Forensic Anthropology Team to lead the forensic efforts of an international team charged with investigating violations of human rights and humanitarian law in the Democratic Republic of Congo.[30] The team was called the UN Joint Investigative Mission for Eastern Zaire, and its work was to be a short-lived and frustrating exercise. As MacDonald reports, the team ultimately abandoned plans for a major exhumation in the city of Mbandaka, Congo, in part because of charges from locals that they were desecrating gravesites.

The graves in question were believed to hold the remains of more than 550 Hutu refugees, part of a wave of more than one million such refugees who fled Rwanda to Congo, at that time called Zaire. During the 1994 Rwandan genocide, militant Hutu groups murdered at least five hundred thousand Tutsis and Hutu moderates. In July of that year, the Tutsi-dominated Rwandan Patriotic Front (RPF), led by Rwanda's current president, Paul Kagame, captured the capital, Kigali, and brought the genocide to an end.[31] As the RPF gained control of the country, millions of Hutus, fearing reprisals, fled to Burundi, Congo, Tanzania, and Uganda. Their fear was not baseless, as the massacre of Hutus in places such as the Kibeho camp in southwest Rwanda—"in full view of aid workers and U.N. peacekeeping troops"—would prove.[32]

The UN camps erected to shelter Hutu refugees in Congo wound up being home to a difficult-to-discern mixture of civilians, combatants, and genocidaires,[33] sitting in the midst of another nation that was also embroiled in conflict. Zaire's dictator, Mobutu Seso Seku, had well-known links to the Hutu Power movement in Rwanda. The Tutsi-led powers in Rwanda had watched in frustration as the UN High Commissioner on Refugees arranged for Mobutu's army—the natural allies of the Hutu genocidaires now based in the camps for any future military incursions back into Rwanda—to serve as refugee camp security forces. In 1997, a coalition of militant groups, led by the rebel fighter Laurent-Désiré Kabila and enjoying significant support from Rwanda, succeeded in forcing Mobutu into exile. Kabila proclaimed himself president of the newly renamed Democratic Republic of Congo. His forces attacked groups of Hutu refugees and other villages—"Despite the presence of civilians, including women, children, and the elderly."[34] The refugees in Mbandaka, where the UN Joint Investigative Mission for Eastern Zaire would attempt exhumations, included babies and children who, according to witnesses, were bludgeoned to death against a wall.[35]

As reports make clear, the politics behind the aborted UN forensic investigations in 1997–98—much like the warfare and refugee crisis that instigated them—were often not what they appeared at first glance. Along with flagrant obstruction of the investigations, the team had to contend with fears for its safety as armed men blocked them from talking to witnesses or examining gravesites.[36] As the UN gradually came to terms with Kabila's control over the country, the political weight it was willing to put behind the investigations seems to have evaporated.[37] Members of the Argentine team traveled to the region five times, interviewed witnesses, and mapped out 210 possible massacre sites, but Kabila's government in Kinshasa used disputes about the time period that should be under investigation, and complaints about the personnel in the investigative body, to keep investigators away from the graves.[38] The Argentines' reports on the Congo investigations are exercises in diplomatic restraint, the frustration simmering beneath cool phrases about the planning and logistical tasks completed during weeks marked by waiting to get through bureaucratic red tape. The team traveled from one continent to another multiple times, frequently finding itself obligated to recruit new forensic experts as the investigation stretched out over multiple trips and beyond anyone's planned timetable. When they finally did begin to exhume some of the graves at and around Mbandaka—before their work was again cut short by protests, threats, and extortion attempts[39]—the sites had clearly been tampered with already, many skeletal remains removed by government forces in what the team calls a "clean up" operation.[40]

Perhaps most crucially, what MacDonald portrays as an eruption of religious feeling against exhumation among civilians in Mbakanda was actually part of a centrally coordinated program of obstruction. As the New York Times reports, "One investigator on the way to a suspected massacre site saw officials handing out banners protesting the inquiry to villagers, who then promptly held a protest."[41] The Argentine team points out that the "timing and location" of the protests held against the forensic team "corresponded closely with the mission's itinerary, which only the government knew";[42] they also note that the signs were printed in three languages, including French and English—not something that would normally be expected in a provincial Congolese city.[43] The concern over desecration of the graves, made in this context, appears to have been exaggerated or concocted in order to keep a lid on an inconvenient history. Perhaps the Kinshasa government was consciously playing on a set of stereotypes of African villagers, and a media all too eager to cast them as superstitious and benighted, to lend the appearance of legitimacy to an ersatz demonstration.

Human rights debates have long been marked by a dichotomy between the universality of human rights and the particularity of "local culture." Yet the unraveling of the exhumations in Congo demonstrates how unwise it may be to assume that every claim of the sacred is "local" in nature. The local and the international, furthermore, are not opposite sides of a binary, but rather points in a complex web that also includes national, ethnic, and other levels of loyalty and command.

Even in Jedwabne, where the religious nature of the rabbis' objections is harder to dispute, the drama unfolded against the backdrop of a tense national situation that would have been hard to ignore. In the years before the publication of Neighbors, Poland had begun to experience a largely unforeseen "renaissance" of interest, among many ordinary Poles, in the Jewish culture that had nearly been extinguished in their country. Growing numbers of people were rediscovering Jewish roots, which had sometimes been concealed for survival, and committing themselves to religious observance.[44] The controversy over *Neighbors*, which stirred up painful memories of the Jewish past in Poland and some vigorous expressions of anti-Semitism,[45] threatened to upset, or even derail, this new phase of Jewish-Polish relations.

Rabbi Michael Schudrich, the most high-profile representative of Orthodox Polish Jewry to visit the Jedwabne mass graves,[46] is a leading figure in Poland's Jewish renaissance.[47] Schudrich has expressed discomfort about the political and cultural effects of Gross's work: "Gross writes in a way to provoke, not to educate, and Poles don't react well to it. Because of the style, too many people reject what he has to say."[48] The forensic anthropologist Haglund hypothesizes that fears of upsetting the fragile reconciliation between non-Jews and Jews in Poland played a part in the rabbis' eagerness to shut down the Jedwabne exhumations.[49] Rabbi Polak, from Boston University, disagrees. Though convinced that the case in favor of exhuming the mass grave in Jedwabne is "unassailable," he is nevertheless convinced that those who voiced religious objections had the best of intentions: "Their respect for Jewish law, for *Halakha*, is worthy—but they don't have the skills to work [the correct interpretation of the law] out."[50]

Regardless of the potential political motivations behind the rabbis' intervention, the question of what counts as "local culture," in Jedwabne as in Congo, requires a closer look. Schudrich is a Jew of Polish descent; born in New York, he moved to Poland in the 1990s to work for a Jewish foundation. No stranger to Jedwabne's history, he helped the Institute of National Remembrance locate relatives of the victims and solicit testimonies from them and officiated at recent ceremonies there.[51] Yet at the time of the exhumation efforts in Jedwabne, Schudrich was serving as the rabbi of Warsaw and Łódź,[52] both hundreds of miles away from Jedwabne (in 2004, he rose to the post of Chief Rabbi of Poland). Schudrich's authority to speak on behalf of Polish Jewry, especially at an historic site such as Jedwabne, is itself a divisive issue for this complex, diasporic community. In Jérémie Dres' nonfiction graphic novel exploring contemporary Jewish life in Poland, *We Won't See Auschwitz*, a member of the Jewish Social and Cultural Association in Poland (TSKZ) refers to Schudrich dismissively as "an American with Polish citizenship who speaks revolting Polish! And he's the rabbi for the whole country!"[53] Another interview subject refers to the renaissance so closely associated with Schudrich as "a Disneyland financed by the Americans to enlighten the little Poles about the Jews who lived amongst them."[54] The other rabbis who visited the Jedwabne exhumations to express their objections had flown in from Israel and London.[55]

These rabbis' fears about desecration of the Jedwabne graves were not unanimous among Jewish authorities, as Rabbi Polak's article makes clear. Nor is it certain that these figures could be said to speak for the religious beliefs of the murdered Jedwabne Jews themselves, or the many Jews in diaspora, many of them highly secular, who have relatives buried in Polish soil.[56] After the Holocaust, questions of authority and victim/survivor voice are greatly complicated by scale: both the extent of Nazi mass murder and the size and complexity of the Jewish diaspora. At an even deeper level, it can be argued, the perennial question of what Judaism *is*—a religion, culture, or ethnicity, how important those different forms of identity have been in the historical persecution of Jews, and how necessary it is that they all be present in contemporary Jewish identity—remains an undercurrent beneath all questions of memory, desecration, and who speaks for the dead at Holocaust sites.

The true extent of religious conviction, and the sources of authority through which it is expressed, are important variables when post-conflict graves are declared to be sacred. Another is whether these objections or prohibitions are unique to *mass* graves, to the special context of violence. MacDonald's *Christian Science Monitor* article portrays the special circumstances of human rights violations ("Our loved ones have suffered enough") as the primary reason religious people have opposed international forensic exhumations. In fact, as Renteln writes, many cultures and religions (including the Hmong, Orthodox Jews, Muslims, Mexican Americans,[57] and the Navajo/Diné) observe prohibitions on interfering with the physical integrity of *any* dead body. These beliefs lead to complex situations when domestic authorities want to perform an autopsy, even when no human rights violations have occurred. Melanie Klinkner, exploring the possibility of forensic investigations of Khmer Rouge atrocities in Cambodia, mentions as one potential obstacle the belief "that the spirits of those who die unnatural deaths cannot rest and therefore may cause misfortune among the living."[58] This belief sets the victims of violence apart from the "normal" dead, making it particularly dangerous to disturb their rest. One of Klinkner's Cambodian informants, however, tells her that exhuming dead bodies is not, generally, "acceptable for the Cambodian people,"[59] suggesting a more widespread prohibition.

It is also possible, in some cultural systems, that mass graves will be *less* subject to religious prohibitions than normal graves. In Guatemala, priests drew upon the resources and rituals of their faith to "ask permission" of God for the victims of violence in their villages to be exhumed. The prohibition against disturbing graves remained generally in effect, but divinity also showed itself to be flexible, sensitive to a particular context in which means that are normally forbidden (exhumation) could contribute to sacred ends (providing a Christian burial). Rabbi Polak's article claims, even more firmly, that exhuming the dead from mass graves is not only permitted but *necessary*: in other words, he sees the rabbis in Jedwabne as having misinterpreted the demands of the sacred.

As much as these perspectives among religious leaders differ, they are united in treating *sacredness* as the primary value at stake in the fate of mass graves. Though embedded in complex textual interpretations, the debate between the rabbis in Jedwabne and Rabbi Polak boils down to the question of which is more sacred: the location of an original grave and undisturbed rest of its inhabitants, or the religious laws and rituals governing burial that were violated by those who created the mass graves. It is important to distinguish this shared sense of the sacred, which can exist even among parties disagreeing over the fate of a mass grave, from other uses of the term. When a reporter asked Laura García-Lorca, the poet's Federico García Lorca's niece, if she was disturbed at the thought of leaving her uncle's remains in the ditch where his killers dumped him, she replied, "What *ditch*? It's a sacred place. They're all [García Lorca and his fellow victims] in good company there."[60] García-Lorca frames her claim that the grave is sacred—and thus her family's opposition to the exhumation—in terms of solidarity and justice. Religion is implicated far more obliquely.[61]

If you believe that to disturb a grave is a *religious* offense against the sacred and a disturbance of dead souls, you believe so regardless of whatever other interests might favor an exhumation—unlike García Lorca's family, who ultimately consented to an exhumation out of respect for the wishes of the families of other victims most likely buried with him.[62] Even Rabbi Polak argues against his colleagues with a competing interpretation *about the demands of the sacred*; he does not say that other considerations can temper or alter those demands. A religious objection to the disturbance of mass graves is, in its absoluteness and the internal consistency of its logic, as firm as the logic of "aparición con vida" was in Argentina.

Gathering Information, Marking Boundaries

Earlier I highlighted the recent, rapid development of international codes of ethics for forensic teams involved in human rights investigations. What do these codes tell forensic experts to do in situations like the ones in Cambodia, Congo, or Jedwabne? One crucial document to look at for answers is the International Committee of the Red Cross's report on "The Missing and Their Families."

The conference that preceded the report, convened in three meetings over the course of 2001, was prompted in part by the challenges and controversies that arose during the massive, complex, and bureaucratically burdensome forensic investigations in the former Yugoslavia in the mid-1990s. But it was also, more specifically, a response to shattering experiences that were unique to the International Committee of the Red Cross.

Since World War I, the Red Cross's mandate has included documenting and searching for missing persons,[63] as well as coordinating the exchange of bodies between opposing armies. Originally the Red Cross's lists of the missing and the dead included only men in uniform; however, as a new era of intracountry conflicts and heavy civilian casualties dawned in the second half of the twentieth century, the Geneva Conventions adopted additional protocols to reflect these realities.[64] The Red Cross, the Geneva Conventions' greatest champion, thus found itself increasingly in charge of the search for missing civilians. With this role came a whole new set of dilemmas, eloquently phrased by Marco Sassòli and Marie-Louise Tougas:

> In many contexts the ICRC knows soon after the war that nearly all the missing are dead. . . . Should a humanitarian organization like the ICRC destroy hope when it is often impossible to be absolutely certain that a missing person is dead? May the ICRC conversely perpetuate suffering, if only by omission, simply because absolute certainty does not exist? Should the ICRC leave it to the families to decide what they want? Their first choice, to cling to the hope that their loved one is alive, is not in their genuine interest if there is a high probability that the person is dead. Their second choice, to insist upon absolute proof of death, likewise prolongs their suffering in the many cases where such proof will never be available.[65]

Eric Stover, one of the key players in bringing forensic expertise to Argentina in the 1980s, traveled to Bosnia and Croatia during the war that broke Yugoslavia apart. He was, at the time, the director of Physicians for Human Rights and served, along with Clyde Snow, as a consultant to a UN commission looking into mass graves and other violations of international humanitarian law. Stover remembers the 1991 siege of Vukovar, a Croatian town, as a defining moment for the Red Cross, as well as for the broader story of the former Yugoslavia's violent dissolution.

In the summer of 1991, both Croatia and Slovenia declared their independence from Slobodan Milošević's government. Milošević promptly sent the Yugoslav National Army (JNA) into both territories to regain hold over them. As the Croatian National Guard, out-manned and out-gunned, began to lose ground to the JNA, civilians, patients, and Croatian fighters converged for safety on the centrally located Vukovar Hospital.[66]

Red Cross representatives in Croatia initially secured permission to evacuate sick and wounded patients from the hospital. The JNA commander reneged on his promise, however, and Red Cross staff wound up forced to stand by and witness as busloads containing patients, hospital staff, civilians, and combatants rolled past them.[67] Most of these people would later be found in Ovčara, a farming area south of Vukovar, buried in mass graves.

The Red Cross's status as a neutral observer and humanitarian actor has always been a difficult balancing act, with the definition of "neutrality" being more an art than a science.[68] Yet finding itself in the role of impotent bystander to a massacre in Croatia was, according to Stover, a source of grief and consternation for an already heavily taxed organization, which was facing tensions between field staff and Geneva-based officers, a lack of resources, and a world with no shortage of terrible conflicts.[69]

Peace in the region would not ease these challenges for the organization. After the signing of the Dayton Accords in 1995 and the cessation of hostilities, the Red Cross began compiling its lists of missing people and trying to find an answer for the wives and other family members now stuck in a limbo of uncertainty. Its "death attestation" program matched witness accounts with information about missing people gathered from the former Yugoslavia's various new governing authorities. The program was intended to give widows and other survivors legal certifications of their losses and allow them to move on. Instead, it caused outrage. In the region's "ethnic cleansings," family members were frequently separated from one another, the men and boys massacred while the women's lives were spared—often so that they could be subjected to systematic rape.[70] Despite these patterns of family displacement and regrouping, the Red Cross permitted only immediate family members to add a missing person to their list, excluding testimony by neighbors and other witnesses.[71] For many women who believed persistent rumors that their husbands were still alive, the Red Cross' plan to declare their loved ones dead based on hearsay and official records, without a body or any other material sign, was "unacceptable" at best, monstrous at worst.[72] Stover writes, "While the Red Cross delegates could have delivered the death notifications in a more sensitive and appropriate manner, they were also the hapless victims of circumstance. Aside from the NATO troops, the ICRC was the most visible of all the international agencies and thus an easy target for scorn."[73]

Whether the Red Cross deserved this scorn or not, the organization emerged from its experiences in the former Yugoslavia with evidence that its role as a coordinating body in the search for missing people required more direct involvement in the fate of the material remains of those people—in other words, in forensics. The conference it convened on "The Missing and Their Families" constituted a rare attempt to gather nearly all of the organizations involved in international forensic investigations. Its findings and recommendations are among the best reflections available, to date, of a consensus within the field on matters both ethical and practical.

As a humanitarian response to the terrible and conflictive things witnessed in the former Yugoslavia, the report on "The Missing" is a remarkable document. It combines practical advice with deep reflection about post-conflict realities, grief, and the ethics of exhumation and autopsy. It largely delivers on Lola Vollen's hope to "capture the accumulated wisdom of past efforts worldwide and begin the process of developing a comprehensive model for recovering and identifying the remains of the victims of large-scale atrocities."[74] When the report briefly addresses the religious beliefs of mourners, however—and especially the belief that graves are sacred—it unintentionally reveals both the difficulty of the subject and the ever-present temptation of evasive abstractions.

"Despoilation and desecration" of the dead, the report suggests, should be made a crime under international law, even when occurring during a conflict within a nation's borders.[75] For those working at graves, with remains, and with families of the missing, it also recommends best practices for interviewing relatives, creating databases of antemortem information about the deceased, and handling bodies in systematic ways that preserve evidence, a record of chain of custody, and any clues to individual identity.[76]

Most of the report's recommendations, in other words, are about *gathering and preserving information.* They locate the point of convergence between a complex mix of influences: the methods of forensic science, the desire of human rights organizations to create an accurate historical record, the importance of ending uncertainty for families of the missing, and the Red Cross's own long-standing mission to gain access to prisons and other sensitive conflict areas as a neutral fact-finder.

Other recommendations, however, are more philosophical in tone. In a section on "Considerations on the meaning of death and recommendations for appropriate behaviour," the report tells forensic experts and other humanitarian aid workers to "Respect the remains; they are part of the deceased person and as such are in some way sacred."[77] In a document published by a secular organization,[78] this is a surprisingly unequivocal statement. Rather than merely suggesting that many of the people Red Cross workers assist in the field happen to believe that dead bodies are sacred, it is declarative: dead bodies *are* (in some way) sacred. The language suggests not just respect for the beliefs of mourners, but identification with their perspective. It abandons the usual distance we see, in humanitarian texts, between people in need and those who come to their aid—experts and relief workers whose own beliefs and cultures are usually rendered invisible.[79] By way of contrast, in its own set of recommendations, the Argentine Forensic Anthropology Team takes a more dispassionate tone, preserving this distance: "The relatives' cultural and religious practices with regard to the dead and reburial ceremonies should be respected and taken into account as the investigation proceeds."[80]

The report then outlines a set of specific injunctions for forensic experts: "Respect the remains. . . . [T]o mutilate them is to desecrate them"; "The body must never be presented naked"; "If the corpse has been mutilated, the mutilations must so far as possible be hidden."[81] Indeed, there is nothing to be gained, from a forensic perspective, in presenting dead bodies naked to their families (provided they can be unclothed when they are examined in the morgue) or in gratuitously mutilating them. However, by offering no definition of "mutilation," the text skips over a major area of controversy. A forensic expert such as Clea Koff may find "things like extract[ing] pubes for sexing, or saw[ing] out bits of femur for DNA sampling" to be unpleasant or even "horrific";[82] but she will ultimately justify them as nongratuitous, necessary evils in the service of a much greater, and ultimately much more *respectful*, effort to tell the full story of what happened to these bodies. She may see only intentional damage, inflicted with malice (such as the bulldozing of graves by Serb militants) as mutilation. If, however, you believe—as many religious people do—that dead bodies should never be disturbed or autopsied, then the men with bulldozers and the pathologists with lab coats are not so sharply distinguished: what forensic experts see as "necessary evils" you see as another form of mutilation. Only if the forensic community puts itself in charge of defining "mutilation" can experts rest so assured that their methods are respectful.

Defining "mutilation" and concealing its effects from mourners may be tasks for humanitarians and forensic experts, but the report does offer other, important roles for religious leaders, whom it refers to as "representatives of what is sacred."[83] It is an apt designation given the importance, over and above any particular religious doctrine, of the *category* of the sacred as a force working around mass graves. According to the report, these representatives of the sacred may guide families through the mourning process, officiate at funerals, and mediate between forensic experts and survivor communities.[84] Echoing anthropological insights about belief systems in which the dead can spiritually contaminate the world of the living,[85] the report acknowledges that funeral rites can be "dangerous" to a community if not performed by a knowledgeable person.[86]

Yet a conundrum remains. While "The Missing and Their Families" envisions religious leaders working alongside forensic experts in complementary roles, in Jedwabne, it was precisely these "representatives of what is sacred" who shut down the exhumations. On the one hand, the report suggests that religious leaders must interpret or "represent" the sacred on behalf of their communities. On the other hand, it also affirms that forensic teams arrive at the scene with their own ethic, perhaps even their own conception of the sacred, which they see as compatible with their scientific techniques. Perhaps because the clashes around mass graves in places such as Congo and Jedwabne were still new at the time of the report's writing, it leaves unexplored the possibility that these two groups—and two very different ways of thinking about the sacredness of the dead—will be in conflict.

Even the Argentine Forensic Anthropology Team, known for its sensitivity to families of the missing and local context, falls back on hopeful projections when faced with the question of religious prohibitions. Its recommendations on "Exhumations and Respect for Cultural and Religious Funeral Rites" read:

> There are often non-conflicting ways to respect the victims' families' decision in the extreme case of their total opposition to exhumation. From a legal standpoint, this is often possible as (1) most Tribunals and Commissions will order forensic work in a very selected number of cases; and (2) to prove a massacre, for example, not all the bodies need to be found and examined. From historical and documentation standpoints, we can often still provide an estimation of the non-exhumed individuals.[87]

Like the Red Cross, the Argentine team focuses on "nonconflicting" situations—the very situations where other forensic experts are least likely to need the recommendations of these experienced and thoughtful practitioners. As early exhumations in the former Yugoslavia illustrated, moreover, the two types of resolution described in the Argentine team's recommendations—selective sampling of "representative" graves for a tribunal and partial exhumation of the bodies in a given grave—can result in tremendous discontent among survivor communities. In Jedwabne, replacing a full exhumation with calculated estimates about the number of individuals in the graves—the only option left for the Institute of National Remembrance after the rabbis' intervention—has clearly left those hoping for a precise history of the massacre far from satisfied.

Some forensic experts have expressed a healthy humility about their status as visiting experts rather than mourners or survivors. To dedicate oneself to this work, however, goes hand in hand with a basic conviction that the bodies of victims of atrocity, if left unidentified in a mass grave along with evidence of the crimes committed against them, are suffering an ongoing injustice. It is a conviction forensic experts share with human rights activists around the world, and often families of the missing and other local stakeholders. Victims and mourners may have many different opinions of what constitutes desecration and how to show respect for their dead. The work of forensic teams is so complex because they not only offer scientific expertise, but through the exhumation and identification process also become a voice for particular beliefs about what the dead are owed.

What comparative value do these human rights imperatives have in the face of sacred claims? Is there any way to reconcile these two different attitudes toward mass graves, or, where reconciliation fails, an honest way to decide which one has a greater claim over the gravesite? Though these questions largely beg for practical solutions, there is some conceptual confusion behind them too. In what follows, without endeavoring to craft a new set of guidelines (something only practitioners are prepared to do), I attempt to clarify the relationship between human rights and the sacred in the very unique, highly charged context of the mass grave.

Sacred Foundations

The relationships between religion, the sacred, and human rights have been contentious from the start. The process of drafting the landmark Universal Declaration of Human Rights, adopted by the United Nations in 1948, was long and sometimes quite rancorous, nearly breaking down at a number of key moments.[88] The original United Nations Human Rights Commission, led by

Eleanor Roosevelt, entertained the notion of including a reference to "God" or "the Creator" as the source of human rights, echoing the American Declaration of Independence's statement that men "are endowed by their Creator with certain unalienable Rights." They ultimately rejected the idea, however, because they saw these terms as threats to the "universality of the document."[89] The commission was concerned that not only atheists but also those whose religious cosmology did not include a single God-creator would not accept the language.[90] The declaration's preamble and first article are thus filled with well-known secular language, much of it drawing on the French *Déclaration des droits de l'homme et du citoyen* and other Enlightenment precedents, about the inherent dignity of the human person, equality, freedom, peace, "brotherhood," and the "human family."[91] It stitches together normative views about human nature, family and community, the rule of law and international relations while also carefully avoiding any religious language of justification.

Among the commission's representatives, there were significantly divergent interpretations of how this language came to be chosen. Roosevelt herself, along with P. C. Chang, a Chinese playwright-diplomat and one of the commission's "intellectual leaders," felt that "Those who believed in God . . . could still find the idea of God in the strong assertions that all human beings are born free and equal and endowed with reason and conscience." By speaking to shared values without specifying any particular religious foundation for those values, Roosevelt wrote, the declaration "left it to each of us to put in our own reason."[92]

By contrast, Charles Malik—a Western-educated philosopher who served as the Lebanese representative to the Human Rights Commission (which he would chair after Roosevelt)—initially supported a reference to a "Creator" in the declaration. The original language he drafted for Article 16, protecting marriage and the family, stated that "the family deriving from marriage" was "endowed by the Creator with inalienable rights antecedent to all positive law."[93] The commission rejected the phrase, and Malik's position seems to have evolved, to the point where he not only assented to Roosevelt and Chang's proposed language, he even defended it from a late attempt, in final committee meetings, to add a reference to the divine.[94]

Mary Ann Glendon, in her detailed account of the declaration's drafting, claims that Malik's ultimate support for the text in its now-familiar form, with no references to a Creator, meant that he had "come around to Chang's and Mrs. Roosevelt's view,"[95] but in the process she elides an important difference. Chang and Roosevelt proposed that the relationship between human rights and belief in God could be *resolved* through the declaration's broad evocation of values such as dignity and equality. These values could be, but did not *have to* be, religious: both possibilities, a religious grounding and a nonreligious grounding for rights, were equally valid and accessible to individual reason.[96] Malik was far less satisfied. The debates over theological references, he wrote, "are often concluded silently by sheer sensing that the prevailing climate of opinion will never admit such terms."[97] In his view, the question of the religious foundations of human rights was not *resolved*, but rather deferred for pragmatic reasons.[98] In a 1949 speech reflecting on the writing of the declaration, Malik still seemed dissatisfied with attempts to articulate international ethics without reference to the divine. He emphasized the equal importance of "the joyous liberties of the Greek city-states" and "Christian charity" as "authentic sources" of the Western tradition, and criticized as "superficial" the nineteenth-century attempt to "emancipate . . . man of the possibility of any dogma or faith."

Malik's dissatisfied view lives on. In a chapter of his book, *The Idea of Human Rights: Four Inquiries*, the philosopher Michael Perry sets out to prove that human rights are "ineliminably religious." Like Malik, Perry seems to feel that leaving the relationship between human rights and religion unspecified is not so much a satisfying compromise as an ongoing strategy of avoidance, depriving human rights of a full justification. Furthermore, it contributes to a larger form of intellectual impoverishment, whereby religious questioning (which is different from religious dogma or ritual) is banished from the public square by severing the link between morality and cosmology. Gone is the sense that an account of what to do about human suffering is bound up with answering questions about who we are and why we are in this world in the first place.[99]

The broader project of critiquing secularism is not likely to be of immediate help to the forensic experts trying to figure out just how far into the ground they can dig. But Perry's arguments are worthy of attention for the way in which they help characterize the confrontation between the human rights imperatives of forensic teams and religious prohibitions, especially by raising the crucial question of the place of *morality* in that confrontation.

Perry starts his chapter with an epigraph from the economic historian and social critic R. H. Tawney (1880–1962): "The essence of all morality is this: to believe that every human being is of infinite importance, and therefore that no consideration of expediency can justify the oppression of one by another. But to believe this it is necessary to believe in God."[100] Though Tawney wrote the passage in 1913, before the development of the human rights framework in its modern form, he captured an idea close to the heart of human rights: every individual human person has an importance at odds with utilitarian calculations.[101] For Tawney (and Perry), you simply cannot proclaim the "infinite importance" of the human person, in all situations and against all challenges, without explaining the source of that importance. "Inherent dignity," like reason and many of the other qualities listed in human rights declarations, moreover, merely begs the question: Where does that dignity come from?[102]

The answer, for Perry, is not only a religious worldview but, more specifically, the concept of the *sacred*. The sacred gives voice to the fundamentally religious idea "that every human being is the beloved child of God."[103] Malik was thus right to feel that a reference to a "Creator" was lacking from the Universal Declaration of Human Rights, for this connection to the divine source of all life is the thing that gives each human life its intrinsic value. Unlike Laura García-Lorca, who ascribes "sacredness" to her uncle's grave in secular and even political language, Perry is careful to specify that the religious core of the sacred is not adaptable or negotiable: "The conviction that every human being is sacred—*sacred in the strong/objective sense, sacred because of how the world really is, and not because of what we attach value to in the world*—is inescapably religious," he writes.[104]

If human rights themselves are based on an irreducible, universal conception of the sacred—as Perry forcefully argues—this philosophical insight has direct relevance to forensic teams facing religious prohibitions against exhumation. In the spirit of the Red Cross report, which straightforwardly states that human remains are "in some way sacred," forensic teams might find they at least share a common language with people such as the rabbis in Jedwabne. Though scientists, priests, imams, and rabbis do not share all the same traditions or texts, they can at least approach the issue as a matter of disagreement between different "representatives of what is sacred" over what exactly the sacred demands. An easy resolution might still be hard to reach—after all, even rabbis still disagree about the application of Jewish law to mass graves. But gone would be the sense of scientists and believers gazing at each other, bitterly, across a gulf—the sense that is hard not to take away from the partial exhumation in Jedwabne.

Yet there is another gulf here that must be bridged. It lies between the way human rights theorists such as Perry talk about the sacred, and the types of sacred claims people doing the daily work of human rights actually encounter.

In the theoretical debates about human rights, the sacred appears as a *moral* category. Part of what drives the perceived need to resolve its relationship with the ascendant moral vocabulary of human rights, then, is the sense that the two vocabularies share, and perhaps even compete over, the same terrain, defining the moral value of human persons. Nowhere is this link made clearer than in Perry's argument that we simply cannot get to a defensible claim that *"certain things ought not to be done to any human being and certain other things ought to be done for every human being"*—his elegant encapsulation of the idea of human rights—without basing it on "the conviction that every human being is sacred."[105]

Mass graves lead toward a very different understanding of the relationship between human rights and the sacred. The basic religious objection against forensic exhumations is not that forensic experts undervalue or disrespect the dead. Rather, it is that in exhuming a grave they will disturb a certain order. The dead body, for the rabbis who halted the Jedwabne exhumations, is sacred, and the space it occupies, the mass grave, is a world apart. To enter into that zone with latex gloves, backhoes, and shovels is to profane the most sacred of places. Thus Haglund's report on Jedwabne and similar accounts focus on the risk of disturbance rather than immorality or even disrespect. The Maya priest who intervened on behalf of exhumations in Guatemala, as Sanford describes, "ask[ed] permission from God to disturb the bones." In his criticism of the below-ground path being dug at the Holocaust memorial in Belzec, Poland, Rabbi Weiss writes, "The project has already disturbed—and will continue to disturb—the ashes and bones that cover the entire surface of the camp and the human remains that lie underneath. . . . We [Jews] sanctify the dead by covering them, not by digging into them."

To the extent that moral issues arise from this disturbance, they are not centered on the value of individual persons, alive or dead. Nor do they specify what we ought to do, or not do, to one another—things that Perry rightly identifies as the true subject of human rights. The violation that occurs when forensic teams dig into a sacred space is categorically different from a violation of human rights. It is not an attack on a human person, but rather on a set of rules or agreements that certain places are not proper to enter, that they belong not to the living community but to the dead and possibly the divine.

Though absent from the theorizing of Perry and many of his interlocutors, there is in fact a long tradition of sociological and anthropological thinking that has more accurately captured this reality. It defines the sacred not so much as a moral link between the human and the divine, but as a social category establishing boundaries. In the opinion of the influential early sociologist, Emile Durkheim, the sacred is actually more universal to human culture than any morality. Moreover, the division it marks—between the sacred and the profane—is starker, more "*absolute*," than the moral division between good and evil:

> In all the history of human thought there exists no other example of two categories of things so profoundly differentiated or so radically opposed to one another [as the sacred and the profane]. The traditional opposition of good and bad is nothing beside this; for the good and bad are only two opposed species of the same class, namely morals, just as sickness and health are two different aspects of the same order of facts, life, while the sacred and the profane have always and everywhere been conceived by the human mind as two different classes, as two worlds between which there is nothing in common.[106]

For Durkheim, the sacred is more closely intertwined with epistemology—questions about the nature and scope of human knowledge—than with morality.[107] The profane encompasses the world we can know, touch, and understand; the sacred is the unknowable and untouchable.[108]

Unlike the arguments in which the sacred defines the intrinsic and infinite importance of human persons, and thus comes to overlap with human rights, Durkheim sees the sacred in spatial and material terms. He writes, "A rock, a tree, a spring, a pebble, a piece of wood, a house; in a word, anything can be sacred."[109] While the Red Cross report refers vaguely to the dead body as being "in some way sacred," Durkheim is more specific: "The dead man is a sacred being. Consequently, everything which is or has been connected with him is, by contagion, in a religious state excluding all things from profane life."[110] The dead body may be feared, revered, or both. The important thing is to recognize the distance it has traveled from us, and the sacred charge of the space around it. Later studies taking a historical, anthropological, or even literary approach have emphasized that to call someone sacred is not to establish his intrinsic value or inviolability; rather, it is often to signal his marginality to the community that has marked him as sacred.[111] The pyre or altar is usually the next and final destination for this sacred being.[112]

The encounter between forensic science and religious prohibitions thus has little to do with the value placed on human persons, clashing moralities, or even the ethical status of the dead body. One of the reasons the authors of the Red Cross report can so casually remark that the dead body is "in some way sacred," in fact, is that the forensic, human rights, and humanitarian communities have mostly avoided philosophical questions about what dead bodies mean or what we owe them. So there is no alternate vocabulary from humanitarian or forensic practice that competes with the religious idea that dead bodies and graves are sacred. The sense of shared terrain—of some necessary but unarticulated link between human rights and the sacred—that motivates so much theoretical discussion turns out, in a concrete situation where human rights and sacred claims intersect, to be completely absent. Gone, along with it, is the optimistic view that the sacred might establish some new, shared language for forensic teams and representatives of what is sacred.

Two Trees, Different Roots

At first glance, it may seem strange for the Red Cross report to place its observation that dead bodies are "in some way sacred" in the midst of a discussion of mutilation, which calls up images of the most violated, fragmented, and least recognizably "human" bodies found in mass graves. For those who normally associate the sacred with beautiful shrines, museum objects, or stunning landscapes—or with lofty ideas of the infinite importance of human lives—the focus on these abject bodies is jarring, to say the least.

In fact, in this key portion of the report, the authors echo the nuanced, ambivalent version of the sacred found in the writings of Durkheim and others. Sacred objects, places, and bodies inspire respect and horror, awe and distance.[113] If the sacred is defined purely in the unequivocal, positive ways Perry offers—as a connection to the image of a divine Creator—the decaying, mutilated dead body becomes difficult to recognize as sacred.

The Red Cross report opens the door to a fuller conception of how the sacred actually operates; in the process, it also suggests the limits of human rights as an ethic for dealing with mass graves. Throughout most of the report, the forensic process is explicitly linked to the quest for historical accuracy, legal accountability for the perpetrators of violations, and to the rights and needs of victims and mourners. Yet when they begin to speak of practices that center on the *material fact* of the dead body itself, the authors shift from human rights to another language: the ambivalent language of the sacred. The sacred, the report seems to say, is more suited to the dead body and the ways we experience it—the stench, the abjection, the reverence, the need for ritual—than human rights. Though not a philosophical text, the Red Cross report lends significant support to the view that the sacred is not the secret root of human rights, but rather another tree entirely.

What happens at sacred graves in the aftermath of atrocity is an encounter between an expanding, searching ethic and a language concerned with drawing boundaries around knowledge. Despite all of their scientific and organizational complexity, there is a unifying feature to the practices of human rights forensic teams: whether focused on putting perpetrators in jail or constructing a revisionist-proof history, they all demand action. The teams must *find* the grave, *gather* the evidence, *identify* the bodies, *document* their findings. The response to the unknown, in forensic ethics, is to find answers (even if these answers, produced through a particular set of technologies, can only capture certain kinds of truth—for example, a name but not a nuanced account of the dead person's political beliefs). When obstacles to that search appear, experts marshal new technologies, find new methods, and work to make the unknowable knowable—except, of course, in cases like Jedwabne, where they have reluctantly agreed to leave behind graves that were designated as sacred.

The sacred marks off certain spaces as inaccessible to human knowledge: not because of technical constraints but because the activities and knowledge of the living community require limits, both voluntary and involuntary.[114] In the face of ever-expanding human knowledge and technologies, it works to preserve a horizon line.

Negotiations

The Red Cross report is correct when it indicates that knowledge of the sacred and the profane has its own representatives, whose expertise is often as exclusive as the forensic anthropologist's ability to tell the age of a skeleton by examining its bones. Forensic teams seem to understand that contesting the basis of sacred claims would not only fail, it would also breed charges of arrogance, even cultural imperialism, that can only hurt the mission and reputations of their organizations.

For all the genuine wisdom and tantalizing suggestions in the Red Cross report, however, it and similar manuals for forensic investigations generally fail to anticipate much of the real complexity of interactions between forensic science and religious belief, between sacred graves and human rights. In one place, the Red Cross report warns of the power relations that exist between humanitarian workers and those they assist.[115] Yet it abandons this analysis of power when it comes to the subject of religious leaders. The report's authors seem prepared to concede full authority to these leaders over what spaces are sacred or profane, and what kinds of practices are allowed there. However, the

most easily identifiable or audible religious figures do not always have an un-
questionable claim to represent the interests of the dead (which can never really be determined with any certainty) or the desires of survivor communities.
Nor should the differences between the cultural, the religious, and the "local"
be underestimated: Rabbi Schudrich, for example, may have a form of religious
authority that empowers him to speak for Polish Jews, but his historical perspective and religious worldview do not represent all of the people—Polish,
Jewish, or both—who feel an investment in the fate of the Jedwabne graves and
others like them.

Sacred mass graves, and the attempts to exhume them, are not just another
human rights story where "justice clashes with culture."[116] After all, forensic
experts in this highly internationalized field have their own cultures, as well as
the shared culture of their profession. Survivor communities and other "locals,"
moreover, have proven to be well versed in the vocabulary of justice, whether
they are expressing the desire for an accurate history of atrocity or for prosecutions against war criminals. To give up on petitions for justice too readily because the people making them do not wear priestly robes, are not "foreign" or
"cultural" enough, would be its own form of damaging cultural caricature—an
exaggeratedly philosophical, and underpoliticized, understanding of the differences between religious claims and the claims of human rights.

Forensic teams are right to take very seriously the belief that graves are sacred and should not be touched. They also owe it to other stakeholders to investigate sacred claims carefully and weigh them against other priorities, including
the ones the teams themselves bring to the field. As Mercedes Doretti (of the
Argentine Forensic Anthropology Team) and Jennifer Burrell write, "We anthropologists do not dictate the rules of engagement although neither do we
passively accept them, especially when they prevent us from being able to fully
investigate a crime."[117] An ethic of listening can be combined with a healthy
sense of the extraordinary potential of forensic human rights work. Most forensic experts are aware of the hazard in arrogantly imposing their methods
on people who do not want or believe in their work, but there is equal hazard
in thinking that every voice raised in opposition represents all of the people it
claims to represent, is based on a good understanding of forensic practices, or
is automatically entitled to stand between scientists and mass graves containing
both evidence of crimes and bodies that might be returned to their mourners.

There is an important difference between sacred claims and the conditions
in which they are made. Sacred claims in Cambodia, Congo, and Poland may

all share the same basic features. They differ significantly in their political context, however, and in the category of religious or political actor who advances the claim: whether the rabbis and congregants in Jedwabne, King Norodom Sihanouk and other royalists in Cambodia,[118] or Laurent Kabila's bloodied and triumphant regime in Congo. Forensic teams cannot fruitfully question the source of the sacred, but they *can* and already do analyze the on-the-ground politics of the places where mass graves are found—in fact, no other field of professionals or scholars has amassed as much knowledge about these politics.

In the case of Jedwabne, different "representatives of the sacred" disagreed about whether an exhumation could be performed and under what conditions. What has been treated as an unresolvable conflict between the state and religion, or justice and culture, appears to have been far more complex. For instance, why were an American-born rabbi, his colleagues from Israel and London, and his congregants judged to be greater authorities—or simply more important stakeholders—than the Jedwabne-born Rabbi Baker and Rabbi Polak, who approved of the exhumations? The "compromise" exhumation in Jedwabne, sadly, seems to have lived up to the standards of *neither* the sacred nor human rights. No one has reason to celebrate: not the rabbis and congregants who believe that even the partial exhumation was an unwanted desecration, not those who feel that the massacred Jews still deserve reburial, and certainly not Gross, Chodakiewicz, or any other historian hoping for a definitive account of a terrible massacre. The conversation about exhumations in Jedwabne seems, to borrow some of Charles Malik's eloquent and frustrated phrasing, to have been "concluded silently" due to the "prevailing climate" rather than brought to a resolution.

Looking at these issues and negotiations on a case-by-case basis will only take the field so far. Some valuable comparative work could be done to understand what makes the difference between places where forensic teams and religious leaders have worked together and places where they have been at odds. Why could satisfying compromises be found in Guatemala and Indonesia but not in Poland? Is Jewish religious doctrine more stringent than the faiths in these other places, or are there political or historical factors that tend to affect the extent to which exhumation-friendly religious interpretations are or not available?[119]

Sadly for forensic teams, there is no escaping their role as political actors operating within a landscape of competing stakeholders. Even where they defer to the claim that graves and bodies are sacred, that decision is *political* in the sense that it creates winners and losers among the communities with a stake in the exhumation (or in there being no exhumation). If authorities can sometimes use religious prohibitions to mask other interests, or if the views of the most vocal religious figures do not reflect a consensus among mourners, then there may be times where, as Doretti and Burrell suggest, passive acceptance may not be the best course of action. In these cases, forensic teams will need the best possible toolkit to explain, without donning a false mantle of universal authority, why the demand for human rights investigations must be heard as loudly as sacred claims, and why these investigations may sometimes require the danger of committing what some people will consider to be a desecration. They may have to mobilize local stakeholders who want exhumations, asking them to speak up for the cause of human rights, and this process may come to feel unpleasantly like a public relations campaign.[120]

The unpleasantness seems worth bearing. Where sacred claims have the force of sincerity—where mourners, descendants, and others with the most intimate connections to the dead share a belief that graves should remain untouched—forensic teams would be right to fly home. Where these conditions are not met, to give up on an exhumation without getting their hands dirty (a specialty, literally and metaphorically, of forensic experts) would be to abandon not only their own mission, but also the desires of families, mourners, and others who view mass graves not as a forbidden world, but as a hellish part of our own world—a part that calls out to be known and, in some limited way, to be repaired.

Chapter 4

Dead to Rights

"nobody sees essence who can't / Face limitation."

—Louise Glück, "Circe's Power"

The Silent Stakeholder

It was my final question for Clyde Snow. We had already spent a long morning in his living room, drinking Guatemalan coffee he roasted at home and talking about the possible sources of scientific error in identifying Chile's *desaparecidos*, the frustrations and lessons learned from forensic investigations in Bosnia and Congo, ways to prove that chemical weapons had been used against the Kurds in Saddam Hussein's Iraq, and many other things. Before we broke for lunch, though, I asked if I could bother him with a question of a more philosophical nature than the topics we had covered so far—a question I had been saving for this face-to-face encounter with the most important figure in the forensic science of human rights.

"Do the *dead* have human rights?" I asked. "If you were presented with a scenario where you knew that the legal evidence from a grave wasn't going to go anywhere, and that there were no surviving family members who could be located for whom the identification could be meaningful, would you still feel a sense that it was worth spending time, effort, resources on getting people out of a mass grave just for their sakes, even though they're dead?"

Snow politely told me it was a good question and then entered the longest pause of the interview. When he began to speak again, he worked his way around the question a bit, first touching on the importance of knowledge gained from studying human remains ("The last thing that the dead can do is teach us"), and then the limits of anyone's ability to exhume and identify all of the dead in mass casualty events such as the Indian Ocean tsunami of 2004 or the January 2010 earthquake in Haiti. "I think you have to look at things from what is feasible," he said, firm resolution creeping back into his drawl. "If you're going to spend millions of dollars repatriating the dead, in situations where you have to ask the question, could those resources be better spent in schools and clinics? And maybe that's a better way, in many of these situations, to memorialize the dead. Plant a tree, plant a thousand trees. . . ."[1]

It was a practical, even humane answer to a big, abstract question. Yet it was also strangely modest, coming from a scientist who spent a long and storied career exhuming and studying dead bodies—a man sometimes called the "bone sleuth" and often quoted paying tribute to the dead body's authority in speaking against murderers and criminals.[2] The person who had pioneered the investigation of mass graves at some of the twentieth century's worst massacre sites was telling me, in effect, you have to know when to look away from the graves to the conditions that surround you. You have to know when to plant trees.

I was not entirely surprised by the response. In all of my time working alongside forensic experts, interviewing them, studying their reports and brochures and websites, I had never heard them speaking about the dead victims of atrocity as having human rights. While Snow's pragmatic nod toward the needs of the living and the scale of disaster is undoubtedly a crucial piece of this story, it still deserves a fuller exploration. The silences in discourse, after all, can teach us as much as what is said. Exploring the question of whether the dead bodies in mass graves have any human rights requires thinking about the dynamics of forensic investigation and the contexts in which it takes place, as Clyde Snow did during our interview. But it also requires careful consideration of the nature and scope of human rights.

Human rights, alongside the scientific method, are the most crucial organizing concept in the field of international forensic investigation.[3] Along with an obvious starting point for many mass grave investigations (which are usually triggered by reports of human rights violations), human rights are now increasingly also seen as part of their *outcomes*. The right of families to know the fate of missing persons, the importance of worldwide concern for human rights victims, and perhaps even the activities of human rights institutions (such as international tribunals) are reaffirmed through the processes of exhumation and identification of the dead.

The idea of human rights is closely tied to a series of assumptions about the legitimacy of intervention in conflicts around the world and in the affairs of sovereign states.[4] Human rights issues also tend to have certain common *narrative* elements,[5] and thus make an impact on how the evidence collected in forensic investigations is used and publicized—for example, with the importance of establishing certain categories of people as perpetrators, victims, and sometimes bystanders, or in the sorting of what are sometimes quite fuzzy distinctions between combatants and civilians. Despite the unavoidable presence of human rights law, human rights organizations, and human rights rhetoric in their work, however, forensic experts have largely avoided a troublesome question: Do dead bodies actually *have* human rights?

Perhaps any sensible person would avoid such a head-scratcher. Yet it is worth remembering that forensic experts have elsewhere proved very adept at interpreting and even innovating human rights concepts for the work they do, most notably in their forceful articulation of the right of families to know the fate of their missing relatives.[6] Human rights are the connective tissue that is supposed to link the forensic expert testifying in front of a war crimes tribunal, the geneticist working to reunite disappeared children with their birth families, the investigator digging up the bodies of liberation-minded guerrillas, and many others. All of these experts, in different contexts, are pursuing the rights of victims, survivors, and loved ones to know what really happened, to see justice done, to have their stories acknowledged, and to mourn. In an era where "rights talk" occupies a privileged place in justifying humanitarian action, the human rights of the dead seem like a natural place for forensic teams to seek moral and political authority for the work they do. Yet this crucial part of the circle that human rights makes around international forensic investigation remains undrawn, beyond the reach of both the scientific and the moral-political vocabularies employed in the field.

For the most part, in publications by international forensic teams as well as media reports, mass grave investigations are described as an avenue toward some ethical or political goal ultimately meant to benefit *living* people: the end of uncertainty for families of the missing (who may not even know if their loved ones are dead or alive), prosecutions of war criminals, or political stability for a post-conflict nation. The dead body is an "object of study" or "object of mourning,"[7] sometimes even an object of political negotiation,[8] but rarely is it described as directly benefiting from the activities of forensic teams. The dead person is beyond pain or joy, as per the rationalist assumptions of the scientist; he or she can be memorialized, even honored—but not *changed*. The dead body, unlike living mourners (who can progress through various stages of grief, eventually achieving "closure") is static—an *object*, but not subject, of the forensic process. Derek Congram and Dominique Austin Bruno declare, with confidence, "We are, after all, excavating the dead solely for the sake of the living."[9]

This logic stands in tension with the beliefs of many people that dead bodies inhabit a sacred space separate from the world of the living, but not wholly passive in its effects on that world. Perhaps this is a gap that cannot, and should not, be bridged—there are, after all, productive ways for forensic scientists and mourners to work together without sharing all of the same assumptions. Yet the silence about the rights of the dead also introduces important and unanswered questions for the human rights organizations that carry out mass grave investigations.

Of course, there is no proof of the concrete, independent existence of human rights for *anyone*, let alone the dead. No pathologist will ever cut open a body and find, hidden behind the appendix or curled around the heart, her human rights. Some philosophers have reached for an independent proof of the existence of human rights based on rational arguments,[10] while others, in the tradition of "natural rights," have called them as self-evident as the fact that telling the truth is better than lying.[11] Still others, such as Michael Perry, think that if we believe human life "*really is*" sacred, we can also justify the existence of human rights independently of the vicissitudes of where and when those rights are, or are not, respected.[12] Any glance at the troubled world around us, however, seems to support Hannah Arendt's view that human rights only gain *practical* currency for people who are part of a political community capable of hearing their claims and acting to protect their rights.[13] The debates about whether human rights have a logical "foundation" are intriguing. However, they seem rather less urgent than a conversation that acknowledges the clear influence of human rights on the international, national, and grassroots levels, while acknowledging the ongoing failure of the highly developed human rights framework and its associated institutions to alleviate many of the horrors they were designed to prevent. With this reality in mind, there is much work left to be done in probing what kinds of projects human rights translate into: coherent or contradictory, liberating or hegemonic, adaptable to new challenges (such as climate change), and so on.

Arendt sees an essential connection between human rights and the suffering person's ability to *claim* those rights before an audience. Those who "no longer belong to any community whatsoever" have particularly faint hope of enjoying any human rights.[14] The dead are not completely beyond the reach of various meaningful kinds of "belonging," not all of which are religious or based in organized ritual. But they are not, in most cases, members of the political communities created by the modern nation-state,[15] which is—most of the time—the accepted guarantor of human rights. Nor are they taken into account, beyond a few rules regarding the treatment and repatriation of remains during times of war, in the international laws and treaties that provide legal recourse to those whose rights nation-states have violated or ignored. The question of whether the dead have human rights, in the rare cases where it has been addressed, tends to generate either a firm "no" or a tentative, convoluted defense.[16]

To ask whether the dead bodies in mass graves have human rights, following Arendt's logic, is really to ask whether they are still part of the various political communities around them. The language of belonging and not belonging is among the most central determinants of what constitutes a community, and human rights is now the most far-reaching moral language of belonging that is used on the international stage. What does it mean for organizations and individuals that travel the world unearthing the dead victims of atrocity to see their work through the lens of human rights? What questions do human rights help them answer, and what new ones do they raise? There is nothing theoretical or quixotic about studying how forensic teams talk about or do not talk about human rights, about the dead bodies in their midst, and what lines they draw between the two. The endeavor is, in fact, essential to understanding forensic teams as political communities, and what role the dead themselves play in a growing global project of exhumation.

The Paradox of Human Rights for the Dead

There is a basic paradox involved in talking about mass grave investigations as a form of human rights work. The paradox is that international forensic teams arrive at mass graves only *after* the people in the graves have already had their most fundamental rights violated, irrevocably. They operate in a setting that is painted with failure: the failure of governments to preserve democratic institutions and protect basic rights; the failure of other nations to intervene against genocide in a prompt and effective manner (if, in the particular context, such an intervention would even be possible); and the everyday moral failure of human beings who slaughter, rape, and torture in the name of destructive ideologies. Rony Brauman, the former president of Doctors Without Borders, says, "When one speaks of a failure, one implies that there could be success. I have a hard time imagining what a humanitarian success would be in situations where violence is itself the sign of failure. As humanitarians we inscribe ourselves in failure."[17]

In the case of the scientists and humanitarians who work for international forensic teams, working long days amidst the material evidence of irreversible human suffering may cause a particularly acute sense of being "too late for human rights." Forensic experts generally measure their work in terms of how many perpetrators have been convicted or how many individuals' remains have been identified and returned to family members. Convictions, identifications, and published reports provide concrete benchmarks to present quantifiable goals to donors and keep people motivated to do this grueling work, even as they also explain some of the most important political and moral reasons to exhume mass graves.

Yet, as issues from school reform to financial crises illustrate, those variables that are easiest to quantify and measure are not necessarily the only or most important ones. Furthermore, there is a politics to every kind of measurement. We tend to proceed from the assumption that the act of measuring is what comes after the process being measured—you plant a bulb and then watch as shoots spring up from the earth inch by inch. But in reality, especially in a complex institutional setting, measurement tends to create a feedback loop in which the original action, now that it is measured, is increasingly influenced by the rubric of measurement itself. A famous example of this phenomenon is the controversy over "teaching to the test" in US schools, where in recent decades a proliferation of new assessments have been implemented to measure student learning. The measures, designed as ways of examining how well schools and teachers were doing their jobs, have often come to reshape the curriculum and daily life in the classroom, and even the purpose of teaching itself—as well as creating incentives to cheat.[18] "Even if the measure, when first devised, was a valid measure, its very existence typically sets in motion a train of events that undermines its validity. Let's call this a process by which 'a measure colonizes behavior,'" writes political anthropologist James C. Scott.[19]

The benchmarks currently used to measure and evaluate international forensic investigations capture much of what is important to living stakeholders, as well as what could reasonably be supposed to matter to dead victims of human rights violations. Helping families find out what really happened to the missing, convicting war criminals and human rights violators, and establishing a historical record backed by science are each, in their own way, indirect forms of respect for the dead.[20] But forensic experts also work for and *with* the dead in much more direct, concrete ways. There is an important ethical dimension of international forensic investigations that, in Michael Barnett's phrase, still "falls outside the model."[21]

Mercedes Doretti, of the Argentine Forensic Anthropology Team, describes gluing the pieces of a skull back together and seeing that small, almost mechanical task as a form of "reparation."[22] In the past decades, forensic teams have expanded their activities out from the gravesite, offering psychosocial assistance to families and training to local health professionals, but their most unique feature is still that they dig up the dead. They do so in a way that requires special skills because the forensic process is both *conservative* and *transformative*. Evidence must be preserved, photographs taken, body positions and clothing associations recorded, but at the end of the day, ideally, anonymous remains will change into named bodies and mass graves into marked gravesites, tombs, or memorials. Does this complex, deeply ethical activity correspond to some form of human right? If not, what other language captures it? Can it be measured, and should it?

The dead have legal rights in certain political jurisdictions, such as the right not to be trafficked, dissected without consent, or used sexually.[23] But all of the complexities one finds when dealing with dead bodies in the domestic context are magnified many times over in the relationship between the dead victims of atrocity, global projects of transitional justice and truth telling, and universal human rights. Human rights are explicitly intended to transcend local laws and to demand international concern, if not immediate international action. Do dead bodies flung into anonymous graves suffer "crimes against humanity" like the living—meaning their fates concern all of us, no matter how far we are from their graves? Are their rights to dignified treatment in death—a standard that, just to complicate matters, varies enormously across and even within cultures[24]—of the same order and magnitude as the human rights that were violated while they were living? Is it a human rights violation when perpetrators encase a body in cement, as security forces did in Argentina,[25] or bulldoze bodies from one grave into another in order to make them nearly impossible to identify, as Bosnian Serb forces did to mass graves in Bosnia?[26]

Respecting Rights, Understanding Their Limits

There is truth in Hannah Arendt's claim that we learn, from the rights a given group of people does or does not enjoy, what place they have in a political community. This does not mean, however, that every violation of a particular individual's human rights is an argument that the social consensus around the human rights framework is nonexistent, or crumbling.[27] Arendt herself differentiates between the particular historical groups that are the subject of her own argument about the limits of human rights (refugees and stateless people deprived, over lifetimes and even generations, of meaningful membership in any political community), and the many people who suffer, every day, from human rights violations within existing political communities that are failing their highest purposes when those violations occur. Arendt's point, in looking at refugees and stateless people, was that the entire world could deny them their rights without anyone being directly responsible for this failure. There was no one to call a hypocrite because no political community claimed these people as its members. The vocabularies a leader such as Martin Luther King Jr. was able to draw on—in which he continually contrasted the "promise of democracy" and the "goal of America" with the reality of its color line[28]—show how the idea of membership, even when continually violated, provides the oppressed with some ground to stand on, some public claim to make.

A living person can suffer the worst violations of human rights and still *possess* those rights. My grandparents were the victims of a long-term and constant violation of their rights when they were held prisoner in Nazi concentration camps. But after their liberation, in Sweden, they once again enjoyed many human rights, from the most basic (the right to life) to the very complex (the right to freedom of movement across borders, which they eventually used to recover a few possessions from their native Poland and settle in the United States).

The danger in calling refugees, stateless people, prisoners, and others "rightless," a term used by Arendt and many contemporary critics,[29] is that it renders static and hopeless a situation that is open to change. In this way, it seems to naturalize the violence of perpetrators and the indifference of the world. "Rightless" is a description of the *person*, whereas rights violations are *actions* that can be protested, acknowledged, and reversed. It can be extremely difficult, in practical and legal terms, to provide the victims of serious and ongoing rights violations the chance to enjoy their rights again. Daily, hard work of all sorts, from grassroots activism to major institutional reforms in national and international governance, is the only way to recognize once again the basic rights of generations of people living in refugee camps, women and children trafficked for prostitution, or the people still held without charge, at the time of this writing, at the US prison in Guantánamo Bay, Cuba. But so long as a person has a future, it is always possible that her rights will again exert some force, no matter what she has suffered.[30] This is the point of saying that human rights are *inalienable*: they can be violated, but not taken away.

Dead bodies can be lost. They can be burned to ash and spread to the winds as they were at Auschwitz, vaporized as they were at Hiroshima and Nagasaki. While it still might be legitimate to talk about certain claims these dead people make on the institutions that outlive them (for example, to have their estates distributed according to their wishes),[31] it seems nearly impossible to imagine that a vaporized person, a person turned to ash, a person whose body is irrevocably lost, can have human rights. In the most basic, material sense, the subject of rights is gone—it is, indeed, too late for human rights. I think of my grandfather's three-year-old daughter Miriam, murdered by the Nazis in Poland. I have no idea where her remains might be. I can mourn her, "remember" her in my indirect way, and seek what little information is available about her. But there is no way in which I can respect her human rights.

This is what the violation of the dead really means. Perhaps it is not morally equivalent to violations of the living because we do not know what suffering, if any, it causes the dead. But it has its own special horror. The violation of the dead can render them permanently "rightless" in a *definitional* sense—precisely the sense we cannot and should not use for the living. Gas chambers, atomic bombs, and cruder forms of violence can take things away from the dead that can never be put back: their identities, their places in the world, their bodies. The crucial element of the moral vision of human rights is that they are inalienable—that the untouchable, the concentration camp prisoner, the person locked in a squalid hotel room or the back of a van can still hold onto them as a claim, hope, and rebuke. The fact that the dead can be so clearly and utterly past any hope of restoring their rights means they never had human rights in the first place.

This horror, the horror of permanent violation, haunts the practice of international forensic investigation. Forensic teams work with limited resources, in places where weather, the boundaries of conflict, landmines, and the decay of remains over time can all make it impossible for them to find and exhume every grave. Even in Bosnia, home to an unprecedented multidecade, multimillion-dollar effort to identify the dead, not every grave has been exhumed and not every body identified.[32] In many of the graves that have been exhumed, the bodies—which perpetrators moved from grave to grave in an effort to hide and destroy evidence—are fragments, ripped apart and mixed together. Describing the challenges facing forensic experts trying to identify the *desaparecidos* at Patio 29, Chile's most infamous mass grave, Paco Etcheverría asks us to imagine an airplane full of unregistered passengers that crashes on a mountaintop, and everyone dies. The airplane catches fire as it crashes, irreparably damaging the remains of some of the passengers. The mountaintop itself, it turns out, is actually a cemetery, full of older bodies whose deaths had nothing to do with the plane crash. When investigators discover the crash site a decade later, they face an underground landscape containing the bodies they are searching for, and other bodies of people who died under nonviolent circumstances.[33]

In circumstances such as these, some of the dead may eventually be identified; many will not. Is there something to be gained by continuing to use the language of human rights as a promise, even where it can never be fully realized? Should we talk of dead people having the right to be identified when so many never will?

Human rights theorists have taken a number of different positions on the importance of "feasibility" to human rights, in other words, on whether something must be achievable to be a human right. Michael Ignatieff writes:

> The rights and responsibilities implied in the discourse of human rights are universal, yet resources—of time and money—are finite. When moral ends are universal, but means are limited, disappointment is inevitable. Human rights activism would be less insatiable, and less vulnerable to disappointment, if activists could appreciate the extent to which rights language itself imposes—or ought to impose—limits on upon itself.[34]

Too large a gap between human rights principles and the world in which they are carried out, Ignatieff says, is damaging to the project of human rights as a whole. This warning seems particularly pertinent to international forensic investigations, burdened as they are with the tenuous hopes and deep grief of families of the missing, as well as the difficult tradeoffs required for political stability in post-conflict scenarios.

"Feasibility" is, in most cases, a description of what human institutions and communities are or are not capable of accomplishing: some mixture of facts on the ground and background political and social factors. There are immutable conditions of the world: in Etcheverría's analogy, the airplane catching fire is one example. Then there are background political and social factors, such as the failure to register the passengers aboard the plane. It is crucial to recognize the difference between these two kinds of phenomena, for only then can a line be drawn between human rights as a set of statements about what we can (or have a right to) hope for, and human rights as a list of impossible and self-defeating expectations.[35] Erring in either direction has its cost: if Ignatieff is correct that human rights should be accompanied by a pragmatic acceptance of limits, he should also acknowledge that the presentation of social realities as "natural" facts is the principle mechanism of ideology, and the greatest obstacle to a genuinely liberating practice of human rights.

A world where no one is tortured, or a world where we all have basic health-care, seems far off given the current prevailing circumstances. But there is no specific limit on human agency that prevents us from achieving these things. We all have the free will not to torture, and though global basic health care would be an unprecedented institutional and redistributive project, no natural barrier makes it impossible. Articulating these things as rights, then, is the transformative spark without which the human rights project would lose its meaning.[36] It serves the dual purpose of expressing hope and delivering a rebuke: it is in our power as humans not to torture, and no one should be tortured, so why do we still torture?

By contrast, it is not within the collective agency of the living people on this earth to grant every dead person, people washed away by tsunamis and people burned by marauding armies, a respectful burial or other ritual. The problem with articulating universal rights of the dead, and perhaps one reason forensic teams avoid such bold use of human rights language, is that the hope those rights would express is impossible to fulfill, and the rebuke that accompanies those hopes unfair. There is thus a logic behind the limited place human rights have in describing what forensic teams do: the sense that human rights are at the beginning of a path that slowly disappears into wilderness.

Conclusion: Injuries and Indignities of the Dead, in Context

Work on behalf of the dead may be one of those places where it is easier to recognize and respond to injustice than to completely theorize the conditions of justice. Forensic ethics emerge, often quite literally, from the ground up.

It can be stated unequivocally that the bodies in mass graves have been violated, that what they have suffered is a basic form of injustice. But how? What is the exact structure of the injustice?

The violence against the bodies in mass graves reaches across the boundaries of life; it is committed first against living human beings and then against their dead bodies. It carries out these transboundary attacks on three major fronts:

Identity

Amor Mašović, the head of the Federation Commission for Missing Persons in the former Yugoslavia, points out that the perpetrators of human rights violations can strip their victims of their identity at three successive stages.[37] First, while the victims are alive, their soon-to-be murderers force them to give up identity documents, personal items, and clothing. Then, after the massacre, the killers heap the dead together in piles or in mass graves, their resting places and bodies undifferentiated. Finally, in places such as Bosnia and Argentina, perpetrators bulldoze the bodies into secondary graves or otherwise damage them in an attempt to render their identity irrecoverable through forensic methods. In this way, unfortunately, the global spread of human rights forensic investigations has sometimes prompted preemptive violence against the dead.[38]

People who conduct and study forensic investigations have rightly been suspicious that certain aspects of modern Western death rituals, especially the emphasis on discreet resting places for individuals with a personalized tombstone or other marker, would be treated as a standard even for cultures where various other forms of collective burial and remembrance are the norm.[39] Yet the deprivation of identity is a violation whether or not it takes place in a cultural context in which each grave is marked with a name and date. Even in cultures that cremate bodies or send them off to sea, the community carrying out these practices knows the identity of the dead person whose remains are the object of the ritual. Stripping someone's identity from her is a violation whether or not all cultures choose to mark or preserve those identities in the same way once the person is dead.

Location

The makers of mass graves do not only strip bodies of their individual identities; they also leave those bodies in an unwanted, unchosen place. The idea that there is a proper *place* to be buried is at least as old as the idea that there are rituals to conduct for the dead, older than Israel's dying request to his son Joseph: "bury me not, I pray thee, in Egypt: but I will lie with my fathers; and thou shalt carry me out of Egypt, and bury me in their burial place."[40] In the forensic context, even in those instances where survivors believe that people must remain buried in the place where they were killed, they have taken steps such as gaining control over the land, practicing rituals of purification, and sometimes working with forensic teams to exhume the dead, identify them, and then *re*bury them at the same massacre site.[41] In other words, these communities have transformed and claimed ownership over the location where the bodies will remain.

Care

The care that relatives and other mourners offer a dead body, whether it takes the form of washing, cremation, viewing, or any other practice, cannot be carried out when that body is in a mass grave. Forensic experts themselves have personal and professional ethics that guide the treatment of dead bodies, offering them some of the care they did not receive from their murderers. They also return those bodies to their mourners, who can care for them in a more intimate and culturally appropriate setting. The violation of the dead, in this case, is not just the failure to offer them any care. It is also the targeted attempt to place them *beyond the reach of care*—an attempt that, in the thousands if not millions of cases where bodies are lost and destroyed, is sadly often successful.

To other stakeholders, including international tribunals, families of the missing, and transitional governments, forensic teams offer a complex mix of different benefits, from evidence collection to historical truth to credibility. What they offer to dead bodies is much simpler and more specific: they name and identify these bodies. They relocate or "repatriate" them from unchosen places to places selected and recognized by a community of mourners, restoring them to the physical and social worlds from which they were violently torn. Finally, they provide the bodies with care: directly, during their various contacts with them, and indirectly by handing them over to families and other mourners. Trying to see these actions in terms of human rights, based on an unelaborated set of associations between international forensic investigation and "human rights work," opens up the chasm between what forensic teams can actually accomplish and the overwhelming number of lost bodies from millennia of human history—an underground map of atrocity that stretches across the planet's surface. Understanding forensic investigation instead as a set of specific, partial, but powerful answers to very particular forms of violence shifts the focus away from failure and unrealistic expectations. It opens the way toward an ethical orientation that is almost as concrete, as tactile, as the work forensic teams do in mass graves.

Chapter Five

Caring for the Dead

"The first thing I do with the bones is touch them."

— *Patricia Bernardi, member of the Argentine Forensic Anthropology Team*

Double Vision

The dead bodies in mass graves are violated, rightless, and sometimes fragmented beyond recognition. They have already lost their lives, a loss that can never be repaired. However, these realities do not end the conversation about what can be done—what is *being done*—for the dead victims of atrocity. Dialogue about the ethics of international forensic investigations has both broadened and deepened significantly over the few decades since Clyde Snow and his Argentine students began exhuming the *desaparecidos* in the mid-1980s. Forensic experts have had to look beyond the origins of their field in the medico-legal effort to document crimes, paying ever more attention to the needs of families of the missing, as well as the goals of transitional justice, collective memory, and social repair. Yet the conversation has featured surprisingly little reflection on the changes, physical and otherwise, that these experts make to *dead bodies*—changes that go far beyond identifying them by name, as powerful an outcome as that may be.

Philosopher Maurice Hamington points out that tactile experiences of care are often implicitly present where we tend to focus on other forms of knowledge and action. Recalling how he taught his daughter to ride a bike, he writes:

> Our conscious attention is on the task at hand—learning to ride a bike—so that the subtext of the dance between my body and my daughter's goes largely unnoticed. She wobbles and reaches for me, and I grab her. She falls and cries. I hold

her, comfort her, and inspect the scrape. My daughter is explicitly learning how to ride a bike and implicitly learning how to care.[1]

The forensic anthropologist or archaeologist who exhumes a skeleton from a mass grave, separates its bones from the soil and from other bodies, and assembles it as a unique individual—taking pains to wash and clean each bone, to note every mark of trauma new or old, and fit each piece together in the proper anatomical order—is explicitly practicing science, as well as contributing to larger goals of human rights activism and transitional justice. Implicitly, she is also caring for the dead.

Clea Koff, the forensic anthropologist and author who participated in mass grave investigations in Rwanda and the former Yugoslavia, spends much of her memoir, *The Bone Woman*, puzzling over this missing piece of forensic ethics. She calls it her "double vision": the ability to see the implicit alongside the explicit, quantifiable results alongside more elusive feelings and ideas that she struggles, and ultimately fails, to articulate fully. Koff's failure is not hers alone. Rather, when she does try to voice a care perspective on her work, she finds many obstacles thrown in her path.

In one particularly illuminating passage from the memoir, a Reuters reporter, Elif Kaban, visits the Kibuye church in Rwanda, the site of a brutal massacre of Rwandan Tutsis whose graves Koff and her teammates are in the midst of exhuming. Kaban asks Koff what is going through her head while working in a mass grave, surrounded by massacred bodies. Koff replies that she is thinking, "We're coming. We're coming to take you out."[2] Her teammates, she writes, subsequently mocked her: "We're coming . . . we're coming to take you out to dinner," was their joking refrain. Koff reflects, "For me, the conundrum was that I was capable of both scientific detachment and human empathy, but when I revealed the latter, I was made to feel I had revealed too much."[3]

Koff now says that the teasing was mostly a result of the unexpected media exposure her remark received. She and the other forensic experts working at the site had been instructed not to share any concrete details of the investigation with the press, but they were told that personal reflections about their emotions would be acceptable. So, according to Koff, she was one of a number of people present that day to share a "solemn" perspective on their work. After Kaban's article came out, however, the quote from Koff was repeated in multiple venues, a rare bit of human feeling coming from a tightly controlled gravesite. The wave of requests coming in from journalists, who now wanted to speak directly to Koff, upset the established protocol—which Koff says she never set out to question—in which Bill Haglund and Robert Kirschner, the leaders of the team, would be in charge of speaking to the press.[4]

Yet where there is mockery, there is also discomfort, and where there is discomfort, there is a story to be told. Koff's remark trespassed in at least three sensitive areas. First, she injected raw emotion into a fragile system where scientific detachment is the norm. Second, the sentence "We're coming to take you out" creates a narrative of rescue, one that puts the forensic anthropologist in the position of the hero and the dead body below as the needy subject. Humanitarians have good reasons, based on the history of their field (especially what Barnett calls "imperial humanitarianism"), to fear narratives of rescue; and most (though not all) forensic experts are cautious to avoid openly proclaiming themselves heroes. Third, Koff *describes the dead bodies themselves as beneficiaries of her work.* Koff's teammates' discomfort with this aspect of her remarks is particularly palpable in the teasing, as they poke fun at her for "hearing voices" and joke about her dining with the dead. The function of their ridicule is to take Koff's affective, nontechnical description of a relationship between the forensic expert and the dead victims of atrocity, and turn it into a metaphysical parody. It is as if Koff were revealing that she believed in ghosts, rather than voicing the powerful feelings that come with unearthing missing, beloved, sought-after bodies.

Forensic ethics have yet to make the important distinction between what Koff was trying to express and the exaggerated metaphysical conjecture into which her words were twisted. Yet Koff's direct address—her promise—to the dead bodies beneath her feet was not metaphysics. It was a simple statement of fact: dead bodies are the principle objects of a forensic expert's search, and the stakeholders who undergo the most dramatic transformation throughout a forensic investigation. The task of this final chapter is to pay close enough attention to this transformation—to the tactile, caring parts of the forensic process—that it no longer appears as secondary to trials or laboratory DNA identifications, but rather takes its rightful place in the constellation of ethical meanings that go along with exhuming dead victims of atrocity.

Care, Location, and Repatriation

The previous chapter ended by identifying three forms of violation experienced by the dead bodies in mass graves. They are stripped of their identities, abandoned in unchosen and unwanted locations, and placed beyond the reach of care. Each of these violations has some corresponding form of redress in forensic practice. The importance of identifying individual bodies after human rights violations (rather than treating them purely as evidence) has already received significant attention, scholarly and otherwise; in recent decades, it has been enshrined in the mandates of organizations such as the International Commission of Missing Persons and the International Committee of the Red Cross. There is something lost from an account of forensic investigation, however, when—as is often now the case—the exclusive focus of attention is the dichotomy of prosecutions and identifications, the body as evidence and the body as individual person. Recent efforts to distinguish between a humanitarian and a human rights model of international forensic investigation, furthermore, relegate human rights to the courtroom and place the "humanitarian" label on identification efforts that are imagined (often inaccurately) to be less political than trials in their effects. This categorization promotes a narrowly dualistic view of the forensic process.[5]

With all of the attention now being paid to the most highly technical, computerized methods of forensic science, especially DNA analysis, dialogue within and about the field threatens to become even more narrow, goal-oriented, and less humanistic. As Sarah Wagner eloquently states:

> This effort [of DNA identification] requires collecting, cataloguing, and storing massive amounts of data—that is, the re-presentation of bits and pieces of individuals' lives into Excel spreadsheets and computer database windows. . . . But placing the statistically sound DNA evidence above other forms of human knowledge, including more traditional forensic techniques, draws too strict a line between the realms of science and humanism at work within the identification process.[6]

Various aspects of forensic work are irreducibly tactile: exhuming the grave; lifting out, sorting and assembling individual bodies; matching them with their clothing and other personal objects; and extracting the samples that are used for DNA analysis, for example. Beyond their contributions to the identification process, these activities have ethical dimensions, as well as their own forms of moral hazard. These practices are forms of care. They are also, significantly, places where acts of care and repair that are acceptable to forensic experts can clash with mourners' own ideas about how the dead should be treated.

In fact, identification, location, and care—the three key elements of violations against dead victims of atrocity—are intertwined in important and often underappreciated ways. To understand the ethical importance of physical location in the forensic process, a fruitful comparison can be made between international forensic investigations and efforts to repatriate dead bodies and artifacts from museums and scientific collections to indigenous peoples. While articles about forensics occasionally use the term "repatriation" to refer to the process of returning identified remains to family members,[7] surprisingly little has been written comparing the politics, ethics, or procedures of these two different forms of repatriation.

Location is a central concern in repatriation claims. The Cheyenne word for repatriation, "Naevahoo'ohtseme," literally translates to "We are going back home";[8] it thus makes reference to native people's historical displacement from their ancestral lands as well as their contemporary demand that bodies and objects be returned to the places they now call home. Repatriation advocates have said that putting things "in their rightful place" is part of a larger effort to see that their ancestors are "well cared for."[9] Along with ascribing an important ethical value to location, indigenous repatriation shares with international forensic investigations a concern for violence that affects both the living and the dead. The sense that violence continues posthumously, affecting both the dead and survivor communities, translates into a call for some new model of repair. The repatriation of bodies and objects to indigenous peoples, like international forensics, features complex politics of expertise and hotly debated questions of who "owns" this material.

There are also important differences between international forensic investigations and indigenous repatriation. First, the idea of nationhood tends to play a very different role in these two contexts. The word "repatriation" refers to a "*patria*," or nation, to which bodies and objects are returned. For most indigenous communities, the claim of sovereignty—of being a politically distinct nation, even if its territory is embedded within the territory of another nation—has been a key facet of repatriation claims. The contemporary mass graves that forensic teams investigate, by contrast, appear in nations that are breaking apart as well as those that are being reassembled—in fact, in cases such as Iraq, ambiguousness about the future of the nation where the graves are located forms part of the tense backdrop to the investigations. Forensic investigations can exacerbate long-standing boundary disputes, as the locations of the dead or the massacres they suffered are used to establish claims upon a particular territory.[10] In places such as Argentina and South Africa, dead bodies are "repatriated" to small family units, and in some broader sense to political communities that are committed to the transformation of their nation-states, but they are rarely collectively owned by a group that conceives of itself as a distinct "nation." In fact, in these cases, it was the murderers who wished to purge their victims from the national community, and the victims and survivors who have sought to reclaim their place in that community.

In the human rights context, moreover, the emphasis is on identifying *individuals* by name and returning them to their families (with some exceptions, such as Rwanda, where collective burials of genocide victims have been common though controversial). In the indigenous repatriation of historical remains, for both practical and cultural reasons, there has been less emphasis on individual identifications and more on the idea of a nation reclaiming its unnamed ancestors.

Finally, science plays a much different role in indigenous repatriations than it does in international forensics. Forensic science offers genocide victims a new "technology of repair."[11] Meanwhile, for many indigenous peoples, "the interests of science" have long been used to justify the ongoing abuse of their dead. Though the debates between scientists and repatriation activists have gradually become less heated and more collaborative, in many cases the principle demand of indigenous peoples is for scientists to renounce their claims of ownership over bones and artifacts.

Taking a body out of a mass grave and to a place where it can be visited, recognized, and mourned can be seen as a form of care. However, a change in location is only one of the transformations this body undergoes, and the vocabulary of "repatriation," alone, does not capture all of the ways in which forensic experts and others care for the dead.

A Care Perspective

"Care" seems like an oddly simplistic, unsophisticated term to employ in the face of the tremendous scientific and political complexity of forensic work. As a term of analysis, care—a word appearing so often in corporate slogans and on Hallmark cards—is vague, even debased. This is in part because, in English, the term glosses over distinctions made more easily in other languages. For example, in Spanish, I can speak of the *cariño*—the tender, caring feeling—that I bear for my children, and I use an entirely different term, *cuidado*, for the daily "care work" I put into feeding, bathing, dressing them, and attending to their other needs. While these two meanings often braid together—the *cariño* I feel for my children, home, or pet motivating the *cuidado* I perform for them—they are not the same. Tenderness does not always result in effective and sustained caring activities, or vice versa. Forensic care is emphatically of the latter type, a form of labor rather than a sentiment.

Care, despite its fluidity, does have some central and repeated features. Perhaps the most important of these features is that care has an object: to care is to care for *someone* or *something*.

In fact, one of the strange things about some prominent philosophical investigations of care is that they have a tendency to state, early on, that care is focused on the other rather than the self,[12] yet they proceed to spend most of their pages extolling the value of a "life ordered through caring,"[13] the satisfaction that care brings to the caregiver, and all of the sensitivities he or she must develop,[14] while devoting comparatively very little space to a discussion of what happens to people and things that receive care. These works thus tend to reflect, in their very structure, some of the narcissism they reject on philosophical grounds. I aim to avoid this tendency by defining forensic care as object- rather than subject-centered. It is focused on material changes in dead bodies, as well as the social relationships between them and other people, places, and objects.

Care is oriented to specific others, and while it often expresses hopes for various outcomes (that the child will be healthy, the plant grow, the artwork be preserved for future generations) it is fundamentally *process-focused*.[15] If it were possible to ensure that a child would discover his passions merely by having him swallow a pill, or a garden take shape by pouring a special solution on a patch of ground, some people might choose to do these things, but they would no longer be forms of caring. Care as concept and as process are inseparable. Caring is thus closely connected to repetition and ritual: reading a bedtime story to a child, pruning a plant, applying a dab of paint and letting it dry before approaching the painting again.

This attention to process is one of the areas where a care perspective has the most to offer to the current conversations about ethics among forensic experts. Even as the ethical guidelines produced by forensic experts and organizations have gradually become more complex and holistic, they have remained relatively focused on *outcomes*, and even then, outcomes of a particular sort.

You cannot care for children if you do not spend time with them; you can only admire them. And you absolutely cannot care *for* dead bodies (as opposed to caring *about* dead people and their memories) without touching them,[16] performing rituals over them, or some other form of direct engagement. In the contemporary West, in fact, there are very few people, forensic experts among them, who have the chance to care for dead bodies.[17] By shedding light on *process*, care illuminates a hidden world of forensic ethics: a world of intimate touches, glued fragments, and regretful cuts.

The final reason to use the term "care" is a bit counterintuitive: I use it because it is inadequate. There is something about other terms, such as "respect for the dead," that implies coherence and consistency even where a precise definition eludes us. Respect, we think, is something we at least know when we see it. I am not certain that we feel as secure about care.

Care *surprises* us. Often when we offend our friends or loved ones, it is because we have failed to perceive how much they cared about something: the coffee date we failed to keep, the lovingly prepared dish we forgot to praise. To spend time with small children, similarly, is to be constantly thrown off your guard by what they do and do not care about. You spend an hour building a sandcastle with them only to have them knock it down with glee and prance away, then you cause a flood of tears because you have brought the red rather than the blue towel. What we tend to call children's "irrationality" is often really the fluidity and extreme dynamism of their care, a care that has not yet settled into the comparatively more predictable rhythms and channels of adulthood.

To care for others, young or old, is thus to be constantly acquiring knowledge about *their* cares, just as forensic experts must collect knowledge about the needs and concerns of mourners. It requires getting used to being wrong: observing, listening, rethinking, and revising. Meyeroff writes, "One important reason, perhaps, for our failure to realize how much knowing there is in caring is our habit sometimes of restricting knowledge arbitrarily to what can be verbalized."[18] Many of those who write about care seem conscious of the inadequacy of their own vocabulary, since care is a passive description of a process that can only be lived. To write about care is to posit in advance that you are tracing outlines on the page but do not have all the colors necessary to fill them in. Though my description of forensic caring, I believe, fills in parts of the picture that Koff and others have yet to draw, it is still far from full-color.

Bodies, Gender, Rights, and Paternalism

Over the past few decades, ethicists, psychologists, and other scholars have made significant efforts to articulate a theory of "care ethics." Many of these efforts have been part of a wider attempt to bring feminist perspectives into moral theory.[19] Decades after Carol Gilligan and Nel Noddings wrote influential early books of care theory, it now has proponents working in moral, political, and feminist theory, bioethics, and other fields.[20]

In essence, what these authors and theorists have done is to construct a language to describe the sorts of intuitions that Clea Koff gestured at in her answer to Elif Kaban's question in the morgue—this difficult-to-articulate side of her "double-vision." It is a language that emphasizes relationships and processes, partly as a reaction against the long-standing dominance of abstract reasoning in Western moral philosophy.[21] Some of the established language of care theory fits well with post-conflict forensic investigations; other elements do not. Four issues closely examined by care theorists that have direct relevance are the importance of bodies, gender roles, the relationship between rights and care, and the dangers of paternalism.

Industrialized societies tend to accord far more economic and social value to professions that maintain distance between bodies than those that are organized around bodily contact.[22] A medical specialist who prescribes pharmaceuticals and interprets radiographic images is paid more than a nurse who "reads" pain and discomfort on the bodies of her patients, applying moisturizer, adjusting pillows, and emptying bedpans of their bodily waste. A university professor, lecturing from a podium, is more esteemed than a preschool teacher reading a story to three children sharing the small space of his lap. Furthermore, the special knowledge of how bodies can be made comfortable, heal, and learn new tasks—possessed by the nurse and preschool teacher, and not necessarily by the more "specialized" doctor or professor—often lacks a name and widely recognized ways of discerning between an unqualified, qualified, or outstanding professional. It is far easier to know who is the best podiatrist in your city than who is the best hospice worker to help a loved one pass in comfort and peace through the threshold into death.

In response, care theorists have emphasized the importance of touch, of acknowledging the experiences of pain, pleasure, and difference in one's own body and those for whom one cares.[23] This "embodied" aspect of care is crucial to forensics. As a field, international forensic investigation shares the same partitioning of the technical, abstract, and scientific from the embodied and relational. The annual reports of forensic teams list identifications made, testimony delivered in courtrooms, grants won, and the acquisition of new laboratories and equipment. Only in memoirs such as Koff's or the occasional heart-to-heart interview do we hear about bodies passing through different stages of care.

It seems far from accidental that these emotive memoirs and interviews—much like the traditional "caring professions"—are places where women predominate.[24] The data on participation in human rights forensic investigations, by gender, is limited. Steadman and Haglund's 2005 survey of four major forensic organizations—which measured only participation by forensic anthropologists, not other specialties—found that 55 percent of anthropologists involved in this work were male.[25] Women appear to make up a majority of those entering the field in recent years.[26]

Gender certainly plays a role in shaping the public personae of different forensic experts. Clyde Snow was consistently portrayed as a tough "bone sleuth," whereas Clea Koff's memoir labels her a "bone woman," her gender highlighted right in the title. In fact, it seems possible that Koff's "We're coming to take you out" comment went viral not only because of the rare glimpse it afforded into the affective life of a forensic investigator, but also because of the novelty of a female voice (a young one, at that) coming out of a field whose spokespeople and authority figures were nearly uniformly masculine. So much the better, for media narratives, that Koff's remarks seemed to offer what might be considered a feminine, emotional take on mass grave investigation.

Forensic work can yield information that requires gender-conscious analysis. Massacres in Srebrenica and other parts of Bosnia targeted military-aged men and boys for murder, while women were kept alive to be systematically sexually assaulted and sometimes imprisoned in rape camps. In Argentina, pregnant women were targeted for kidnapping in part so that their babies could be "adopted" by military families. These cases make plain not only how rape and reproduction become instruments of war, but also how the ideology of the Argentine junta and Serbian nationalists intertwined their misogyny with eugenics, imagining that a particular race or subversive strain could be bred out of existence.[27]

Around mass graves, the legal and scientific outcomes some care theorists might see as traditionally "masculine" are actually inextricably woven together with the care of the dead. For example, having relatives view the clothing found on dead bodies can be a crucial aid to the scientific effort of identification. But there is no way to separate that purpose from the fact that washing and preparing the clothes for viewing is also an intimate act of care.

Human rights are, and I believe will remain, among the most powerful ways to describe both the violations experienced by victims of atrocity and the claims for redress that can be made by survivors and mourners in its aftermath. The role human rights play in forensic investigation is neither exactly like care nor radically opposed to it.[28] The rights to knowledge, truth, and mourning that are increasingly invoked around mass graves and in courtrooms reflect a caring, contextualized, relationship-focused view of the experiences of families of the missing:[29] a desire to provide them with opportunities to express grief and come together as a community. Care can clearly be embedded in or intertwined with other ethical imperatives, including human rights, and one need not treat care as a competing theory in order to see its value.[30]

Yet caring for dead bodies is different, in important ways, from according them human rights. Human rights are intended to be absolute: one either tortures a person, or respects his right not to be tortured. There is simply very little if any middle ground. To posit a middle ground, in fact, is nearly always to ally oneself with the torturers, as lawyers for the George W. Bush administration did when they argued that brutal treatment not causing "serious physical injury so severe that death, organ failure or permanent damage resulting in a loss of significant body functions" did not qualify as torture.[31] Arguments can be waged over the *definition* of torture—for example, whether solitary confinement constitutes a form of torture.[32] Once this practice becomes part of torture's definition, however—soon, hopefully, in international law as well as in a shared global understanding—there should be no "solitary lite." The practice in all its forms must be seen as a human rights violation.

In this respect, care describes areas of human experience and human action that are qualitatively different from rights. Care, of all sorts, exists not in absolutes but on a continuum. When a patient has an illness that can be cured, the first imperative of care is to cure her. If her condition is chronic and cannot be cured, then caring for her requires alleviating her symptoms and allowing her to participate, as much as possible, in the life of the world (through wheelchairs, pain-relief medications, acupuncture, or physical therapy, for example).[33] If her illness is fatal and in its late stages, she and her family may choose hospice care, implying a focus on pain-reduction and, ultimately, on dying with dignity. Care moves through ladderlike stages, realigning its priorities from what seemed an absolute good—the cure—to what is still left to do when that good cannot be achieved. Most importantly for the forensic context, the possibilities for care do not end at death. Caring actions create real changes in the conditions and status of dead bodies, bodies that are and sadly must remain beyond the reach of the absolute guarantees of human rights.

Another issue calls out for attention from anyone writing about care ethics, no matter the context: the specter of paternalism. Care work of all kinds is shot through with difficult decisions about when to hang on and when to let go, when the cessation of care is a failure and when it is the only way left to respect another's autonomy—a respect that can, in itself, be a form of caring. How long can refugees be housed in camps and eat food rations before the integrity of their own foodways—meaning the way they grow, gather, and store food, as well as their recipes and the social structures built around their eating—are irrevocably destroyed? Michael Barnett argues that "humanitarianism is defined by the paradox of emancipation and domination."[34] Among the many dangers of paternalist domination, he lists:

> Those that presume the authority to represent the suffering of others frequently (mis)appropriate the pain in ways that celebrate the deliverer and limit the capacity of victims to express in their own words their suffering and sorrow. The very cultivation of compassion can generate little more than feel-good moments that immunize onlookers from real action that can have more tangible effects. The "gift" often comes with obligations and generates new forms of dependency and obligation. The passion of compassion can lead to a "politics of pity" that creates a distance between the observer and the suffering object.[35]

This danger will not go away. Nor is it, as Barnett argues, an airtight case against humanitarian action. Neither the blind imperialist nor the armchair critic makes particularly good company for anyone trying to understand the real texture of humanitarianism or international activism. There are a great many excellent arguments for erring on the side of caution and skepticism whenever the subject of international interventions is raised, whether military, humanitarian, scientific, or some combination of the above. But there are also some very bad arguments, which are, in their own ways, as hostile to evidence-based thinking as the worst, "white savior industrial complex"-style humanitarian adventurers.[36] The most strident critics of humanitarianism often make it seem as if the geopolitical power dynamics that exist between wealthy nations and the various countries they assist are played out, in an exact microcosm, on the ground where humanitarians meet those in need. This is not the case: humanitarian aid workers are not governments (though they may sometimes participate in "governance"),[37] and the relationships formed in the refugee camp or emergency hospital are fraught with danger but also different from any grand narrative of domination and subordination.

In the Introduction, I described different reactions to the disparity between efforts to identify victims of the genocide in the former Yugoslavia versus in Rwanda. In some experts' eyes, caring for victims and survivors of the Rwandan genocide required respect for their cultural integrity: to force a highly technical process of individual identification on people who were in the midst of sanctifying collective graves for their dead would be the very definition of destructive paternalism. To others, the claim that Rwandans' "culture" made it permissible not to offer them the same technologies of truth that were being employed in Europe smacked of condescension and paternalism combined, a resurrection of the image of the childlike and superstitious African. In this latter interpretation, caring for the victims and survivors of genocide entails offering them every technique and capability you possess, and letting them and their descendants decide what meaning they wish to make out of the science. Wearing lenses that can see only opportunities for care and rescue, or on the contrary only the moral hazards of paternalism, exempts one from having to consider and even balance the competing interpretations available in most situations. To say that care plays a role in international forensic investigations, furthermore, implies nothing about whether those investigations should be conducted in any given case.

Forensic Caring

One of the most damaging accusations mourners and critics (including many forensic experts who had worked in the region) leveled against the tribunal-sponsored forensic investigations in Bosnia and Kosovo was that they were concerned too narrowly with legal outcomes, in the process failing not only to make adequate plans for identifying the individual dead but also to treat them with sufficient respect or care. The response has been a movement to put families of the missing at center of forensic ethics,[38] reviving and expanding the approach the Argentine Forensic Anthropology Team developed in the 1980s, when amnesty laws drastically curtailed their ability to contribute evidence to trials. This family-centric model, now sometimes referred to as a "humanitarian" approach to forensic investigation, asserts that forensic experts have the duty to accompany families in their grief, using both forensic science and psychosocial support to help them exchange the trauma of uncertainty for the sad resolution of mourning and remembrance. Collecting information from families, informing them about the details of a case, and arranging for the return and reburial of remains are now seen, by many, to be as central to international forensic investigation as exhumation or autopsy.

The humanitarian model goes a long way toward a care perspective on forensic investigations. Along with its attention to relationships of various sorts (between families and their missing loved ones, families and their broader communities, forensic experts and families), it crosses over the professional barriers often erected between scientific experts and caring practices.

However, a fully articulated care perspective, while in many ways complementary to the humanitarian approach, goes further in establishing continuity between the forensic expert's work at the gravesite, in the lab, and with families. So long as we are open to the idea that not all of the objects of care must be *sentient*—a significant departure from most versions of care ethics—we can see how care shapes the practices of forensic workers as they interact with families as well as when they handle dead bodies in the relative privacy of the lab or morgue. Washing the clothes of the dead, piecing together tiny bones into a recognizable hand, allowing a woman who has just received incontestable proof that her son is dead to get up from the sofa and serve you lunch (thus asserting her dignity and correcting, in subtle ways, the balance of power between forensic expert and mourner): all of these activities radiate out from a common project of care. True, various parts of this long process require different skills. The person who repairs the hand may not also be the best person to inform the mother of her loss; though there is something particularly powerful about examples where a small group of investigators have taken all of these interactions with the living and the dead, from the start through the end of the investigation, upon themselves.[39] Regardless, intimate and precise forms of care are required from everyone involved at every point in a forensic investigation, and a lack of care in one place—disrespectful storage of dead bodies, or a brusque and impatient death notification to a relative—will be felt elsewhere.

From a care perspective, it is of equal importance that once the bodies of the dead are repatriated to their mourners, these mourners have the opportunity to care for their dead through their own chosen rituals. Unlike the dead, living mourners are not only *objects* of care; forensic work ultimately empowers them to take over from the experts, to care for their dead in ways that only they have the knowledge, preparation, and feeling to do. The forensic archaeologist Richard Wright, describing a reburial ceremony after the excavation and analysis of a Holocaust-era mass grave in Serniki, Ukraine, writes:

> Out of the woods, like deer, emerged a few hundred villagers from Serniki. They stood uncertainly around the grave. Some Jews from Rovno gathered inside the grave with shovels. An American rabbi studying in Minsk conducted the ceremony. That was the moment when the technical team felt awkward and unnecessary. *A new regime had taken over.*[40]

Forensic care is involved in the *creation of more caregivers*. Unlike DNA identifications or other aspects of the investigative process, it does not concentrate expertise in the hands of the few, but rather naturally seeks to end the monopoly
of the forensic expert to spread the activity of care out from the gravesite into
the community.

This activity can spread in different ways, and there is no single prescrip-
tion for how communities of mourners will undertake the work of caring for
the dead. In her ethnography of Spanish Civil War exhumations, Renshaw
notes that due to the length of time between the conflict and the exhumations,
"there is a very limited history of intimacy or bodily knowledge between the
living and the dead" at the sites she studied.[41] It is usually the grandchildren
of the civil war victims who are most active in exhumation efforts, and their
memories of the dead—if they have any—often come through photographs
and stories rather than vivid, embodied memories. While in Spain, Renshaw
did not witness the types of intimate interactions between living mourners and
the remains of dead that she had seen in Kosovo (and that are recounted in
stories from Bosnia, Chile, Guatemala, Kosovo, and other places). Yet she did
notice more subtle, indirect ways in which relatives of the dead took ownership of care work:

> The primary way in which relatives physically engaged with the dead was by as-
> sisting in nonexpert manual tasks. This work might include digging the topsoil,
> sieving the grave fill, or washing the soil from disarticulated remains. . . . It was a
> physical manifestation of care and affection for the human remains, but not a re-
> enactment of physical gestures of affection from a remembered in-life intimacy.[42]

One of the central principles of the humanitarian approach to international
forensic investigation is that it considers identifying individual bodies to be at
least as important as collecting evidence on behalf of courts and tribunals. Its
most vigorous supporters argue, "The overwhelming desire of relatives from all
religions and cultures is to identify their loved ones."[43] In this view, the human
universal that makes forensic work "humanitarian" is the desire for individual
identification of the dead.

Yet there remain important questions about what constitutes forensic
"identification." In some cases, such as Rwanda and Timor-Leste, communities of mourners have cultural and even political practices of identification
that, while acceptable to them, do not meet the standards of forensic science.
In other cases, forensic anthropologists may be able to identify only a skull

or fragment of bone, and be unable to locate or identify the rest of the body. Through DNA analysis, positive matches can now be made between living family members and tiny fragments of an individual. The forensic anthropologist Bill Haglund thus wonders: "Is [identification] to prove the person died, or to collect as much as possible of remains for a family?"[44] In other words, is identification a search for *facts* or for *material*?

While most of his colleagues would acknowledge the importance of both facts and material, the former is still very much the dominant paradigm in which identification work is viewed. Stephen Cordner and Helen McKelvie, in an article on evolving standards in international forensic ethics, begin with the following statement:

> Forensic expertise in human rights investigations serves four purposes. On a humanitarian level, the aim is to help families uncover the fate of their loved ones. The investigation also serves as documentation to set the historical record straight. The purpose is furthermore to uncover legally admissible evidence that will result in the conviction of those responsible for the crime. Ultimately it is hoped that such investigations will deter future violations by demonstrating through forensic documentation and litigation that those responsible will be held accountable for their actions.[45]

The quotation eloquently captures the complex mixture of priorities forensic investigations have taken on as they have unfolded in post-conflict areas around the globe. Note, however, the focus on facts and other intangibles: the fates of the dead, documentation, evidence, deterrence. *Bodies*—as physical entities whose mourners long for them, and perhaps even as direct beneficiaries of the forensic process—are nowhere to be found in this otherwise very rich list of the things international forensic investigations can accomplish.[46]

Michael Barnett, reflecting on a wider trend within humanitarianism, writes:

> The desire to measure places a premium on numbers—for instance, lives lost and saved, people fed, children inoculated—to the neglect of nonquantifiable goals such as witnessing, being present, conferring dignity, and demonstrating solidarity. Is it possible to quantify, for instance, the reuniting of families, the providing of burial shrouds, or the reducing of fear and anxiety in individuals that are in desperate situations? If these activities and their impacts cannot be operationalized, will they be left outside the model?[47]

Somewhere between the vocabularies of legal accountability and humanitarian need, along with occasional gestures to the importance of "symbolically significant measures" such as memorials and official apologies,[48] the physical work of digging, brushing, washing, and assembling fades into the background. We are left with no vocabulary for the activities of forensic teams that are neither legal nor merely "symbolic": forms of repair directed toward dead bodies themselves, not only to their mourners.

A care perspective in no way contradicts the goals enshrined in the humanitarian approach. However, it has a different answer (or simply a longer answer) to Haglund's question about the search for material remains. The forensic investigator, from a care perspective, seeks the integrity of the dead body *as a body and a beloved*. She sees the work of care as a form of repair and knows that a few bones or locks of hair—however useful for ascertaining the identity of the deceased—are far less adequate, as objects of care, than a full body. Of course, as Haglund pointed out in the same conversation, the demand for complete bodies often far outpaces the limitations of forensic teams' resources and the conditions under which they work—especially in the former Yugoslavia and other places where graves have been subjected to tampering. Yet families have repeatedly voiced their feeling that even one bone of a missing loved one is significant,[49] which logically also means that *every* bone is significant. The absent pieces of a body are missed just as much as the found pieces are cherished and mourned.

A care perspective, in addition to articulating underappreciated aspects of forensic work, also provides a new way to talk about limitations, potential hazards, and the work that remains undone. In one of her most candid passages, Koff recalls a series of reactions she had while examining the body of a teenage boy her team had exhumed from a mass grave in Bosnia:

> I felt so awful, so full of hurt and emotion, and mixed in with that was a knee-buckling sense of privilege that I was touching the bones of someone whose family was out there and wanted more than anything to have him back, no matter what condition he was in, and yet I was the only one holding him. I felt like I was betraying him, or his mother—I couldn't work out which.[50]

Koff later faults herself for losing "an element of self-control" in this moment. Perhaps this loss of control was emotionally hazardous for her, yet it also offers a powerful view of the delicate balance necessary for a care perspective on forensic investigation. Koff highlights the importance of "touching" and "holding" to both herself and the boy's mourners, the bodily reality of her work.[51] Yet she is also conscious of the almost perilous privilege that her expertise confers on her: the responsibility she has as the first person to make this intimate contact with the remains of a displaced and violated person, and the possibility that his mother might feel betrayed, or at least disempowered, by the process. Finally, she voices a sense of obligation to the dead body itself, again fraught with potential dangers ("I felt like I was betraying him").

This last aspect of Koff's remarks, the relationship she articulates between herself, her work, and the dead body, is still a far too unexplored facet of the conduct and meaning of forensic investigation. It is also a place where the conceptual framework provided by care theorists often falls short. In their focus on relationships and reciprocity, care theorists tend to assume life and sentience on the part of the recipient of care. In contrast, the world of forensic investigations, especially of mass graves, is one of living mourners, lost objects, and dead bodies that exist somewhere in the hazy middle ground between objects and persons. Mass graves thus demand a new perspective on care work, particularly in terms of what counts as an object of care and what care achieves for those objects.

What Forensic Care Does for the Dead

Care is fundamentally other-oriented. The caregiver's achievement is not in the consistency of his own behavior or the rewards for it, but rather in the extent to which the person, animal, or thing being cared for benefits from the care received. Care theorists thus tend to emphasize the value of "reciprocity" in caring. By "reciprocity" they do not mean that all relationships must be equal in terms of how much care is given and received, but rather that the recipient or object of care plays an active role in the caring process. As Joan Tronto writes, "The final phase of caring recognizes that the object of care will respond to the care it receives. For example, the tuned piano sounds good again, the patient feels better, or the starving children seem healthier after being fed. It is important to include care-receiving as an element of the caring process because it provides the only way to know that caring needs have actually been met."[52]

Unlike children, students, patients, pets, and many other "objects of care," the recipient of a forensic expert's acts of care at the gravesite and in the morgue—the dead body—cannot acknowledge the care it is receiving. Though important changes take place in the dead body as it moves through the forensic process, it does not grow or flourish in any traditional sense.

Reciprocity narrrows when care is directed toward nonspeaking and even nonsentient others. Virginia Held, contemplating the example of a "severely mentally disabled person," says that the caregiver must "imagine a relation" with the patient,[53] while Tronto, in the passage quoted above, gives us the example of the tuned piano whose reciprocation of care is its musical sound.

Much of the language used in media reports about forensic investigations follows Held's suggestion, "imagining a relation" between forensic experts and dead bodies. This is the central theme in Koff's remark about "coming to take you out," as well as the oft-repeated claim that forensic experts "make the bones speak."[54] The latter metaphor operates in part by blurring an important distinction between *information* and *speech*. Speech, unlike the information that forensic experts collect from bodies and interpret, asserts agency. It is unpredictable. It can reveal, but also conceal or mislead.

All of this metaphorical language may also be beside the point. Forensic experts *do* enter into a relationship, of sorts, with dead bodies, and not merely an imagined one. This relationship is a unique one in which the affective and ethical concerns of the forensic expert—ones she feels herself, and ones she represents on behalf of families, mourners, and her teammates—can only elicit *material* responses from the body. This is not to say that the dead body is only a "thing," but simply that, like things, its outward expressions are limited and not under any kind of conscious control. They are not verbal, developmental, or forms of healthy flourishing. They do not resemble real speech or agency.

Tronto's piano-tuning example thus may be an appropriate parallel to the dead body, an inanimate object which can nevertheless "respond" to care in outwardly visible/audible ways. However, while the tuned piano is fully restored to its original sound and state, the dead body is permanently lost to life. In the case of forensics, while caring practices can accomplish important things, including limited forms of repair, they can never fully reverse the effects of violence or of time. Forensic care treats as valuable whatever material vestiges remain of a life, even as it continually exposes just how much has been lost.

Any definition of forensic care, then, must be extremely modest: modest, yet able to convey how much is at stake. There are important differences between a well-tuned musical instrument and a mourned body. A body is the home of, or coextensive with, a self; a musical instrument, even the most treasured, rare, or antique one, is not a self but rather a tool for the expression of selves—selves that manipulate it but that it can never wholly contain. The forensic context does not obliterate the distinction between person and thing (though for many people dead bodies fall somewhere between or outside of those categories). Rather, mass graves and forensic investigations create much more complex relationships between person and thing than most care ethicists have contemplated.

Mourners may attach great importance and meaning to the bodies of the missing and disappeared, but this is not always the case. They may find the bones of their dead woefully abstracted from the person they once knew, unrecognizable, or too traumatic a reminder of the tortures and disfigurations inflicted on a loved one.[55] Often these same relatives, however, react differently to the clothing and objects associated with their dead. As Koff reports:

> I was told that many of [the Mothers of Vukovar] wouldn't accept anthropological identifications, didn't care that the body matched their relative down to the number of teeth missing from years before or a healed fracture, on top of being the right age, height and sex. What those women did respond to were the artifacts—again, items forensic scientists consider only presumptive identifiers. One woman believed [in the identification] when she saw the front-door key to her old apartment, found in the pocket of the trousers worn by the man anthropologically identified as her husband.[56]

An article about life after the Srebrenica massacre alludes to "one case where the mother kept her son's jar of Nivea cream because it had his fingerprints on it. 'That was all she had left,' she said."[57] Robin Reineke of the Colibrí Center for Human Rights remarks that everyday objects collected from the bodies of people who die crossing the US-Mexico border are "really representative of personhood in a way that the bodies and the bones aren't necessarily. They can also be the single most compelling item for families to believe that this unrecognizable thing is their missing person."[58]

Forensic investigations can serve as much to reassemble a world of people and objects as to lend scientific certainty to identifications. As the best-known scientific means for identifying people become more technical, less dependent on reading the anthropological "signs" on bones than on sending DNA samples to labs for analysis,[59] families may make even louder demands for the tactile certainty of a recognizable object. This need falls outside of the "information, accountability, and acknowledgement" model of humanitarian concern for families of the missing,[60] and shows that individual *identity* is just one piece of a larger, material world—a world that once belonged to the dead and is still inhabited by their mourners. This does not mean that individuals—with their bodies, names, and histories—are not still central to a care perspective. Just the opposite: of all the objects remaining in the Bosnian woman's house that had been touched and used by her son, the most treasured was the Nivea cream that bore a direct imprint of his body—a trace, the fingerprint, that is known to be among the body's most unique identifiers.

The following elements, in combination, are unique to caregiving in the forensic context: limited reciprocity between caregiver and object, the irreversibility of the worst forms of damage done to the dead, and ties of concern and affection that connect bodies to objects, occasionally even making objects nearly as "representative of personhood" as the bodies to which they were once attached. All of these features inform my definition of what forensic care does for the dead victims of atrocity: *Forensic care aims to restore the dead body's own integrity, and its place within the social and material world from which it was violently torn. It seeks, in every touch, examination, and technical practice to which the dead body is subjected, to respond to, reverse, and/or repair the violence suffered.*

The first part of my definition bears a strong resemblance to Zoë Crossland's description of the Argentine Forensic Anthropology Team's exhumations as "an attempt to relocate the disappeared in society; re-establishing them within the network of human relationships that was ruptured when they were abducted."[61] However, the networks being reassembled include not only ties between people but also between people and places, people and objects, and even places and objects.[62]

A care perspective describes concrete changes in a body's status that are brought about through exhumation, autopsy, repatriation, and reburial, without needing to resolve questions of the eternal soul or the relationship with ancestors—questions that can only be answered by individuals and communities of mourners themselves. A care perspective need not specify when or if we cease to be persons and become bodies or things; instead it exposes the areas of overlap and transformation. It also testifies to the continuity of the violence that robs people of their lives and violates them after death. When I refer to bodies that have been "violently torn" from their social and material worlds, I include not only the circumstances of abduction to which Crossland refers—the destruction of identity documents, the clandestine prisons, the unanswered habeas corpus petitions filed by relatives—but also the placement of dead bodies in unmarked graves, and the lies and rumors spread about them after their deaths.

Embedded in the second part of the definition (forensic care *seeks, in every touch, examination, and technical practice to which the dead body is subjected, to respond to, reverse, and/or repair the violence suffered*) are two different forms of value that can be accorded to the dead bodies of victims of atrocity. The first depends on the presence of mourners, who confer value on the body based on their desire to recognize it, claim it, and perform rituals over it. The second acknowledges that the call to care now often extends beyond the immediate community of mourners: to forensic experts, human rights organizations, and others who believe the violation of bodies and creation of mass graves require some response, even from afar. International forensic investigation is not only the scientific study of human rights violations but also the ongoing search for avenues by which these violations can be acknowledged and answered.

Since care is not absolute, a body does not fall beyond the reach of care just because it is fragmented, partially destroyed, or even lost. One can care for the living, the dead, and even for fragments of the dead. The care offered to one bone of a dead woman stands in for the years of loving touches that have been robbed from her and her mourners.[63] Even if a body is disappeared or destroyed, the connections between that dead person and a world of people and objects—connections mourners have long been making visible to forensic teams—ensure that the possibility for care still exists. The jar of Nivea cream, treasured by the boy's mother for his fingerprints, is a worthy object of care, and it is capable of the same powers of substitution.[64] In these cases, the dead body's place in a social and material world is still restored, but through a more complex process of substitution, exposed connections, and marked absences.

While the hands-on, material aspects of forensic investigation are highlighted in my description of forensic care, the most cutting-edge technologies also make an important contribution. For example, DNA analysis is useful not only for identifying a particular set of remains, but also for matching disassembled or dispersed body parts to *one another* correctly—in other words, restoring not only the identity but also the integrity of the dead body.[65]

While forensic care is a discreet set of practices, that set of practices has a limit. There comes a moment when the body, or whatever parts of it have been recovered, are placed back in the care of loved ones—and when those people take charge of the caring process. Once in the hands of mourners, care may take a sharp turn away from the forensic paradigm. A forensic team may go to great pains to identify and assemble a skeleton correctly, only to find that the dead person's mourners believe he should be cremated. The seeming irony here is a shallow one: the eventual cremation of the body does not undermine the importance, for the mourners, of receiving the right set of remains and knowing that forensic experts treated it with care. How families and mourners themselves define "caring" treatment of the dead, once the forensic process has reached its conclusion, will inevitably be rich with cultural and contextual variation, but by the time these decisions are made, the forensic expert has already made a contribution by aiding the body's journey back into the social world. The mourners take up the work not only of caring but also of defining what care means to them and the people they mourn.

The violence visited upon the dead bodies in a mass grave was an attempt to place them beyond the reach of care. Even in the most extreme cases, however—the bulldozed and commingled remains of the Srebrenica massacre, the bodies thrown from planes into the waters of Argentina—the attempt ultimately fails because of the networks of affect, touch, and meaning that care creates both in life and after death. It is indeed possible to violate the dead in such a way that they are beyond the reach of human rights. The perspective outlined here, however, supports the conviction that there is no real way to place the dead beyond the reach of care. Where the full body is missing, a hand or skull may be found; where there is no hand or skull, there is a jar of Nivea cream or a favorite, often-borrowed, often-mended shirt. Among the most important tasks of the forensic expert who exhumes bodies and objects, matches this bone with that skeleton and this skeleton with that mother, are the unearthing of these networks of affective connection and the expansion of opportunities for care. Against violence that attempts to place the dead into a black hole where memory and care cannot penetrate, the forensic process proves Hannah Arendt right: "The holes of oblivion do not exist."[66]

The Scalpel's Edge of Care

A care perspective opens up new ways of seeing the forensic process and measuring its successes. But an ethical lens that only measures the good tells us about as much about real human conduct as a national anthem tells you about a particular country's political realities. Care is, crucially, a way of seeing and interpreting the dangers, flaws, and frictions of forensic investigations, as well as their successes.

Various forensic techniques, such as extracting samples from bodies for DNA analysis, can conflict with religious and cultural prohibitions against disturbing or profaning the body. Practices that forensic experts undertake in a respectful attempt to identify a body and tell its story may look, to others, like a form of mutilation. Similarly, classic anthropological techniques for identifying the dead may involve treating their bodies in ways that seem uncaring and even quite violent.[67] In a passage from her journal worth quoting at length, Koff recalls cringing at the way Bill Haglund, while working in a mass grave in Rwanda,

> would exhume a child and then literally rip its mandible off to get a look at dental age for our grave form. . . . I mean, it is horrific that we have to do things like extract pubes for sexing, or saw out bits of femur for DNA sampling but the goal is about restoring personal identity, and it comes at that price. Intellectually, I know that Bill isn't ripping the mandibles out with force because he wants to look possessed but rather, it's the bones adhering with just the last bits of mummified temporal muscle, and a bit of elbow grease is what it takes to get a look at the teeth and thus, preliminary age. And is our process more horrific than the actual cause/manner of death? After all, we wouldn't even be here if these people hadn't been attacked by machete-wielding assailants while they prayed to some god for protection.[68]

Despite her own attempts to place Haglund's action into an explanatory framework, Koff cannot quite displace her discomfort. Nor can she help but notice when other experts behave differently. Working at a morgue in Kosovo, more than four years later, Koff admires the work of a pathologist who seems to touch bodies "with compassion,"[69] even in situations that could prompt humiliation or disgust: for example, while trying to locate a bullet in the buttocks of an old man's corpse.[70]

There are important circumstantial differences in these two situations that appear in Koff's memoir. Haglund was working inside a mass grave filled with hundreds of bodies, which were packed so tight that "there was barely any soil left between them."[71] In contrast, Eric Baccard, the pathologist in Kosovo, conducted his examinations in a morgue with a single dead body before him. While Haglund is a forensic anthropologist, trained to deal with skeletal remains, Baccard is a pathologist with a background in general practice (with living patients) and accustomed, in the forensic context, to working only with fleshed remains. The motions, cuts, and other practices each one considered "normal" and respectful thus most likely differed by discipline and long experience.

It is also important to note that, while there were critics of Haglund's work on mass graves in Rwanda and the former Yugoslavia, Koff was not one of them. In fact, when a panel met in San Antonio to review allegations of misconduct on Haglund's part, Koff gave testimony as a "staunch supporter" of his leadership. Revisiting her journal entry about this incident with the mandible, Koff said in an interview:

> The Office of the Prosecutor wanted information about the demographics of the graves, some sort of indication of what was going on. They were expecting potentially two thousand bodies. We were only several hundred bodies in. Bill [Haglund] was under terrible pressure to give them some sort of preliminary information. . . . My feeling was that it was inappropriate that Bill would some-times jump in the grave only to get preliminary age estimations . . . as opposed to telling the Tribunal, 'You're going to have to wait.' Well, he probably didn't feel like he was in a position to tell them [that] . . .[72]

For Koff, Haglund's behavior in the grave in Kibuye cannot be separated from the pressures that were on him as a team leader, and the calculations that, for better or for worse, only he had the information to make: "He was the one receiving the phone calls; he was on the helicopter back to Kigali. He was the one talking to people who didn't know what we were dealing with, and he was the one trying to get some demographics."[73]

Nearly two decades later, Koff is still discomfited by the conduct she wit-nessed in Kibuye, but she has now incorporated it into a broader reflection on the different ethical lenses she and Haglund may have brought with them to the gravesite:

> I felt like the whole thing didn't really fit in with how we do forensic work. We don't rip anything, I mean, there's no . . . we have scalpels, we have tools, we have ways of doing things. . . . Standing around in our grave were people from Kibuye town who were working with us, and they used to stop and put their hands on top of their shovels and their chins on their hands, and they used to watch Bill. And I used to be thinking, 'I hope they don't think this is the way we do things.' I used to think, if we had a CCTV camera here that showed footage of what we were doing to a roomful of people who believe that their relatives might be in this grave, would Bill do anything differently? Or would he still actually rip off a mandible of a five-year-old child? Well actually, knowing Bill, I think he *would* [rip the mandible]. Because Bill believed that if we could go faster, that would be better. But Bill didn't see that, I don't think, as an *ethical* issue. This is just, like, what it took to get the mandible off . . .[74]

In *The Bone Woman*, double vision appears a way to describe Koff's strug-gles to balance two sides of her own experience as both a scientist/expert and a feeling person. Now, reflecting on her Kibuye journal entry, she looks beyond the self and through the imagined eyes of mourners at the gravesite—or via an imagined television camera, an idea she returned to multiple times during our interview:

> If you are wondering if you're outside of your ethical code . . . as a forensic anthropologist, one of the ways of examining that is: Would you do anything differently if the people who were related to this body were present right now? Would you work slower, would you be more careful, would you be more cautious? Would you go faster, would you try and hide something? . . .[75]

Three central features sit at the heart of Koff's double vision: first, she calls attention to the *process* of exhumation.[76] Second, she views that process from the perspectives of two different stakeholders: forensic expert and mourner. Third, she inflects both of those perspectives with ideas about care. Notably, she doesn't fault Haglund for not sharing her double vision, nor does she think he was unconcerned with the needs of mourners. It was just that, in the particular circumstances of his work in the grave in Kibuye, Haglund was seeing those needs exclusively in terms of *outcomes* (getting demographic information from the graves). Haglund was not *un*ethical, but his ethical lens was narrower than Koff's in this moment, either through temperament, the position he had been placed in, or both. The criticism expressed in Koff's journal should be taken, therefore, as a meditation on a particular, highly charged moment in a forensic investigation—one not governed by explicit rules, but subject to affective judgments.

As someone who takes a care perspective on her work (whether or not she would choose that particular label), Koff continues to struggle with the ways in which forensic science can require destructive, even seemingly violent treatment of material in the service of extracting information. Her exculpatory reference to the "elbow grease" required from Haglund as he removed the boy's mandible resembles Albert Howard Carter's description of autopsy: "a specialized kind of touch, one that destroys in order to promote understanding."[77] Midway through the passage from her journal, she embraces this sort of utilitarian calculation: "The goal is about restoring personal identity, and it comes at that price." Immediately afterward, however, she follows up with a lesser-of-two evils argument that betrays how deep her discomfort remains: "And is our process more horrific than the actual cause/manner of death? After all, we wouldn't even be here if these people hadn't been attacked by machete-wielding assailants while they prayed to some god for protection." This comment sounds an odd note because forensic experts are not simply less violent and "horrific" than the perpetrators; they are supposed to *repair* some of the effects of violence. To even compare forensic work to a massacre, as Koff does in this journal entry, only accentuates the sense that something is amiss, that her gut reaction has not quite been assuaged by all of her intellectual work of justification.[78]

Koff's continuing, deep discomfort with the occasionally destructive nature of forensic work resurfaces even more dramatically in a mystery novel she authored after *The Bone Woman*. The book, *Freezing*, follows two forensic anthropologists as they assist in the search for a serial killer. The anthropologists met years before as colleagues on the post-genocide forensic investigations in Rwanda (thus allowing Koff to weave significant aspects of her own personal experience into her tale), and now they own a small nonprofit agency that seeks to help the families of missing persons in the United States.[79] The killer is eventually revealed to be a former colleague of the anthropologists, who made his first kill while on the UN mission: "It was the ideal place to do it," he says, "what was one more dead body in Rwanda?"[80] His method involves using his forensic training to dismember, with clinical skill, the remains of his victims, and then scatter and hide them—embracing the very destructive aspects of forensic science that Koff herself seems so hard-pressed to accept.

Frozen also features a minor character that is romantically obsessed with the corpse of a woman he has murdered. He keeps her frozen, completely intact, for years. When he is caught, this man's greatest preoccupation is with the state of his victim's remains,[81] and he is horrified to learn that investigators have had to "cut her up" in order to identify her.[82] Koff thus stages an uncomfortable, ironic role reversal, in which the woman's killer is desperately pained by the investigators' "violence" against his victim.

In Koff's fiction, then, both extremes—care for the dead body's integrity, and joy in its destruction—can be linked to violent pathology. In the meantime, the book's forensic anthropologists and their allies in law enforcement busily search for every single body part of the missing women, while also accepting the occasional, inevitable need to cut them open or remove a mandible. They thus point toward a place of uneasy sanity between the two extremes, though it is a "sanity" complicated by the fact that at least two of these major characters are plagued by post-traumatic stress disorder symptoms such as nightmares, panic attacks, and flashbacks.

The very real destructive processes where bits of bone must be sawed off of the body, or mandibles removed, create a potential conflict in forensic care. Though technological solutions to this dilemma may eventually be found,[83] sometimes the methods used to identify a particular body—and thus restore it to a web of connections among people, places, and objects—result in violations, permanent or temporary, of the body's integrity.[84] In this case, a process of *reversal*—transforming the anonymity of a discarded body back into a named person—conflicts with a process of material *repair*. Just as human rights sometimes come into conflict with one another, so too practices and imperatives of care can point in different directions.

These conflicts cannot be resolved in the abstract. Rather, they constitute a challenge built into the very process of forensic care, as Koff herself indicates in another interview: "There is always the uneasy feeling that one is undoing the natural order of things, that one is a scalpel's edge away from actions that could be seen as disrespectful to the bodies and therefore hurtful to the surviving families."[85] Koff posits, convincingly, that while this unease may be intrinsic to the work, the solution in each given case—the types of care that are most valued, the price that is worth paying for them—must be part of a dialogue between forensic teams and mourners.

Caring Too Much

Another major theme in Koff's memoir is the importance (and difficulty) of maintaining some psychological distance from the gruesome realities laid out before her every day at the gravesite and in the morgue. In an article about forensic specialists who study animal cruelty, Charles Siebert writes, "Those whose compassion compels them to confront and combat daily its utter absence are, of necessity, often forced to affect a passionless pose."[86] Forensic experts must sometimes suppress their own empathy—their personal, emotive experience of empathy, not the empathy built into the very structure of the work they do—in order to control their reactions to acts of unfeeling violence.

Negative emotions, such as empathy and grief, may not be the only ones forensic experts find themselves concealing. In a speech at the Sydney Jewish Museum, the forensic archaeologist Richard Wright wondered if he should "feel guilty" for having "found the work interesting," "enjoyed the camaraderie of others in [his] team," and taken comfort in "the occasional black humor." For Wright, the most stressful part of an investigation is the preparation phase, and "the finding of the grave and the bodies is a release from stress."[87] In a similar vein, Derek Congram and Austin Bruno describe the satisfaction and even elation that can come along with finally locating a mass grave, or having one's hypotheses confirmed by the evidence that emerges along with human remains. They remark that "to be seen as enjoying one's work is an unspoken taboo in forensic science."[88]

Yet perhaps Siebert errs in so confidently calling the forensic experts' detachment a "pose" and implying that it is always "forced" upon them. The forensic expert's professional detachment may possess a social and even ethical element that is not visible when it is described in terms of the lone scientist managing his or her own stress—an element we might even associate with care. As uncomfortable as Koff was with Haglund's rough handling of bodies in a Rwandan mass grave, she remembers being at least as ambivalent about a different encounter: this time, with a Swedish anthropologist in a Kosovo morgue. The anthropologist, an expert in medieval human remains, was new to the investigation of "fresh" or recent graves. She began to weep over the first skeleton she was supposed to examine, breaking unspoken rules of comportment and professionalism on which, Koff realized, she too had come to depend. Koff comforted the anthropologist, but confesses in her memoir:

> And yet I was angry with her—so angry—why had the Swedish government sent an anthropologist who'd never seen 'fresh' bodies to a forensic mission in a country [Kosovo] where the victims had been dead for less than two years? Why was she here if she couldn't take this? . . . As I was rubbing her shoulder, I was thinking, "Don't do this to me. Don't start me crying, because I might never stop."[89]

Courtney Brkic, who also wrote a memoir after working on exhumations in Bosnia, recounts that her own teary breakdown prompted a sympathetic but firm response from the Peruvian anthropologist José Pablo Baraybar: "'You're too close to it,' he told me, almost groaning, 'And it's hard on everyone because you are.'"[90] These scenes of commiseration and sometimes gentle suppression on the part of forensic experts are part of "a constant negotiation between emotional detachment and emotional engagement" that Layla Renshaw also observed among the members of an exhumation team in Spain.[91]

The often-silent rules of conduct at the mass grave or forensic lab are not merely protective "poses" each expert dons for his own sanity or protection. They are, in fact, an important part of the social life of the forensic team. As both Koff and Baraybar make clear, managing your own stress—and knowing to step back when you cannot—can be a way of caring for your teammates, respecting the boundaries that others around you need to continue with their work. There is thus an alternative explanation for the forensic expert's carefully maintained detachment. The seeming lack or suppression of care may in fact be nothing of the sort: instead, it is part of the complex balancing of care required of a professional who is embedded in multiple caring relationships at once—with dead bodies, mourners, and teammates, among others.

Beloveds in the Earth

Clea Koff never quite resolves the problem of her double vision. Fear of losing the professional distance she finds necessary for her work cuts her exploration short, as do the social pressures she faces. The unfinished project of her memoir, then, is to find a sustainable care perspective on the forensic investigation of mass graves. For Koff, there is something unsatisfying about the current state of affairs, something that makes her end the book still contrasting the part of her that is a forensic anthropologist with the part of her that is a *"person"*[92]—not exactly a ringing endorsement of the profession.

Other forensic experts might have less interest in thinking about their work in this way: they might have alternative languages of professionalism and duty, or be content, as Clyde Snow advised his Argentine students, to "work during the day and cry at night."[93] Those experts nevertheless continue to make changes in dead bodies, graves, and associated objects that are consistent with the idea of forensic care. An absence of care in the *actions* of a forensic expert might raise alarms, but not every forensic expert must enter the field for identical reasons or describe their work in the same language. For those who do share some of Koff's doubts and discontent, however, her memoir begins an important conversation that I have tried to continue here.

A care perspective on forensic ethics has the potential to reconcile the forensic anthropologist and the person. It also offers a richer understanding of forensic investigations to a broad swath of the public: mourners, scholars, human rights activists, humanitarians, observers, and practitioners. As indigenous peoples have struggled to reclaim dead bodies and artifacts from museums and collections, "repatriation" has served as a powerful rhetorical tool and a conceptual rubric under which a number of different kinds of political, spiritual, and other claims come together: claims of ownership, cultural and moral equality, the continuity of indigenous presence in colonized lands (against the idea that indigenous items are "relics" of dying or extinct peoples), and contemporary nationhood. Repatriation has also changed how scholars, curators, scientists, and the rest of us conceive of the objects in question. Indigenous remains and artifacts, many of us now perceive, are important, even beloved, and have potential homes other than the museums where they were long displayed behind glass along with the skeletons of extinct species. Similarly, a care perspective on international forensic investigation is ultimately a set of reasons why this work can matter to anyone. It is about the world of difference between a body tossed into a mass grave and a body that can be mourned.

The procedures of forensic investigation are necessarily grounded in the presence of dead bodies: at the gravesite, in the lab, and as they are returned to mourners. Much of the "best practices" talk among practitioners has thus included recommendations about how to treat human remains in these settings.[94] In the meantime, however, the nascent field of international forensic *ethics*— the guiding statements about what post-conflict and post-disaster forensic investigation can do and why it matters—has largely treated the dead as people with stories to be told, with unanswered claims for justice, and as sources of information. These views are all true, but incomplete. Forensic ethics have yet to fully account for the fact that the dead victims of atrocity are also *bodies* still present in the world.

In her memoir of her mother's life, *The Exile*, Pearl S. Buck writes:

> Once I heard someone say of another's dead child, "The body is nothing now, when the soul is gone." But Carie said simply, "Is the body nothing? I loved my children's bodies. I could never bear to see them laid into earth. I made their bodies and cared for them and washed them and clothed them and tended them. They were precious bodies."[95]

These feelings about bodies—that they are precious things we make, and to which we must tend—are not just facets of some "humanitarian need" that forensic experts must acknowledge on the path toward the *real* goals of convicting criminals, revealing histories, and contesting the lies of tyrants and murderers. The cluster of techniques and technologies used in forensic investigation are the most reliable way, after the worst violence, to recover bodies that have been treated as trash and make them precious again. If we cannot recognize the centrality of this effort, it seems to me, we have missed the boat somewhere. Our vocabulary has been too narrow, our focus too limited. Perhaps we have begun to confuse expertise—the things *only* forensic experts can do, such as analyze DNA samples and conduct ballistics tests—for ethics. The latter includes many projects that depend on the skills of experts, but quickly move out from laboratories and morgues into homes, churches, and cemeteries. Far from layering some new theoretical language over forensic work, a care perspective allows forensic *ethics* to reflect more accurately things that are already central features of forensic *practice*.

Tremendous progress has been made, in a few short decades, in crafting norms and priorities for this entirely new sphere of human rights work. The family-centric, "humanitarian" approach currently gaining wide acceptance in the field represents a significant leap forward in accounting for the new demands and possibilities that emerge as forensic experts travel outside of domestic morgues and crime labs, across national boundaries, to mass graves and other sites of atrocity. Yet perhaps because international forensic investigation is so new, and because its realities constitute such a terrifying world apart for those who have not seen them firsthand, the dialogue about ethics has remained relatively enclosed within a small group of organizations and practitioners. A care perspective may help create new conversations in unexpected places. Discussions about forensic investigation and mass graves should extend outward from the fields of science and law, human rights and humanitarianism, and transitional justice to people involved in indigenous repatriation, hospice care, funerals and burials, and historical preservation. The world is full of precious things, and of people who devote their life's work to sustaining and repairing them. Forensic ethics could use their voices.

In a fragment written soon before he died of cancer, which now appears on his tombstone, Raymond Carver asks:

> "And did you get what
> you wanted from this life, even so?
> I did.
> And what did you want?
> To call myself beloved, to feel myself
> beloved on the earth."[96]

To aid in making the bodies of the missing, murdered, and disappeared beloved on the earth once again—"even so"—is no small feat. Forensic experts' capacity to "repair" the irreparable is limited, as is their ability to restore human rights to those whose rights were so thoroughly violated. Despite—or perhaps because of—these limitations, their work at mass graves is an act of science and humanism, an acknowledgment of the boundless grief and love felt by the living. It is also, and equally importantly, a promise to the dead.

Appendix

International Forensic Teams Pursuing
Human Rights and Humanitarian Investigations

The list below, while not comprehensive, features all of the major organizations that are discussed in this book.[1] It reflects an international community of mostly nongovernmental organizations that have been leaders and innovators in applying forensic science to human rights and humanitarian activism around the world. These groups have historical and organizational ties to one another—one of those ties, unsurprisingly, being relationships with the "godfather" of forensic anthropology, Clyde Snow. These organizations have occasionally worked on the same terrain and even employed the same people at different stages in those experts' careers.

Equipo Argentino de Antropología Forense (EAAF), or Argentine Forensic Anthropology Team: The first independent organization devoted to the application of forensic science to human rights cases, the Argentine team started as a small group of students who Clyde Snow trained in forensic anthropology the early 1980s so that they could recover and identify the victims of political repression in their country. The Argentine team has since helped train other teams throughout Latin America and in South Africa, and it has been involved in investigations in more than thirty countries. The team embraces a family-centric investigation ethic that seeks "to maintain the utmost respect for the wishes of victims' relatives and communities concerning the investigations, and to work closely with them through all stages of exhumation and identification processes."[2]

Equipo Colombiano Interdisciplinario de Trabajo Forense y Asistencia Psicosocial (EQUITAS), or Colombian Interdisciplinary Team on Forensic Work and Psychosocial Assistance: A small interdisciplinary team formed in 2000 by two Colombian anthropologists and an American counterpart, EQUITAS works largely in the search for missing persons and investigation of crimes as a result of armed conflict in Colombia, with a particular interest in exploring special forensic protocols to meet the needs of indigenous peoples and other nondominant groups. The team has collaborated with Physicians for Human Rights and the technology-focused nonprofit Benetech.[3]

Equipo Peruano de Antropología Forense (EPAF), or Peruvian team, formed in 2001, has made important contributions to the investigation of disappearances and other atrocities against civilian populations committed by both government forces and revolutionary guerilla movements in Peru. Because state and guerilla violence has disproportionately impacted Peru's rural, indigenous population, the Peruvian team has begun historical memory and rural development projects in indigenous areas. The team has also conducted investigations and trained forensic investigators through "a model of South-South cooperation" in Somaliland, Nepal, the Philippines, and the Democratic Republic of Congo.[4]

Fundación de Antropología Forense de Guatemala (FAFG), or Guatemalan Forensic Anthropology Foundation: The FAFG was formed in 2001 from a number of groups investigating Guatemala's long civil war and the genocidal massacres of Mayan civilians. It is very much an example of the spread of the "Latin American model" from Argentina outward, sharing the Argentine team's emphasis on psychosocial support for families and long-standing associations with the American Association for the Advancement of Science and Clyde Snow.[5] With the support of the US State Department, the team recently helped to create an internationally accredited DNA lab in Guatemala City, which will aid its forensic identification programs.[6]

Grupo Chileno de Antropología Forense (GAF), or Chilean Forensic Anthropology Group: This short-lived team was founded in 1989 by a small group of anthropologists and archaeologists as Chile was transitioning from Augusto Pinochet's military dictatorship back to democracy. The group, which received initial trainings from Clyde Snow and the Argentine team, worked on many high-profile cases within Chile. In 1994, it disbanded and one of its founding members joined a new identification unit of the state-run medico-legal services. That post-dictatorship identification work has fallen under the shadow of the subsequent revelation of misidentifications at one of Chile's largest mass graves, Patio 29.

The International Commission on Missing Persons (ICMP): Founded in 1996 at the behest of US president Bill Clinton with a mandate to "secure the co-operation of governments and other authorities in locating and identifying persons missing as a result of armed conflicts, other hostilities or violations of human rights and to assist them in doing so,"[7] ICMP has coordinated the long-term effort to identify victims of the 1992–95 war in Bosnia and Herzegovina, pioneering the large-scale use of DNA analysis. In recent years, as part of the peacemaking and transition process in the region, it has gradually turned responsibility for the identification process over to a multiethnic national Missing Persons Institute that it cofounded.[8] The organization has conducted trainings and assisted in missing persons issues in Iraq, Colombia, Chile, and elsewhere.[9]

The International Committee for the Red Cross (ICRC): In keeping with its long-standing role as the "guardian of international humanitarian law" and the major clearinghouse for information about missing persons after armed conflict, the Red Cross has been involved in mass grave investigations since its role as an observer of the World War II-era exhumations in Katyn Forest that proved Soviet responsibility for the massacres there. Morris Tidball-Binz, who was one of the founders of the Argentine team, directs the organization's forensic program. Because of its historical commitment to neutrality, the Red Cross avoids direct involvement in investigations on behalf of war crimes trials and instead has a humanitarian emphasis on locating and identifying the dead on behalf of grieving families.[10]

The Missing Persons Task Team: Founded in 2004 and trained by the Argentine team, the Missing Persons Task Team is committed to the investigation of human rights violations, especially those that occurred during the long period of Apartheid in South Africa. The first forensic human rights team on the African continent, the team is directly sponsored by the post-Apartheid state as a branch of South Africa's National Prosecuting Authority.

Physicians for Human Rights (PHR): Formed in 1986 by a group of doctors who had participated in international human rights work, Physicians for Human Rights has worked on many different issues at the intersection of healthcare and human rights, such as the global HIV/AIDS crisis, maternal mortality, rape as a weapon of war, the political persecution of health professionals, and the participation of health professionals in torture. PHR played a coordinating role in the 1990s mass grave investigations in Rwanda and the former Yugoslavia. The small staff and network of experts affiliated with its International Forensic Program are now involved in investigations, trainings, and missing persons issues in Libya, Honduras, Colombia, and many other parts of the world.[11]

Notes

Preface

1. Heilman 2001, 74.

2. According to Heilman 2001, the logic of Jewish burial rituals holds that "to look directly at the face and body of the dead . . . is to be struck hard by the undeniability of the corpse's passivity, which makes it difficult to believe that a passage to another kind of existence has begun. So the Jewish dead are brought for a brief period before the burial, placed in a casket or enshrouded on a catafalque before all those assembled at the funeral—unmistakable dead yet not altogether visible" (76–77).

3. Joyce and Stover 1992, 143–91.

4. University of Tennessee's Mass Graves Project and Carnegie Mellon's Post-Conflict and Post-Disaster DNA Identification project (which I took part in) are both examples of multidisciplinary, problem-oriented programs with significant involvement from forensic experts.

5. Kinnell 1971, 52.

Introduction

1. Feitlowitz 1998, 6–7.

2. Ibid., 20, 33.

3. McSherry 2005; Klein 2007, 87–128.

4. See Kaplan 2004; Bouvard 2002.

5. According to "Nunca Más," the report of Argentina's National Commission on the Disappearance of Persons, 3 percent of all disappeared women were pregnant at the time of their arrest. Qtd. in King 2011, 542n34.

6. Arditti 1999, 21–26.

7. Feitlowitz 1998, 33.

8. Ibid., 67–68; Klein 2007, 114.

9. Arditti 1999, 69–71; Keck and Sikkink 1998, 94; Lonardo et al. 1984.

10. Stover later served as the executive director of Physicians for Human Rights and is currently the faculty director of the Human Rights Center at the University of California, Berkeley.

11. Weizman and Keenan 2011.

12. See Joyce and Stover 1992.

13. This particular technique has since been discredited. It turns out that pelvic scarring is related more to a particular individual's range of motion than to childbirth. While women generally have more flexible pelvises than men, men can also exhibit pelvic scarring (B. Anderson 1986).

14. King 2011, 542.

15. Arditti 1999, 71.

16. Cohen Salama 1992, 120.

17. A popular account of the Argentine team's formation can be found in Joyce and Stover 1992. For those who read Spanish, Mauricio Cohen Salama's history, *Tumbas Anónimas*, features more detail about specific cases and more on the background politics that often shaped and constrained the team's work.

18. Throughout this book, I often use the terms "human rights" and "humanitarianism" in tandem—though *not* synonymously—when describing the purposes and ethics that drive international forensic investigations. Human rights and humanitarianism are different traditions, each with their own organizations, bodies of international and national law, and activist "cultures" (see Barnett 2011, 16–17). However, international forensic investigations can fall into both spheres, or into the area where they overlap. As the field has grown more complex, organizations are beginning to align, to different degrees, with one tradition or the other; though just as crucially, there are a number of experts who question the way the distinction is being made. For more on the human rights/humanitarian distinction in the forensic context, see Pearlman 2011; and Rosenblatt 2012.

19. See Barnett 2011; Keck and Sikkink 1998; Hopgood 2006.

20. Qtd. in Lucas 1989, 719. The *Oxford English Dictionary*, somewhat more narrowly, defines "forensic" as "of, relating to, or denoting the application of scientific methods and techniques to the investigation of crime." The differences between these two definitions are significant in cases where, for example, the forensic identification of dead bodies after a (legal) violent conflict or natural disaster would satisfy the demands of international humanitarian law, without any "crime" being investigated.

21. See Pierce and Rao 2006.

22. See Wagner 2010; Gupta 2013.

23. See Committee on Missing Persons in Cyprus.

24. Cordner and McKelvie 2002, 874.

25. See Soler, Reineke, and Anderson 2013; Sacchetti 2014.

26. A study of only four organizations found that, during the decade of the 1990s alone, the forensic anthropologists working in these teams had traveled to thirty-three countries (Steadman and Haglund 2005); the Argentine Forensic Anthropology Team alone, on its website, lists forty countries where it has performed investigations, trainings, or assessments (Argentine Forensic Anthropology Team, "EAAF Work by Region and Country").

27. See Stover and Shigekane 2004, 88, 96–97.

28. See International Commission on Missing Persons, "Mandate"; Wagner 2008, 262.

29. See, for example, Argentine Forensic Anthropology Team 2002; Michel 2003, 6.

30. See Kennedy 2004, 26–30.

31. Wagner 2008, 245–50.

32. See Argentine Forensic Anthropology Team 2008.

33. A few examples include the participation of academics and university laboratories in Scotland, Spain, the United States, and Austria in the ongoing identification of Chile's *desaparecidos* (see Comisión de Derechos Humanos, Nacionalidad y Ciudanía 2006), and the Argentine Forensic Anthropology Team's collaborations with Bode Technology Group, a for-profit biotechnology company, to identify remains exhumed by the team (see Syeed and Orellana 2009).

34. Center for Human Rights Science 2011.

35. See Dirkmaat et al. 2005.

36. See, for example, Congram and Steadman 2008; Hunter and Simpson 2007, 271–72; Raino, Lalu, and Sajantila 2007, 58–59.

37. Hunter and Simpson 2007, 279; Juhl and Olsen 2006, 420.

38. Cox et al. 2008, 10; Juhl and Olsen 2006, 420.

39. See Ariès 1974.

40. Juhl and Olsen 2006, 421; Neuffer 2001, 223; Pearlman 2008, 5n33.

41. Haglund, Connor, and Scott 2001, 57. This definition seems to raise the question of what the proper term would be for entire cities or towns, such as Guernica, Dresden, Hiroshima, or Nagasaki, that become littered with the dead bodies of civilians. Is the indiscriminate targeting of civilians more like an execution or a disaster? Can a city become a mass grave?

42. Steadman and Haglund 2005, 3.

43. Juhl and Olsen 2006, 421.

44. There is also considerable disagreement about when to use the term "exhumation" versus "excavation" (see Dirkmaat et al. 2005; Juhl and Olsen 2006, 426–27). Though this particular discussion may be important for scientists learning to work in interdisciplinary forensic teams, each bringing with them a different background vocabulary, it clarifies very little about the goals or methods of forensic investigations for nonspecialists. Throughout this book, I use "exhumation"—the word more familiar to me from my time working at Physicians for Human Rights—as the general term for any activity in which human remains and other objects are taken out of mass graves.

45. See, for example, Cox et al. 2008; Ferllini 2007; Hunter and Cox 2005; Joyce and Stover 1992; Juhl 2005; Zanetta 2009.

46. Cordner and McKelvie 2002, 883.

47. "Ancestry" is not race, and there is significant debate within the field of forensic anthropology about the use of race as a category for identification (see, for example, Hefner 2007; Ousley, Jantz, and Freid 2009; Sauer 1992). Many of our socially constructed categories of race or ethnicity, such as those based solely on skin color, have little correlation with the patterns of variation found in human skeletons. Where there are different

patterns in features such as height and weight based on a person's ancestry, forensic anthropologists must also be cautious not to apply the wrong standards: in post-war Bosnia, for example, some forensic teams investigating mass graves used Western (mainly US) standards for estimating the age and full stature of individuals based on the length and features of certain bones—a necessity because so many skeletal remains there were fragmented and commingled. Because the local population had different physical proportions than the population that had been used to establish the standards, however, many of these estimates later turned out to be erroneous (Steadman and Haglund 2005, 6).

48. See Hunter and Cox 2005.

49. The cause of death is distinct from the manner of death. The latter is a legal designation, limited to a few choices: homicide, accidental, natural, suicide, or undetermined. In many cases around mass graves, archaeological and/or anthropological evidence associated with the grave, not exclusively from dead bodies, can be crucial to this determination. As we will see in one example from the next chapter, rope, wire, or other evidence of binding can establish that people were killed in an execution rather than some sort of mass suicide.

50. See Cordner and McKelvie 2002, 870; Zanetta 2009, 327.

51. See Haglund and Sorg 2001.

52. In fact, one can learn a lot about the ethical and political investments in a particular investigation simply by studying the list of experts who have been brought into the field. The mobilization of social workers and database technicians for the International Commission on Missing Persons' work in the former Yugoslavia speaks to the (hard-won) emphasis on identification and survivor's needs there, as well as the resources available for ongoing forensic work. The seeming lack of any representation from these professionals in recent, US-military–sponsored exhumations in Iraq (see Hinman 2006), by contrast, is a sign of the low priority accorded to the identification of individual bodies or ongoing engagement with survivors.

53. See Wagner 2008.

54. See Brkic 2005; Hunter and Cox 2005, 221.

55. Perhaps one day we will have forensic investigations focused on violations of social and economic rights: detailed accounts of a child's real stature versus accurate projections of what it would have been if she had been better fed, or documenting how she contracted a disease that almost certainly could have been prevented or cured with basic healthcare. Or perhaps someday more of the forensic organizations traditionally involved in investigations of torture and mass graves will join Physicians for Human Rights in studying maternal mortality (Physicians for Human Rights 2007), or take on the problem of mapping, quantifying, and explaining the policies and practices responsible for millions of the world's "missing women" (Sen 2004)—thus creating a new, feminist forensics. There are, of course, many forms of wrongful death, trauma, and human rights violation that occur outside of traditional "crime scenes"—and they, too, can be studied scientifically.

56. What might be thought of as the Minnesota Protocol's "sister document," the Manual on Effective Investigation and Documentation of Torture and Other Cruel, In-

human or Degrading Treatment or Punishment, or "Istanbul Protocol," was also written with extensive involvement from Physicians for Human Rights and colleague organizations and was recognized by the UN in 1999.

57. United Nations 1989.

58. Congram and Dirkmaat, qtd. in Pearlman 2008, n49 and n50.

59. Center for Human Rights Science, Carnegie Mellon University 2011.

60. Snow, personal interview with author.

61. See Boehnke 2013.

62. Koff 13 June 2013.

63. Koff 2004.

64. Koff, telephone interview with author.

65. Ibid.

66. See Hopgood 2006, 97–101.

67. See Raino, Lalu, and Sajantila 2007, 58–59. The dilemma here is somewhat similar to a conflict Hopgood 2006 identifies at Amnesty International, between, on the one hand, the "moral authority" that comes from "privileged access to knowledge that is inaccessible to the ordinary person" combined with a lack of personal investment in the matter at hand (4), versus the "political authority" that comes from identification with a particular group (13–14). In the case of forensic teams, the identification may be with mourners, the local or international human rights community, or even the dead.

68. "Prosecutor Versus Vujadin Popović et al." 2007.

69. Giannelli 2011.

70. Committee on Identifying the Needs of the Forensic Sciences Community 2009, 7.

71. Ibid.

72. Ibid., 7.

73. Paperno 2001, 91.

74. Ibid.

75. See, for example, Baraybar, Brasey, and Zadel 2007; International Committee of the Red Cross 2007; Doretti and Burrell 2007; Stover and Shigekane 2004.

76. Komar 2010.

77. Identifications of this sort are always presumptive, rather than positive, because clothing and objects can be removed and exchanged. In situations of violence and hardship, people may switch garments and even identity documents in the hopes of eluding detection. They may also remove clothing and shoes from the dead if they are themselves in need.

78. Sanford 2005, 233.

79. United Nations General Assembly 1948.

80. See Komar 2008.

81. I have also avoided talk of "impartiality"—often used, somewhat imprecisely, as a synonym for neutrality—because it is less closely related to political autonomy than to a broader vision of moral universalism, discussed here as the third common ethical principle of forensic teams. As Barnett 2011 explains, neutrality is about the identity

of an organization itself—its refusal to take a side in a conflict—whereas impartiality is about the identity of those the organization serves, and "demands that assistance be based not on the basis of nationality, race, religious belief, gender, political opinion, or other considerations" (33).

82. See Forsythe 2005; Harroff-Tavel 2003. In his history of humanitarianism, *Empire of Humanity*, Michael Barnett points out that the International Committee of the Red Cross has risen to such prominence in the humanitarian field that its core principles of impartiality, neutrality, and independence are often treated as constituent elements of *humanitarianism itself*—ignoring a complex history in which other, often more politically committed models of humanitarian action have always been present, including in the pre-1960s Red Cross (see Barnett 2011, 5).

83. Cordner and Coupland 2003, 1325; Hofmeister 2009, 352–53.

84. Neuffer 2001, 223.

85. Cohen Salama 1992, 152.

86. In another context, Sarah Wagner provides a fascinating analysis of how the International Commission on Missing Persons, the organization spearheading the identification of Bosnia's civil war dead for more than a decade, has at times found itself caught between multiple roles, each with a different politics to it. On the one hand, the organization has sought to be a disinterested international arbiter committed to creating an identification process *every* Bosnian could trust. On the other hand, its experts have also been called on to provide testimony and verify evidence for war crimes trials against the former Bosnian Serb leadership (Wagner 2010, 29)—trials seen by many Bosnian Serbs as biased and unfair. Furthermore, many of the bodies identified by the organization are buried in a widely publicized yearly ceremony at a memorial for Bosniak victims of the Srebrenica massacre, which has only highlighted, for much of the public and especially Bosnian Serbs, "the implicit and explicit links between the judicial and identification-commemoration processes" (ibid., 31–32).

87. Baraybar, Brasey, and Zadel 2007, 268.

88. See Wilson 1997; Barnett 2011, 13–14.

89. Barnett 2011, 14.

90. Committee on Identifying the Needs of the Forensic Sciences Community 2009, 112.

91. Scarry 1985, 122.

92. These categories are also deployed with far more "uncertainty and presumption" than is commonly acknowledged (Komar 2008, 1).

93. Arditti 1999, 78; Stern 2013.

94. Goodman 2009.

95. Skinner 2007, 237.

96. Doretti and Burrell 2007, 56.

97. One expert was quick to remind me that there are also forensic scientists focused much more exclusively on their own careers and/or the intellectual challenges of mass grave investigations, and who are not losing sleep over these issues of case selection (Congram, telephone interview with author).

98. The Peruvian Forensic Anthropology Team has begun training a Congolese forensic team to exhume some graves believed to be connected to the "revenge genocide" conducted against Hutu refugees by Rwandan forces in the mid-1990s (de Pablo, Zurita, and McVeigh 2010). An earlier, aborted United Nations forensic project in Congo will be discussed in Chapter 4. Sudan, Sierra Leone, and Iraq are among other nations where many suspected mass graves have been located through satellite imagery and other means, but they remain uninvestigated.

99. See Wagner 2008, 265; Jessee 2012.

100. Meyer 2008.

101. Keough, Simmons, and Samuels 2004, 272.

102. Similar challenges have affected identification efforts in Timor-Leste (Cordner and McKelvie 2002, 874).

103. Steadman and Haglund 2005, 7.

104. Cordner and McKelvie 2002, 881; Fondebrider et al. 2009.

105. The cultural anthropologist Erin Jessee, based on interviews with twenty-four genocide survivors, argues that these accounts paint a false picture, and that there is in fact significant support for further exhumations and DNA identifications of genocide victims in Rwanda.

106. Jessee 2012.

107. Haglund, telephone interview with author, 13 Apr. 2009; see also Wagner 2008, 119–20.

108. Layla Renshaw's research in Spain on civil-war–era graves confirms this sense that a "generation gap" can open up when it comes to attitudes toward forensic identification. She notes "an apparent generational divide between the younger descendants [of the civil war dead], primarily grandchildren, who viewed identification as imperative and had particular confidence in genetic testing, and the older relatives, children of the dead, who were much more ambivalent about the necessity of achieving an individual identification" (2011, 196). Renshaw attributes these different attitudes to both the levels of understanding of forensic technologies and a cultural shift away from "performative acts of public mourning" (including the reburial ceremonies carried out at her field sites) and toward a conception of grief as a private act (ibid.).

109. Parsons, personal interview with author.

110. See Dirkmaat et al. 2005.

111. Jessee's and Robins's interviews and focus groups with families of the missing, while undertaken by individual researchers and thus naturally limited in their scope, are important efforts in this direction.

112. Questions about the distribution of forensic efforts can also come up when graves are thought to contain certain iconic individuals who may have special significance as symbols of victimhood and/or resistance. The graves (or suspected graves) of the Spanish poet Federico García Lorca, the Nigerian activist Ken Saro-Wiwa, and some heroes of South Africa's anti-Apartheid movement have all received a greater share of the attention to missing person's issues in their countries. Is it right for forensic investigators to prioritize those graves that form such an important part of human rights

history in a given country? Or does moral universalism also demand that they work to democratize victimhood, to treat the graves of the famous the same as the graves of the forgotten?

113. See Orentlicher 1991; Rauschenbach and Scalia 2008; Robins 2011.

114. Arendt 1992, 5.

115. See Dirkmaat et al. 2005; Fondebrider et al. 2009.

116. See, for example, Congram and Steadman 2008; Dirkmaat et al. 2005; Koff 2004; Skinner 2007; Steadman and Haglund 2005, 7; Steele 2008; Stover and Shigekane 2004; Vollen 2001.

117. Laqueur 2002, 82.

118. Ibid.

119. Zanetta 2009, 349.

120. G. Sanford 2005, 130.

121. Connor 2009, 249.

122. Paperno 2001, 95–97.

123. Congram, telephone interview with the author. In Thomas Hawley's 2005 account, the US government frequently appeals to the "humanitarian" nature of the search for American soldiers in Vietnam, but it actually approaches the issue in a way that highlights political and economic disparities, treating American bodies as morally privileged (231–34). According to Hawley, the United States has demanded significant Vietnamese investment in the hunt for missing American soldiers while showing little interest in reconstructing a country filled with war orphans, poisoned by US chemical weapons, and dealing with its own much larger numbers of missing and dead (see Kwon 2008; for more on US efforts to account for soldiers missing in Vietnam, see Allen 2012).

124. ZAKA's religious position against autopsy prevents its members from performing or aiding with that extremely important medico-legal procedure (Stadler 2006, 854). Though independent from the Israeli state, the group has participated in public relations stunts meant to gain sympathy for Israel abroad (Berman 2004). ZAKA occasionally adopts the rhetoric of moral universalism: "Wherever the crisis, whenever the need, ZAKA is always there. From the tsunami to Mumbai, from Istanbul to Taba, the UN-recognized international humanitarian organization sends volunteers and paramedics to terror and mass casualty incidents around the world" ("ZAKA International Rescue Unit"). However, this implied moral universalism turns out to be something of a put-on: the missions to these far-flung locales always begin as searches for Jewish dead, Jewish victims, and/or Jewish artifacts (for example, rescuing torahs from New Orleans synagogues after Hurricane Katrina, or collecting the remains of Israeli tourists after the tsunami in Thailand). On some occasions where these rescued objects have been in close proximity to other victims, ZAKA has also lent a helping hand to non-Jews, but Jewish bodies and objects clearly have a privileged status within the group's ethical framework—perhaps appropriately so, given that their treatment of dead bodies is guided by Jewish religious laws.

125. Physicians for Human Rights 2006.

126. Clyde Snow, operating as an independent expert, broke from his longtime col-

leagues and delivered testimony at trials focused on the Anfal Campaign (Salaheddin and Keath 2006).

127. A number of US soldiers have died due to roadside bombs and other hazards encountered in the course of the military-affiliated Iraq Mass Graves Investigation Team's exhumations, undertaken while Iraq was still under occupation and quite unstable (Hinman 13 Sept. 2006). Many forensic experts find the loss of lives in a search for graves both ironic and unacceptable.

128. In an interview, Michael "Sonny" Trimble, head of the Iraq Mass Graves Investigation Team, says: "[A witness in the trials against Hussein regime officials] wants to know if his sister was in the grave we excavated. It's possible to find that out, and we're gonna look into it. She was about eight or nine. I'm gonna run the numbers tomorrow to see how many six- to nine-year-olds we have. We've taken DNA samples; we just haven't run them. That would be a very nice thing if we could do that" (Hinman 29 Nov. 2006). Hofmeister points out that the statement "makes it clear that identifying individuals was not a standard part of the team's work" (2009, 354). At least as worrisome is Trimble's admission that the team was willing to attempt an identification for a specific individual who was serving as a witness for the tribunal, without saying anything about "running the numbers" for other families and mourners, potentially giving the impression of a quid pro quo arrangement in which the possible identification of a loved one is a reward for testimony against the Hussein regime.

129. Cordner and Coupland 2003; Hofmeister 2009, 354; Stover, Haglund, and Samuels 2003.

130. Derek Congram, a forensic archaeologist and anthropologist who worked on the Iraq Mass Graves Investigation Team, offers a thoughtful description his own decision to participate in the effort: "One might . . . be tempted to suggest that the active involvement of many forensic archaeologists and anthropologists from the Americas and the UK in Iraq, the former on behalf of the US government, as a sort of failure to engage in the injustice that was an illegal invasion. These issues and projects, however, are very complex and, notwithstanding the illegality of the war against the Iraqi government (and subsequent, related deaths of thousands), several practitioners . . . determined that there were overriding factors that justified involvement including the search for and excavation of mass burial sites, identification (at the group level) and repatriation of those killed during the Ba'ath Party regime. No forensic context is straightforward and the inability to investigate deaths and clandestine burials created during the NATO-led and UN-sanctioned attack on Iraq in 1991 or the 2003 invasion is a point of frustration for those practitioners seeking to assist with investigation of *all* injustices to which their skills and experience can apply" (Congram and Bruno 2007, 45).

Chapter 1

1. Cornet 2007.

2. For example, during Argentina's period of political repression in the 1970s and 1980s, many families (particularly in the upper classes most sympathetic to the ruling junta) repeated stories of how the disappeared had actually run off with foreign

mistresses to other countries, died in Hollywood-style shootouts with the police, or been eliminated by their own subversive organizations (Feitlowitz 1998).

3. Scarry 1985, 59.

4. See Wagner 2010; S. Anderson 2014.

5. Doretti and Burrell 2007, 46.

6. See Simmons and Haglund 2005, 171.

7. See Crossland 2000; Crossland 2002; Renshaw 2011; V. Sanford 2003; Sant-Cassia 2005; Wagner 2008, 2010.

8. Goodale 2009, 6–7. Goodale sees this dichotomy as a "false one" that needlessly rejects the potential of anthropological observation to construct social theories usefully grounded in the practices of actual people and organizations (7).

9. Baraybar, Brasey, and Zadel 2007; Congram, telephone interview with author.

10. I am not entirely alone in my use of the term to describe groups influencing the politics of forensic exhumations (see Congram and Steadman 2008, 167).

11. Thanks to Kathy Ferguson of the University of Hawaii at Mānoa for raising this question when I presented a paper at the Association for Political Theory meeting in Portland, Oregon, in October 2010.

12. Teitel 2002, 27.

13. Stacy 2009, 59–62.

14. Congram 2014.

15. Wagner 2008, 253.

16. Stacy 2009, 58.

17. See Robins 2011.

18. Congram 2014; Fletcher and Weinstein 2004; Rauschenbach and Scalia 2008; Robins 2011.

19. See discussion in Blau 2008, 2–3; Keough, Simmons, and Samuels 2004, 274.

20. Hereafter referred to as the shortened "Bosnia."

21. Weizman and Keenan 2011.

22. Cuff 2005; Keough, Simmons, and Samuels 2004, 273–75.

23. Cuff 2005, 16; Koff 2004.

24. Stover and Shigekane 2004, 92.

25. Neuffer 2001, 225, 229. Physicians for Human Rights eventually contributed funds of its own, and the US State Department later offered $1 million, but the lack of funds at the outset was a major setback in terms of having the equipment and space necessary to conduct exhumations on a tight schedule before the arrival of intense winter rains that impacted the gravesites (Neuffer 2001, 229).

26. Snow 2013.

27. Ibid.

28. Ibid.

29. Wagner 2008, 95–96; see also Juhl and Olsen 2006, 423.

30. Stover and Shigekane 2004, 91.

31. Juhl and Olsen 2006, 416.

32. Qtd. in International Committee of the Red Cross 2007, 15.

33. Vollen 2001, 339.

34. See Baraybar, Brasey, and Zidel 2007, 268.

35. Hunter and Cox 2005, 171. It is by no means simple to decide what kind of evidence proves that multiple individuals in a mass grave belong to any one of these categories. Congram writes, "Does lack of combat fatigues imply that bodies in a mass grave were all civilians? Not necessarily. Does a leg of cured pork commingled with bodies in a mass grave (the author has actually seen this) mean that those buried in the grave were not Muslim? Not at all. These matters, that fall within the professional purview of forensic archaeologists in the context of medico-legal investigation require critical reflection and often involve a significant degree of ambiguity" (2014). Under international law, a soldier, once taken prisoner, is no longer a combatant (Congram, telephone interview with author)—thus the significance of the phrase "soldiers incapacitated by bindings or blindfolds" in Hunter and Cox's list.

36. Stover and Shigekane 2004, 85, 93.

37. Ibid., 94.

38. Baraybar, Brasey, and Zadel 2007, 269; Hofmeister 2009, 357.

39. Stover and Shigekane 2004, 94–95.

40. Congram, telephone interview with author.

41. French Forensic Mission to Kosovo; Kosovo Crime Scene Group.

42. Congram, email to author, 8 Aug. 2013.

43. See Keough, Simmons, and Samuels 2004, 275.

44. Congram, telephone interview with author.

45. See Nesiah 2002, 825.

46. Fletcher and Weinstein 2004, 32; Stacy 2009, 61–62.

47. Keough, Simmons, and Samuels 2004, 273.

48. "Prosecutor Versus Georges" 1999, 98–99.

49. Reichs 1999.

50. Koff, email to author, 10 July 2013; Koff, telephone interview with author.

51. "Prosecutor Versus Vujadin Popović" 2007, 8929.

52. "Prosecutor Versus Vujadin Popović" 2007.

53. Birkby et al. 1997, VI, "Comments by Colleagues at the Sites."

54. Ibid., VII, "Recommendations."

55. Ibid., VII, "Responses."

56. Ibid.

57. "The evidence of war crimes is overwhelming at each site" (ibid., VII, "Recommendations").

58. Neuffer 2001, 246.

59. Snow 2013.

60. Wagner 2008. In the case of Bosnia, according to Stover, women's activism for the identification of their dead was also influenced by their traditional role, in Muslim societies, as coordinators of the mourning and burial process (Weizman and Keenan 2011).

61. Ibid., 96–98.

62. Bernardi and Fondebrider 2007, 207; Wagner 2008, 265.

63. International Committee of the Red Cross, "The Missing" 35, 56.

64. I explore this horrible symmetry, using Nathan Englander's novel *The Ministry of Special Cases*, in the next chapter.

65. Ghani and Lockhart 2008.

66. See Ferrándiz 2006.

67. I use the phrase "transitional governments"—rather than "democratizing" or "liberalizing" regimes, for example—to capture the specific circumstances of the transition from repressive authoritarian rule, which are different from other moments of reform or political change. As Ruti Teitel writes in her study of transitional justice, "The conception of justice . . . is alternately constituted by, and constitutive of, the transition. . . . What is deemed just is contingent and informed by prior justice" (2002, 6). In other words, while our sense of what it means to be a "democratizing regime" might be largely forward-looking—shaped by whatever we define as signs that democracy has been achieved (fair elections, the presence of civil society groups, or otherwise)—transitional governments must always also be looking backward. Their success at establishing conditions of justice and the rule of law will always be judged with reference to the injustices of the past and how they have dealt with them.

68. Wagner 2008, 262.

69. Juhl and Olsen 2006, 416.

70. Ibid., 413.

71. See Kovras 2008.

72. On the former Yugoslavia, see Wagner 2008; Wagner 2010; and Verdery 1999. On Spain, see Ferrándiz 2006; and Renshaw 2011. On the former Soviet republics, see Paperno 2001.

73. Stover and Shigekane 2004, 99.

74. Kleiser, telephone interview with the author.

75. Wagner 2010, 37.

76. Juhl and Olsen 2006, 413.

77. Jessee 2012.

78. In fact, it is worth wondering why the phrases "healing" and "reconciliation" are so often used in the same breath: if someone hurts me, is it not perfectly possible for both my physical and psychological wounds to heal without my forgiving (or wanting to have anything to do with) the person who hurt me? The demand that healing and forgiveness—or healing and reunification—go together seems rooted in a spiritual, and perhaps more specifically Christian, vision (see Graybill 2001, 7–9).

79. Wagner 2008, 263.

80. Ferrándiz 2006.

81. Tippet 2009.

82. For descriptions of the destruction of gravesites by Bosnian Serb forces, see Stover and Shigekane 2004, 92; Wagner 2008, 51. In Afghanistan, after Physicians for Human Rights documented a mass grave believed to contain thousands of Taliban prisoners, the forces of the suspected perpetrator, General Abdul Rashid Dostum, appear

to have returned to the site with bulldozers and removed almost all of the remains and other evidence (Lasseter 2008).

83. V. Sanford 2003, 44–46.

84. Kennedy 2004, 14–15.

85. See Rieff 2002, 25.

86. The debate about the responsibility "ordinary" Germans, Poles, and citizens of other Nazi-occupied nations bear for the Holocaust rages particularly intensely, as evidenced by the controversy in the 1990s over Daniel Goldhagen's book *Hitler's Willing Executioners: Ordinary Germans and the Holocaust*. In Chapter 3 of this book, I briefly discuss the debate over responsibility for the genocide of Polish Jews, and in particular the forensic investigations prompted by the historian Jan Gross's analysis in his book *Neighbors: The Destruction of the Jewish Community in Jedwabne, Poland*.

87. Juhl and Olsen 2006, 429.

88. See Houck 2006.

89. See Kim and Reinke 2013.

90. Ciocca Gómez, personal interview with author.

91. Eugenio Aspillaga, personal interview with author; Iván Cáceres, personal interview with author.

92. Also see Rosenblatt 2013, "Exhuming State."

93. Bustamante and Ruderer 2009; Comisión de Derechos Humanos, Nacionalidad y Ciudanía 2006.

94. See, for example, Renshaw 2011, 17–21.

95. Renshaw 2007, 241.

96. For one influential discussion on different ideas about international community and their philosophical pedigrees, see Wendt 1999. A healthy skepticism about whether there is such a thing as an international community can be found in David Rieff's *A Bed for the Night*, which argues that international institutions and treaties are "not the expression of community but of power" (2002, 9). Transnational activist networks are the subject of Keck and Sikkink's 1998 groundbreaking study, *Activists Beyond Borders*. For more on cosmopolitanism, see Appiah 2007; and Nussbaum 2002.

97. See Keough, Kahn, and Andrejevic 2000, 74.

98. Wagner 2008, 38–40.

99. Ibid., 42–51.

100. Ibid., 141.

101. In 2013, after a protracted legal battle, the Dutch Supreme Court delivered a verdict with wide symbolic resonance, declaring Dutch peacekeepers responsible for the deaths of three men killed near Srebrenica (Simons 2013).

102. Wagner 2008, 21.

103. Ibid., 17.

104. See Arditti 1999, 78.

105. See Blau 2008, 4; Steadman and Haglund 2005, 7.

106. Having long critical generosity to describe my own research approach, I found that it has also been used by scholars of theater, feminism, and sexuality to describe a

critic who combines scholarly analysis with a sense of direct investment in a particular artwork, production, community, or institution (Dolan 2012).

107. Here are a few fruitful questions for further interdisciplinary scholarship that this book is only able to touch on in passing. I have heard all of these questions, in one form or another, from the mouths of forensic experts themselves: How do the specific traditions and history of the human rights movement—the forms of violence and suffering it to which it has called attention, and the forms that have been less visible—affect which mass graves are investigated and which ones are not? In other words, how does forensic science participate in a questionable process of sorting out which living and dead people gain recognition as victims of human rights violations, and how might this political-scientific narrative be altered? Should forensic teams embrace new forms of scientific activism, such as using their scientific and moral-political capital to give names and stories to deaths caused by poverty, poor public health policies, or corruption? Should they be more publicly telling the story of how their science often contradicts the social construction of race?

108. Physicians for Human Rights 2009.

109. Koff 2004, 86.

110. The concern about revisionism is, as Bill Haglund reminded me, partly a reaction to the persistence of Holocaust denial (telephone interview with author, 13 Apr. 2009). The relatively primitive state of forensic science in the decade following World War II, the poor preservation of bodies and graves in concentration camps and elsewhere, as well as religious prohibitions on exhumation among the Jewish community (described in Chapter 3) resulted in very little forensic evidence being collected after the Holocaust, a problem that has become the impetus for new forensic projects throughout Europe (see Desbois 2008). Haglund sees this lack of forensic evidence as a major reason why Holocaust denial is so persistent, since Holocaust deniers can continue to point (very selectively) to gaps in the physical evidence of genocide.

111. Congram and Steadman 2008, 164.

112. See Laqueur 2002.

113. Congram and Steadman 2008.

114. The exhumations are part of a broader cultural shift toward revisiting Spain's Civil War past, which had been subject to an official "Pacto del Olvido" ("Pact of Forgetting") during the long Franco dictatorship and beyond. The election of Spain's first leftist president since the Franco period, José Luis Rodríguez Zapatero, the passage of a "Historical Memory Law," and the formation of the various associations of family members of Spanish Civil War victims are all part of this shift (J. Anderson 2009; Purcell 2009). Some observers also trace it to the arrest of former Chilean dictator Augusto Pinochet in London in 1998 at the behest of Spanish Judge Baltazar Garzón (who has spearheaded various legal efforts for historical memory within Spain, including attempts to locate and exhume Federico García Lorca's grave). Garzón hoped to prosecute Pinochet for political disappearances during his rule in Chile, including those of fifty Spanish citizens. According to Omar Encarnación, Pinochet's arrest sparked a "lively debate within the national political class about the willingness of the country's judicial

apparatus to go after a foreign dictator while reluctant to examine the legacy of its own dictator," a willingness that to many smacked of colonial-era hypocrisy (2008, 41).

115. J. Anderson 2009; Purcell 2009.

116. Congram and Fernández 2010; Tremlett 2009.

117. J. Anderson 2009, 48.

118. Tremlett 2009.

119. Purcell 2009, 33.

120. She distinguishes this discourse from a more ideological "internal discourse," used privately among the association's members, of historical justice and solidarity with the Spanish left (Renshaw 2011, 247–48).

121. Renshaw 2007, 248.

122. Ibid., 249.

123. See Ghani and Lockhart 2008, 108; Smillie 2001.

124. This focus on empowering *local* institutions is founded partly on the idea that these institutions will ultimately have more trust from local populations and possess important knowledge about the context in which they are working. It is also a response to the long-standing criticism that a large percentage of the donations and governmental support offered to humanitarian and development organizations is sometimes spent on those organizations' own needs (salaries, field offices, equipment, travel, and so on), so that international aid groups are able to build up staff and infrastructure as they move from project to project, while their partners on the ground retain a precarious existence.

125. See Cordner and McKelvie 2002, 882–83.

126. For an example of a recent assessment of this sort, see Physicians for Human Rights 2013. This report on Libya includes data about existing forensic capacity on the ground, as well as the various international organizations that have offered assistance in carrying out post-conflict forensic identifications. In light of this data, it analyzes the "gaps" in on-the-ground capacity and suggests work that Physicians for Human Rights and other institutions can undertake to fill those gaps.

127. Physicians for Human Rights' on-line course in International Forensic Investigation is available on their website, www.physiciansforhumanrights.org.

128. Stover and Peress 1998.

129. See Doretti and Burrell 2007, 47.

130. Equipo Peruano de Antropología Forense 2010.

131. The Argentine team now also runs a yearly field school for forensic investigators from multiple African countries at Wits University in South Africa (van Schie 2013).

132. Snow, personal interview with author.

133. See Doretti and Fondebrider 2001, 140.

134. Ibid.; Gómez López and Patiño Umaña 2007, 189–92.

135. Baraybar, Brasey, and Zadel 2007, 270; Juhl and Olsen 2006, 427.

136. Hunter and Simpson 2007, 276.

137. Hunter and Cox 2005, 220.

138. Hunter and Simpson 2007, 276.

139. See Wagner's chapter "Identifying Srebrenica's Missing," which focuses on the handover of responsibility for forensic investigations in Bosnia and Herzegovina from the International Commission on Missing Persons to the national, multiethnic Missing Persons Institute. Wagner explains how much is at stake in this transition, in terms of redefining forensic identification as a cause uniting families of the missing across ethnic dividing lines, and how difficult it has been in practice to overcome decades of mutual distrust, dependency on international arbitrators, and perceptions that the Institute is being used as political vehicle by one side or another (2010, 35–41).

140. Inforce 2006.

141. Keough, Simmons, and Samuels 2004, 272.

142. Reveco, personal interview with author.

143. "Justicia entregó identidad" 2012.

144. Reveco, personal interview with author.

145. Cáceres, personal interview with author.

146. Padilla, personal interview with author.

147. "Grupo de Antropología Forense" 2005; Sepúlveda Ruiz 2005, 4; Snow, personal interview with author.

148. Browne 1992; Schüller, "Patricia Hernández." One crucial difference, according to Reveco, is that unlike the Argentine team, the GAF's members did not see the group becoming an international actor. Individual members did join forensic investigations outside of the country, but the organization itself maintained a focus on Chilean victims (personal interview with the author).

149. Reveco, personal interview with author.

150. Browne 1992.

151. Caiozzi 1998.

152. Wyndham and Read 2010, 34–35.

153. Bustamante and Ruderer 2009, 37; Wyndham and Read 2010, 34–40.

154. Bustamante and Ruderer 2009, 40–41, 50–51.

155. "Augusto José Ramón Pinochet Ugarte y el Patio 29: '¡Pero qué economía más grande!'" 6 Sept. 2011 (1991).

156. Bustamante and Ruderer 2009, 62–63.

157. Cáceres, personal interview with author.

158. Wyndham and Read 2010, 39–40.

159. Chacón 2006.

160. Bustamante and Ruderer 2009, 92–95; Chacón 2006; Sepúlveda Ruiz 2005, 4.

161. Gallardo 2006.

162. "It's impossible to get [identifications] wrong for 48 skeletons. It's a technical aberration," Reveco remarked in one interview (Rebolledo and Narvaéz 2006).

163. As in many other areas of forensic science, technology has triggered many new developments in craniofacial identification through three-dimensional modeling and other computing techniques (Damas et al. 2011).

164. Browne 1992; Joyce and Stover 1992, 185–86; see Jayaprakash, Srinivasan, and

Amravaneswaran 2001, for explanation of the method's limitations. The identifications were originally made using skull-photo superimposition and complimentary methods such as dental comparisons (Comisión de Derechos Humanos, Nacionalidad y Ciudanía 2006); later, mitochondrial DNA identifications begun by the Instituto Médico-Legal revealed significant uncertainty about these anthropological identifications (Sepúlveda Ruiz 2005, 2). Mitochondrial DNA is both more plentiful in cells and more resistant to degradation than nuclear DNA; it has thus often been used to identify older, skeletal remains like the ones exhumed from Patio 29. However, mitochondrial DNA is inherited from the mother and does not change as it passes from mother to child: it thus requires a sample from a relative on the mother's side for comparison and is far less precise than nuclear DNA (which is unique to every individual)—especially in cases where more than one person from the same matrilineal family has disappeared. New identifications of the Patio 29 *desaparecidos* thus rely on technological advances that have made the study of nuclear DNA gathered from skeletal remains more feasible (ibid.).

165. Joyce and Stover 1992, 185–88.

166. Jayaprakash, Srinivasan, and Amravaneswaran 2001, 123; Snow, personal interview with author.

167. Cáceres, personal interview with author; see also Comisión de Derechos Humanos, Nacionalidad y Ciudanía 2006.

168. Aspillaga, personal interview with author.

169. Ciocca, personal interview with author.

170. Reveco, personal interview with author.

171. Reveco still wonders whether her supervisors' reluctance to involve the Argentines had to do with the cost of bringing them, or with resistance to the notion that a Chilean state institution would be asking for help from a small, activist organization—worse still, an organization from Argentina, Chile's neighbor and longtime rival (personal interview with author).

172. Bustamante and Ruderer 2009, 35, 38–39; Reveco, personal interview with author.

173. It should be noted that Reveco herself, the one member of the GAF who also worked full-time for the state's Identification Unit, rejects any implication that there was pressure to produce results by a certain time (personal interview with author). Patricia Hernández, the director of the Identification Unit, fiercely defended her work until, in 2008, she underwent a surgical treatment for cancer and was left in a permanent vegetative state (Schüller 2011).

174. Another major wrinkle of doubt came in 2001, when Chile's military released a long-awaited list of names of *desaparecidos* that had been thrown from aircraft into the sea. Alarmingly, this new list contained a number of victims whose bodies had supposedly been exhumed from Patio 29 and subsequently reburied by their families (Bustamante and Ruderer 2009, 98).

175. Rebolledo and Narvaéz 2006; Wyndham and Read 2010, 42–43.

176. See Bustamante and Ruderer 2009, 92–101; Comisión de Derechos Humanos, Nacionalidad y Ciudanía 2006.

177. Pamela Pereira, personal interview with author, my translation.

178. Aspillaga, personal interview with author.

179. Qtd. in Bustamante and Ruderer 2009, 75, my translation.

180. Snow, personal interview with author.

181. Reveco recalls that, as the GAF began to dissolve in the early 1990s, Cáceres proposed the group support itself by taking on cases outside of the human rights milieu, working at some of Chile's many historical and indigenous sites. Reveco says she objected because the organization's equipment and start-up funding had all been donated with the understanding that they would be used for human rights efforts, and she felt that veering from this mission would be inappropriate (personal interview with author).

182. Feitlowitz 1998, 5.

183. Constable and Valenzuela 1991, 20–22.

184. Pereira, personal interview with author, my translation.

185. Ibid.

186. Constable and Valenzuela 1991, 136.

187. Comisión de Derechos Humanos, Nacionalidad y Ciudadanía 2006, 119; Rebolledo and Narvaéz 2006.

188. Servicio Médico Legal 2010, 43.

189. The methods developed in the search for the *desaparecidos* also proved useful for the identification of people who died in Chile's major 2010 earthquake (Bryner 2010), and the state's Special Identification Unit is working to integrate humanitarian disaster work into its agenda (Intriago, personal interview with author).

190. "Patricio Bustos Streeter" 2007.

191. This unit has also been in charge of other exhumations related to Chile's late twentieth-century political history: those of former president Salvador Allende, the folk singer Victor Jara, and the poet Pablo Neruda (see Rosenblatt, 2 Dec. 2013).

192. Patricio Bustos, personal interview with author; Marisol Intriago, personal interview with author.

193. See Servicio Médico Legal.

194. Chacón 2006.

195. See Márquez; Rebolledo and Narváez 2006; Schüller, "Patricia Hernández"; Sepúlveda Ruiz 2005.

196. See Leebaw 2008.

197. Blau 2008; Cox et al. 2008, 17; Hunter and Cox 2005, 213, 216; Steele 2008, 420.

198. Stover, Haglund, and Samuels 2003, 665–66.

199. Hunter and Simpson 2007, 270.

Chapter 2

1. The junta referred to its rule by the menacing, Orwellian name "El Proceso de Reorganización Nacional"—the "National Reorganization Process," or simply "El Proceso." For discussion of the ideology and mechanisms of repression in Argentina, see Cohen Salama 1992; Feitlowitz 1998.

2. Feitlowitz 1998, 49.

3. Cohen Salama 1992, 160–61; Joyce and Stover 1992, 244–56.

4. Arditti 1999, 75; Joyce and Stover 1992, 240–41.

5. Joyce and Stover 1992, 245.

6. Cohen Salama 1992, 162–63.

7. In Joyce and Stover's account, it is Ana María Torti's mother, not her sister, who raised these objections (1992, 245). The authors claim Torti's mother was herself a member of the Madres de Plaza de Mayo. Attempts to clarify the events with Stover and members of the Argentine team yielded no firm conclusions. Therefore, I have chosen to follow Cohen Salama's version because of the level of detail and quality of documentation in his book-length history of the Argentine team's early work.

8. Cohen Salama 1992, 165–67.

9. Wherever there is a likelihood of confusion about the particular group of Madres to which I am referring, I follow Temma Kaplan in calling the larger, anti-exhumation group led by Hebe de Bonafini the "Asociación Madres," short for the full name, Asociación Madres de Plaza de Mayo (I drop a "de" that Kaplan inserts between the first two words). I refer to the pro-exhumation, breakaway faction as the "Línea Fundadora," in the original Spanish, for the simple reason that "Founding-Line" (which Kaplan uses) strikes me as a far more awkward phrase in English. One thing worth noticing about the two organizational names is the importance, in each case, of claiming authenticity. De Bonafini's group does so by retaining the group's original name, with "Asociación" added to the beginning; whereas the Línea Fundadora does so by calling attention to the fact that their breakaway faction is composed of many founding members of the Madres de Plaza de Mayo. When speaking about the movement as a whole, or about the organization before it split, I call them "Madres de Plaza de Mayo."

10. Peluffo 2007, 92–93.

11. Bouvard 2002, 108.

12. Cohen Salama 1992, 164.

13. Qtd. in Joyce and Stover 1992, 247.

14. See Crossland 2000; Crossland 2002; Domanska 2005; Edkins 2011; Robben 2000a; Robben 2000b; Stover and Shigekane 2004.

15. See International Committee of the Red Cross 2007.

16. Historical overviews of repression and resistance during Argentina's "Dirty War" can be found in Arditti 1999; Bouvard 2002; Cohen Salama 1992, 15–56; Feitlowitz 1998; Joyce and Stover 1992, 205–18.

17. Kaplan 2004, 114.

18. Keck and Sikkink 1998, 103–10.

19. See Bouvard 2002; Kaplan 2004, 103–51.

20. Kaplan 2004, 116.

21. Keck and Sikkink 1998, 103–10; Klein 2007, 118–24.

22. Cohen Salama 1992, 167. Eventually, according to Cohen Salama, the grave thought to belong to Ana María Torti was exhumed anyway, by cemetery workers who were ill-prepared for the task and who ultimately made it impossible to confirm whether the body inside was hers or not (167).

23. See Cohen Salama 1992, 35–39; Crossland 2002, 119.

24. Feitlowitz 1998, 13.

25. Though this chapter will not focus on the economics of repression and transitional justice, Naomi Klein makes a powerful case that free-market economic programs and their cheerleaders played a crucial role in carving out space for torture and terror, as well as limiting attempts in post-dictatorship Argentina to hold accountable those who steered the country toward both violence and bankruptcy.

26. Ferguson 2009.

27. Cohen Salama 1992, 98, my translation. One of Alfonsín's advisors, the law professor and ethicist Jaime Malamud Goti, argued for concessions to the military with particular bluntness: "Look, this is a fascist society. We have to change its authoritarian structure. . . . And in the process we have to let a lot of people get away with [crimes]" (qtd. in Feitlowitz 1998, 15).

28. For a helpful discussion of the differences between the legal concepts of amnesty and immunity, see the Swiss organization TRIAL's article "Amnesty and Immunity." Impunity, unlike amnesty and immunity, is not a legal concept, but rather a colloquial term for the state of being beyond the reach of the law and/or punishment.

29. I place this popular term for Argentine repression in quotation marks because, as Julio Strassera argued in his role as prosecutor during trials against the members of the junta, it is a euphemism that introduces dangerous distortions. Either there *was* no war, only violence by armed gangs, many of them organized and sponsored by the state; or, if what happened can truly be called a "war," the junta clearly carried out violations of the laws of war that the qualifier "dirty" can do nothing to excuse.

30. Joyce and Stover 1992, 265.

31. Many observers have since pointed out that the law contradicts the precedent set at the Nuremberg trials after World War II, where defendants could not claim immunity from prosecution because they were "following orders" (Kaplan 2004, 139).

32. See Peluffo 2007.

33. Kaplan 2004, 135.

34. Ibid., 116.

35. See Cohen Salama 1992, 52–53.

36. Ibid., 51–52.

37. Kaplan 2004, 139.

38. See Morales's discussion of recent political feuds between Hebe de Bonafini and the leaders of a local chapter of the Madres de Plaza de Mayo in La Rioja: "We'll never take down our slogans of 'aparición con vida' for our children and justice and punishment for the guilty," proclaims one of the organization's spokeswomen.

39. Bouvard 2002, 141.

40. de Young 1998.

41. Joyce and Stover 1992, 254.

42. See Crossland 2002, 121–22.

43. Perhaps the best-known and most articulate spokesperson for this view is Dostoevsky's Ivan Karamazov, who recites a litany of horror stories pulled from news

headlines—largely about cruelty inflicted on children—and rejects the possibility of forgiveness for such actions: "I do not . . . want the mother to embrace the tormentor who let his dogs tear her son to pieces! She dare not forgive him! Let her forgive him for herself, if she wants to, let her forgive the tormentor for her immeasurable maternal suffering; but she has no right to forgive the suffering of her child who was torn to pieces, she dare not forgive the tormentor, even if the child himself were to forgive him! And if that is so, if they dare not forgive, then where is the harmony?" (Dostoevsky 2002, 245, bk. 5, ch. 4). Part of the sense of impossibility that accompanies the demand of "aparición con vida" is that true reconciliation could only be achieved between repentant perpetrators and the *desaparecidos* themselves (even then, if we follow Ivan Karamazov's argument, the *desaparecidos* could forgive only their own suffering and not that inflicted on their families). Since the perpetrators are largely unrepentant and the *desaparecidos* are gone, there is no real possibility for reconciliation, only a vague wish that cannot be fulfilled—a wish that is thus very similar to the demand that the *desaparecidos* reappear alive. In other words, an alternate reading of the slogan says that to the extent the Madres are playing at madness, it is to show that the dream of reconciliation is at least equally mad.

44. Crossland 2002, 121.

45. Robben writes that the Asociación Madres "radically changed the political significance of reburials and the spiritual meaning of the human remains [of the *desaparecidos*]. Body, spirit, and funeral were dissociated. The ossified remains lost their meaning, and so did their reburial. The spirit as metaphor for political ideas was exalted as the only thing worthy of survival in the embodiment of kindred political spirits" (2000b, 106). The Madres, though often secular or atheist in their personal orientations, have indeed always drawn on a heavily religious vocabulary of symbols (Kaplan 2004, 116). "Aparición con vida" itself has a quasi-religious logic: even as the bodies of the *desaparecidos* emerge from mass graves throughout the country, the work of the "faithful" is to wait for them to return alive, as well as to see them reborn in the young disciples who have attached themselves to the Madres. Robben's language, however, is typical in trumpeting the "liminal" quality of the disappeared as something haunting all of Argentina and even reshaping its cultural imagination, when, in fact, one can just as easily find testimonies from Madres and human rights activists who feel that what Feitlowitz calls "the mythic discourse of the missing" (1998, 195) has actually been an obstacle to making concrete progress on addressing past injustices.

46. See Crossland 2000, 155.

47. Kaplan 2004, 131–32.

48. Kaplan 2004, 131; Robben 2000b, 97. In the 1990s, the International Committee for the Red Cross's attempt to institute a "death attestation" program in the former Yugoslavia, which also declared the missing dead without providing physical evidence, met similarly violent resistance. This is not to say, of course, that the Red Cross's motivations shared any of the cynicism of the Argentine dictatorship; few things could be further from the truth. What it signals, rather, is that any attempt to resolve the status of missing people and bodies through bureaucratic means—rather than a search for material

evidence—is likely to be rejected, no matter how well-intentioned it may be (see Stover and Peress 1998, 195–97).

49. Cohen Salama 1992, 87–88.

50. See Bouvard 2002, 140–41.

51. "Many of the forensic doctors had, years before, signed the death certificates for the bodies that they were now asked to examine. This fact, if it does not in fact prove direct participation in illegal repression, at least indicates a close relationship with the security forces and, in some cases, with the murderers themselves. It is easy to imagine that these forensic doctors would be subject to pressures which would make it difficult to do their jobs" (Cohen Salama 1992, 88, my translation).

52. Cohen Salama 1992, 63.

53. During my time at Physicians for Human Rights, I saw this model replicated by some of the authorities responsible for investigating the brutal murders and disappearances of women in Ciudad Juárez, Mexico. An official of the State of Chihuahua assured me that my colleagues and I need not worry too much about the accuracy of the forensic identifications of the murdered women because once families received a set of bones the authorities would provide them with a payment—which, in his view, was all they were really after in the first place.

54. Kaplan 2004, 149.

55. Qtd. in Fisher 1989, 129. De Rubinstein received a set of bones from the armed forces in 1984 that ostensibly belonged to her daughter Patricia, but forensic analysis showed the remains to be those of an adult male (Bouvard 2002, 140–41).

56. Qtd. in Fisher 1989, 128.

57. Madre de Plaza de Mayo 1989, 24, translator unknown.

58. Chile has its own long-running tradition of women's activism, influenced by its Argentine neighbors but also framed and conducted in different ways (see Kaplan 2004, 40–101). The quest to hold the architects of torture and disappearance accountable in Chile, as in Argentina, has been hampered by amnesty laws and other setbacks. It has also had moments of spectacular progress: most notably the former dictator Augusto Pinochet's arrest in London in 1998 for extradition to Spain on charges of torture. Pinochet was ultimately released from house arrest in London, but back home in Chile was stripped of most of his immunities and lived the rest of his years until his death (in 2006) in confinement and under the shadow of prosecutions and corruption scandals. The arrest set off a new wave of human rights trials and other investigations in Chile, and generally helped keep the issue of the *desaparecidos* far from resolved or forgotten, as it is characterized in the anonymous Madre's remark.

59. de Bonafini 1989–90.

60. Cohen Salama 1992, 18.

61. Peluffo 2007, 83–84.

62. The slogan was adapted from the early twentieth-century folk singer and labor activist Joe Hill's letter to a friend just before his death by firing squad: "Goodbye Bill. I die like a true blue rebel. Don't waste any time in mourning. Organize . . ." Ironically, at least in the context of this chapter, Hill's letter then immediately offers instructions for

the disposal of his body, which he wished to have removed from the scene of injustices against him: "Could you arrange to have my body hauled to the state line to be buried? I don't want to be found dead in Utah" ("Joe Hill" 2002). Hill, unlike the Asociación Madres, saw reburial and concern for the fate of his own material remains as compatible with a call for others to keep up his activism. Thanks to Joshua Cohen for suggesting I look into this historical reference.

63. Qtd. in Fisher 1989, 128–29.

64. de Bonafini 1988, 11.

65. Gómez de Aguilera.

66. Bouvard 2002, 198.

67. de Bonafini and Mascia 1999; Marchesi.

68. Muliero 1992.

69. On the applicability of the term "genocide" to dictatorship-era violence in Argentina, see Klein 2007, 106–7, 114–15.

70. Bouvard 2002, 166.

71. Cohen Salama 1992, 211; Crossland 2002, 119; Figueras 2005.

72. Joyce and Stover 1992, 266–67.

73. Ibid., 258.

74. Ibid., 259–61; Snow and Bihurriet 1992.

75. Figueras 2005.

76. Arditti 1999, 21; Feitlowitz 1998, 179.

77. See Keck and Sikkink 1998, 95.

78. Klein 2007.

79. The Asociación Madres published an edited book of Hussein's writings, *Saddam Hussein: Revolution and Resistance in Iraq* (Suleiman 2006).

80. According to Cohen Salama, the "theory of the two demons" owed its success in part to the fact that it allowed ordinary Argentines "to imagine themselves victims of two bands bent on killing each other for reasons alien to the sentiments of 'good people'" (1992, 100, my translation).

81. This tolerant position does not seem to answer the Liliana Pereyra/Ana María Torti dilemma that the Argentine team faced in the Parque Cemetery, where there is uncertainty (as there usually is in the case of N.N. graves) as to whose body or bodies may be in a particular grave, potentially pitting pro- and anti-exhumation family members against one another over the same patch of earth.

82. See Peluffo 2007.

83. de Bonafini 1988, 13.

84. Peluffo 2007, 93–95.

85. Kaplan 2004, 145. While neither group has openly addressed the role anti-Semitism might play in tensions between them, de Bonafini seems to have confirmed the worst suspicions about her personal views. In a set of public remarks after the September 11, 2001, attacks on the United States, de Bonafini praised the hijackers as "courageous" for making "a declaration of war" against imperialism "with their bodies" (de Bonafini 2001). After the respected journalist and human rights activist Horacio

Verbitsky criticized de Bonafini's statements for their dualism—for asking people to choose, in Verbitsky's phrase, "between Bin Laden's explosions and Bush's explosions"— de Bonafini retorted that Verbitsky was "a servant of the United States" and a "Jew" (Marchesi).

86. Gueler 2011.

87. "Hebe [de Bonafini]'s authoritarian style is unacceptable in an organization concerned with human rights," René Epelbaum wrote (1993, 1, my translation). The Línea Fundadora has a decentralized organizational model and few formal leadership positions, features they claim represent the original spirit of the Madres de Plaza de Mayo (Kaplan 2004, 145–47; see also Gueler 2011).

88. The Madres de Plaza de Mayo-Línea Fundadora do occasionally employ the slogan "aparición con vida" (24 Mar. 2010). In recent years, they appear to have done so solely in reference the case of Jorge Julio López, a key witness in the first major human rights trial after Néstor Kirchner's repeal of the Punto Final and Obediencia Debida laws. López disappeared in 2006, just before he was scheduled to finish his testimony against Miguel Etchecolatz, director of a dictatorship-era detention camp (Bradley 2008). The Línea Fundadora meant "aparición con vida" as a very literal demand that everything possible be done to locate López, who they believed might still be alive, as well as an expression of widespread frustration with the slow pace of investigations. They were not, in this case, implying the full range of positions and ideas that the slogan still signifies for the Asociación Madres.

89. Gueler 2011.

90. Ibid.

91. Bouvard 2002, 166.

92. See Renshaw 2011.

93. Domanska 2005, 402.

94. Edkins 2011, ch. 7, para. 43.

95. Ibid. Equally ill-chosen is Edkins's phrase about the *desaparecidos* themselves, which appears in the same passage: "It was their politics that had killed them." It was, of course, the murderous ideology and security apparatus of the Argentine state that killed them, rather than any belief or feature of theirs, political or otherwise.

96. De Mascia 1990, 2–3.

97. Epelbaum 1993, 2, my translation. Epelbaum's confidence in the Argentine team's work received a bittersweet vindication when, in late May of 2014—more than sixteen years after Epelbaum's death—the team successfully identified the remains of her daughter, Lila Epelbaum Stopolsky, one of three of her children who were disappeared (Madres de Plaza de Mayo-Línea Fundadora 2014).

98. For accounts of how Néstor Kirchner successfully courted the support of the Asociación Madres—perhaps as part of his efforts to maintain a broad coalition across both Argentina's center and left—see Asociación Madres de Plaza de Mayo 2010; Petras and Veltemeyer 2009, 79.

99. The rationale the Argentine team offered the National Commission on the Disappeared for its existence, too, was based almost entirely on its differences with the

existing forensic authorities: its scientific capacity to exhume and interpret skeletal remains, its independence, and its dedication "exclusively" to human rights cases (Cohen Salama 1992, 152).

100. Madres de Plaza de Mayo-Línea Fundadora 8 July 2010.

101. Cohen Salama 1992, 112.

102. Kaplan 2004, 148–49.

103. Madres de Plaza de Mayo-Línea Fundadora 8 July 2010, my translation.

104. See Dawson 2011, 257.

105. Joyce and Stover 1992, 243.

106. Peluffo 2007, 92.

107. Cohen Salama 1992, 133.

108. At the time of this writing, years of protracted legal battle were underway over DNA tests conducted on Felipe and Marcela Noble, the adopted children of Ernestina Noble de Herrera, the owner of Argentina's major newspaper, *Clarín*. Some Abuelas de Plaza de Mayo suspected that Marcela could be Matilde Lanuscou—or the granddaughter of another Abuela, "Chicha" Mariani (Ferguson 2009; Goobar 2009). After two rounds of testing on samples taken from the siblings—still considered incomplete by the Abuelas, who continue to add genetic profiles of families of the *desaparecidos* to the state's DNA database for comparison—Felipe and Marcela were declared not a match with the Lanuscou or Mariani families (Goldman 2012, 65).

109. Rita Arditti's book about the Abuelas de Plaza de Mayo is titled, quite appropriately, *Searching for Life*. The painting on the cover, by Claudia Bernardi—the sister of Patricia Bernardi, one of the Argentine team's founders—shows a living person emerging from a skeletal body.

110. Feitlowitz 1998, 67–68; Goldman 2012, 56–57.

111. United Nations General Assembly 1948.

112. H.I.J.O.S. 2010.

113. Kaplan 2004, 139.

114. Rotella 1998.

115. "Argentina's Videla and Bignone" 2012.

116. Qtd. in Fisher 1989, 128.

117. As mentioned earlier, this technique of pelvic analysis has subsequently been shown to be unreliable. Given the knowledge they and their scientist colleagues possessed at the time, however, the Abuelas saw pelvic analysis as an important justification for exhuming female *desaparecidos*.

118. Keck and Sikkink 1998, 94.

119. Goni 2014.

120. Edkins 2011, ch. 7, para. 43.

121. See Hunt 2007, 77–78.

122. See Robben 2000a 87–90.

123. See Held 1993; Noddings 1984; Ruddick 1995; for commentary, see Hamington 2004, 18–19. The question of whether according primacy to the mother-child relationship is feminist and progressive or, to the contrary, essentialist and regressive, will

be discussed briefly in Chapter 5 and seems to have figured into some criticisms of the Madres from feminists in Argentina (Bouvard 2002, 184). It should be noted that, for all of the interest they have incited among feminist scholars, few of the Madres identify as feminists themselves (Fisher 1989, 151; Kaplan 2004, 102).

124. Crossland 2000, 155.

125. Ibid., 152.

126. The Argentine team is, in fact, a rare and historically important exception. Unlike many of the forensic experts who have become involved in human rights work, they had no "day jobs" in forensic labs and no previous medico-legal training, but rather learned the disciplines of forensic anthropology and archaeology while investigating human rights cases.

127. Cohen Salama 1992, 107, my translation.

128. Robben 2000a, 92.

129. Qtd. in Crossland 2000, 154.

130. Many of the students who joined the Argentine team were initially quite squeamish about encountering graves and dead bodies; after their first exhumations with Clyde Snow, however, nearly all of them decided not only to continue with their work but to dedicate the rest of their professional lives to forensic anthropology (Cohen Salama 1992, 148, 151–52). The encounter with remains of the *desaparecidos* did not demobilize them any more than it did their allies in the Línea Fundadora or the Abuelas de Plaza de Mayo.

131. Edkins 2011, ch. 7, para. 43.

132. Mellibovsky 1997, 179.

133. Bouvard 2002, 142.

134. Bouvard 2002, 75–77; Kaplan 2004, 179–80.

135. Madres de Plaza de Mayo-Línea Fundadora 2008, my translation.

136. Ibid., my translation.

137. See Connor 2009, 250–51.

138. Congram and Steadman 2008, 163.

139. Doretti and Burrell 2007, 47.

140. Bouvard 2002, 164; Madres de Plaza de Mayo-Línea Fundadora 2008.

141. Bouvard 1996, 295–313.

142. Compare, for example, Robben 2000b on Argentina and Verdery on the former Yugoslavia.

143. Wagner refers to the Argentine and Bosnian mothers as "parallel social movements" (2008, 250).

144. Koff 2004, 167. According to the journalist Elizabeth Neuffer, in Bosnia some saw the mass graves as "the most searing reminder of how the U.N., the Western powers, and even the Muslim-led Bosnian government had let down the people of Srebrenica. Exhumation, they argued, would be the final 'ethnic cleansing'" (2001, 217).

145. Qtd. in Shin 2005.

146. Koff 2004, 168.

147. Stover and Peress 1998, 210.

148. Pedreño, qtd. in Renshaw 2011, 85.

149. Renshaw 2007, 248; see also Renshaw 2011, 81–88.

150. Pedreño 2004.

151. Federación Estatal de Foros por la Memoria 2007, 3, my translation.

152. Memory versus closure, and justice versus forgiveness, both incorporated into Domanska's phrase, are among these infamous "tradeoffs"—as is the even better-known perceived conflict between truth and justice. The latter is most closely associated, in the transitional justice literature, with the case of South Africa. The South African Truth and Reconciliation Commission famously offered amnesty to perpetrators of human rights violations, largely replacing the model of justice-as-punishment with a restorative model of justice through public confession and victim testimony (see Minow 1998; Rotberg and Thompson 2000; Teitel 2002).

153. Crossland 2000, 155. See also Domanska, who writes that "the junta's crimes would not be forgiven and forgotten as long as the relatives they were looking for retained the status of the *desaparecidos*, situated in the 'between' that separates life and death" (2005, 402).

154. Domanska 2005, 401.

155. Cohen Salama 1992, 104.

156. Aronson 2011, 18.

157. This psychoanalytic conception of closure, like the language of trauma and open wounds, has been particularly influential in the Argentine context. Argentina has had a long love affair with psychoanalysis and is among the world's leaders in the percentage of Freudian and Lacanian analysts within the urban population (Plotkin 2001, 1).

158. If we must traffic in metaphors, it could be pointed out that the dichotomy of "open wounds" and forgetful healing, so often used when talking about the different groups of Madres, actually ignores one of the features of how bodies heal from serious wounds: scarring. A scar is a wound that is no longer in acute danger of being infected (it has achieved "closure") but that remains as a permanent mark—a reminder—upon the body.

Chapter 3

1. Wolentarska-Ochman 2006, 155.

2. See Chodakiewicz 2005; Polonsky and Michlic 2004.

3. Fox 2002, 97–98; Polak 2001, 23; Polonsky and Michlic 2004.

4. See Parry 2012.

5. Oster 2011.

6. Chodakiewicz 2005, 141.

7. Ignatiew 2002.

8. Chodakiewicz 2005, 1, 147.

9. Chodakiewicz 2005, 142; Gross 2004, 359; Polak 2001, 23–24.

10. Barry 31 May 2001.

11. Barry 1 June 2001.

12. Haglund 2002, 2.

13. Chodakiewicz 2005, 250; "Polish Investigators" 2001.

14. Haglund, telephone interview with author, 17 Nov. 2009. Haglund recalls the name of the rabbi pictured as "Rabbi Epstein" (telephone interview with author, 1 Mar. 2011). One of the rabbis present at the exhumations—an expert on the relevant Jewish laws—was Menachem Ekstein (also written "Eckstein"), from Israel (Barry 1 June 2001; Institute of National Remembrance 31 May 2001). However, Ekstein apparently left before the limited exhumation was finished and was then replaced by London rabbi Morris Herschaft ("Polish Investigators" 2001). Despite my efforts to contact religious figures present at the exhumation and conversations with Haglund and Rabbi Joseph Polak, I have not been able to verify who exactly is in Haglund's photo.

15. Ignatiew 2002.

16. Chodakiewicz 2005, 142. "Exact number of victims" is an overstatement. Though a complete exhumation would likely result in a more accurate estimate of the number of bodies in the grave, no responsible forensic expert would claim to be able to provide an exact number, especially for a grave full of fragmentary, burned, commingled remains.

17. Musial 2004, 324–25, 357; Gross 2004, 395.

18. In fact, the Institute of National Remembrance saw its investigation of the site as serving both ethnic Polish and Jewish populations in the common cause of reconciliation. The institute's official statement on the Jedwabne investigation reads: "Publication of a White Book on Jedwabne will become the evidence of clearing of accounts for our share of responsibility for the wartime fate of the Jewish people, whose ancestors have lived with us on the same land for centuries, contributing to the common good and our common history. We would like to stress that the drama of Jedwabne events cannot be the basis of harmful generalisations in assessment of the position of the Polish people during the time of the tragic years of the Second World War" (Institute of National Remembrance 14 Mar. 2001).

19. Berkofsky 1999. Graves uncovered during construction projects and other excavations in Israel have raised the same issues, pitting archaeologists who want time to examine the remains (many of them quite ancient) against Orthodox Jews who claim, in the words of one frustrated archaeologist, that "every bone found in Israel may be a Jewish bone, and they alone have the right to decide what to do with it" (Nagar 2002, 88). In most cases, the archaeologists are permitted to take some measurements, but must quickly rebury the remains. Further laboratory analysis is thus impossible.

20. See, for example, Renshaw 2011, 204–11.

21. Chodakiewicz 2005, 142.

22. Renteln 2001, 1007.

23. Qtd. in MacDonald 2004.

24. V. Sanford 2003, 41.

25. Darewicz 2001; Nowak-Jezioranski 2004, 89.

26. Gross 2004, 359–60; Nowak-Jezioranski 2004, 89.

27. Polak 2001, 24. Polak finds it particularly upsetting that the town's Jewish cem-

etery is just across the road from the mass grave of the Jews burned alive in the barn. About the bodies in the mass grave, he says, "One has a sense of their yearning to cross the street and lie with their forbearers" (telephone interview with author).

28. Ibid., 27.

29. Stover and Shigekane 2004, 88.

30. See Argentine Forensic Anthropology Team 1997, 57–73; Argentine Forensic Anthropology Team 1998, 24–29.

31. Argentine Forensic Anthropology Team 1997, 59; Rieff 2002, 179–81.

32. Rieff 2002, 188.

33. Argentine Forensic Anthropology Team 1997, 59; Rieff 2002, 184–87.

34. Argentine Forensic Anthropology Team 1997, 60.

35. Argentine Forensic Anthropology Team 1998, 26; Maykuth 1997. The ethnic and other tensions fueling the conflict in Congo, it should be noted, predate the conflict in neighboring Rwanda and involve many groups and identities beyond Hutu and Tutsi (see Argentine Forensic Anthropology Team 1997, 57–62).

36. Argentine Forensic Anthropology Team 1997, 64–65; "U.N. Examiners" 1998.

37. French 1998.

38. Argentine Forensic Anthropology Team 1997, 62–63.

39. Snow, personal interview with author.

40. Argentine Forensic Anthropology Team 1997, 64–65.

41. French 1998.

42. Argentine Forensic Anthropology Team 1997, 64.

43. Argentine Forensic Anthropology Team 1998, 27.

44. Dres 2012; Vasagar and Borger 2011.

45. In fact, as recently as 2011, the new memorial to commemorate the massacres in Jedwabne—placed there in July 2001, just after the partial exhumations—was defaced with swastikas and graffiti declaring, "They burned easily" and "Do not apologize for Jedwabne" (Anti-Defamation League 2011).

46. Barry 2001; Polish Radio 1 2001.

47. Lipman 2010; Schudrich 2012.

48. Qtd. in Vasagar and Borger 2011.

49. Telephone interview with author, 1 Mar. 2011.

50. Rabbi Polak, telephone interview with author.

51. Institute of National Remembrance 8 Feb. 2001; Oster 2011.

52. Lerner 2010.

53. Dres 2012, 61.

54. Ibid., 181.

55. Barry 1 June 2001; "Polish Investigators" 2001.

56. I count myself among them. On my father's side, my great-grandparents and all of my great-aunts and great-uncles, save one, died in ghetto liquidations, camps, and gas chambers in Poland.

57. Renteln 2001 does not explain whether the beliefs of Mexican Americans about autopsy differ in any generalizable way from the beliefs of Mexicans in Mexico.

58. Klinkner 2008, 16; see also Cougill.

59. Klinkner 2008, 16.

60. Qtd. in J. Anderson 2009, 48.

61. Laura García-Lorca's sentiments are echoed by those of an elderly countryman of hers who, according to Leyla Renshaw, came to the site of a Spanish Civil War exhumation to admonish the archaeologists for disturbing ground "made sacred by the bones of these martyrs!" (2011, 204).

62. Keely 2009.

63. "History of the ICRC" 2010.

64. Ibid.

65. Sassòli and Tougas 2002, 728.

66. Stover and Peress 1998, 103–4.

67. Ibid., 105; Stover, telephone interview with author.

68. See Barnett 2011; Forsythe 2005; Harroff-Tavel 2003.

69. Stover, telephone interview with author.

70. See Stiglmayer 1994.

71. Stover and Peress 1998, 195; Wagner 2008, 91.

72. Stover and Peress 1998, 196.

73. Ibid.

74. Vollen 2001, 340.

75. International Committee of the Red Cross 2003. The paragraph continues: "Intentionally mutilating the remains before their repatriation as part of a widespread and systematic policy should be considered an aggravated form of the crime. Intentionally obstructing, interfering with, or impeding the process of identification of human remains for the purpose of preventing said identification should be punished as a criminal offence under domestic law." Among many legal precedents cited by the Red Cross, the Statue of the International Criminal Court prohibits "outrages upon personal dignity," including the dignity of the dead (International Committee of the Red Cross 2014, "Customary IHL - Rule 113. Treatment of the Dead").

76. In 2009, the organization collaborated on the even more thorough "Management of Dead Bodies after Disasters: A Field Manual for First Responders."

77. International Committee of the Red Cross 2003, 114.

78. Though the Red Cross's symbol itself has an obvious affinity with Christian symbolism, the organization is not religiously affiliated, and other symbols—such as the Red Crescent, Red Crystal, and Red Shield of David—have been adopted for different cultural contexts.

79. See Dawes 2007, 33.

80. Argentine Forensic Anthropology Team 2010.

81. International Committee of the Red Cross 2003, 114–15.

82. Koff 2004, 57.

83. International Committee of the Red Cross 2003, 113.

84. Ibid., 114.

85. See Durkheim 1965; Douglas 1989.

86. International Committee of the Red Cross 2003, 113.

87. Argentine Forensic Anthropology Team 2010.

88. See Glendon 2001; Morsink 2011.

89. Glendon 2001, 89.

90. The question of the relationship between religion and human rights had already been taken up by a Committee on the Theoretical Bases of Human Rights, commissioned by the United Nations Educational, Scientific and Cultural Organization (UNESCO) and made up of intellectuals from various religious and cultural traditions. However, the list of committee members and the individuals they consulted (including luminaries such as Mohandas Gandhi and Aldous Huxley) notably includes far more "scholars and statesmen" (Glendon 2001, 51) than priests, rabbis, imams, or shamans. The UNESCO committee found significant support for the idea of human rights in various religious traditions (Glendon 2001, 73–78).

91. "Universal Declaration of Human Rights" 1948.

92. Roosevelt 145–47.

93. Morsink 2011, 284.

94. Glendon 2001, 161.

95. Ibid.

96. Johannes Morsink writes, "Most of the religious traditions involved in the drafting allowed for independent access to the basic truths of morality and hence for a secular declaration" (2011, 285). In an elegant later elaboration of this "overlapping consensus" approach to human rights, religion, and cultural difference, Abdullahi An-Na'im writes, "The premise of equality requires that no religious or cultural tradition claim to be the sole foundation for the universality of human rights. Accordingly, when the foundations for human rights differ across cultures, we should view them as interdependent and mutually supportive, not antagonistic and mutually exclusive. The existence of varying foundations for human rights is intrinsic to the enterprise" of articulating and promoting the rights in the first place (2005, 61).

97. Qtd. in Glendon 2001, 161.

98. He had company from the Dutch delegate, Leo Josephus Cornelis Beaufort, a Catholic priest and consistent champion of religious language in the declaration. Beaufort complained that he "did not share the opinion that controversial questions should be eliminated in order to attain unanimity" (qtd. in Morsink 2011, 289).

99. Perry 1998, 13–16.

100. Qtd. in Perry 1998, 11.

101. H. L. A. Hart's essay "Natural Rights: Bentham and J.S. Mill" has an excellent discussion of the ultimate incompatibility of rights and utilitarianism (1982, 79–104); the same sense of incompatibility drives John Rawls's hugely influential critique of utilitarianism, and alternative view of "justice as fairness," in *A Theory of Justice* (see 1999, 27–30). In reality, though, while the Universal Declaration of Human Rights does proclaim the dignity and value of every individual, as well as his or her rights to life and "security of person" (Article 3), it is not actually clear whether it allows for *no* situation in which utilitarian reasoning is brought to bear on the "infinite importance" of every

human life. Though the declaration prohibits willfully abusive practices such as torture, it is generally seen as complementary to rather than at odds with the Geneva Conventions, which permit the waging of war, the killing of soldiers, and even—in cases where appropriate measures have been taken to avoid the needless loss of life—some civilian casualties. In other words, it is likely that the framers of the declaration, writing in the aftermath of World War II, *could* imagine situations where the importance of human life in general, or of basic human values, would require the taking of specific lives. In according "infinite importance"—a phrase not found in the declaration itself—to every human life, Perry may actually go well beyond the claims of the contemporary human rights framework.

102. See Perry 1998, 12–13. In a recent spate of books and articles about dignity, philosophers and historians interested in human rights have sought to answer this question. See Beitz 2013; Kateb 2011; Rosen 2012; Waldron 2012. Moyn 2013, in a review of some of these works, agrees with Perry's sense that a religious worldview cannot be severed from the appeal to dignity in so many modern constitutions and human rights documents. But Moyn emphasizes historical rather than conceptual reasons in his argument. Dignity, he writes, was inserted into global public discourse in the mid-twentieth century largely by Catholic thinkers and politicians. These leaders, far from radically egalitarian, often saw a principle of inherent human dignity as perfectly compatible with social hierarchy, anti-Semitism, and a belief that women's "place [was] within the home."

103. Perry 1998, 26.

104. Perry 1998, 29, emphasis in original. Perry is particularly concerned with the attempt by a fellow philosopher, Ronald Dworkin, to outline a concept of the "secular sacred." Dworkin is not proposing the secular sacred as a foundation for universal human rights; rather, he offers it as a way of rethinking the abortion debate in the United States, which has for so long been stuck in the impasse of "pro-life" versus "pro-choice" positions. Both camps, in Dworkin's view, think the state is right to treat the importance of life—its *sacredness*, in his phrasing—as a public issue. One side ("pro-life") views life as sacred largely because of the "natural investment" God or some other source put into its creation (91); the other side ("pro-choice") tends to emphasize the choices and actions by which all people "shape their lives and, in a sense, create themselves" (Kohen 2007, 9). According transcendent value to this process of self-creation is, Dworkin argues, also a way of treating life as sacred. Since in reality few people on either side value "choice" or "life" to the exclusion of the other, their shared (secular) sense that human lives have sacred importance may allow for a more pragmatic balancing of competing priorities.

105. Perry 1998, 16, 29.

106. Durkheim 1965, 53–54.

107. Mary Douglas, acknowledging Durkheim's influence in *Purity and Danger: An Analysis of the Concepts of Pollution and Taboo*, objects to the distinction he made between magic and religion, which exiled rituals of hygiene from his analysis of the sacred and the profane. Douglas argues that ideas about dirt and hygiene are as central to social organization as religion is for Durkheim. Furthermore, she finds him too absolute in his description of the sacred and the profane: "Holiness and unholiness after all need not

always be absolute opposites. They can be relative categories. What is clean in relation to one thing may be unclean in relation to another, and vice versa. The idiom of pollution lends itself to a complex algebra which takes into account the variables in each context" (1989, 8–9).

108. Durkheim 1965, 55, 62. From the passage above, taken alone, it may seem that Durkheim is impatient or even blasé about morality; however, that is not the case. Nor is he suggesting that there is no relationship between *religion* and morality. While the sacred is not a moral category, the church, he states, is a "moral community" (1965, 62). It is this aspect of religion—its ability to bind and organize moral communities, rather than its attention to the categories of the sacred and the profane—that tends to connect it with the ideas about right, wrong, and the infinite importance of human beings.

109. 1965, 52. Durkheim thus also avoids the anthropocentric tendency in the work of Perry and other theorists focused on human rights. While claiming that his observations on the sacred are culturally universal, Perry privileges cosmologies in which human beings stand at the pinnacle of the order of a divine creation. For Durkheim, the particular object matters less than the "space" it occupies once it has been designated as sacred. A sacred rock participates, no less than a human being, in the sacred and all of the things that go along with it, such as veneration and fear.

110. Durkheim 1965, 435.

111. Girard 1977, 270–71.

112. Kohen 2007, 34; van der Ven, Dreyer, and Pieterse 2005, 272.

113. Among human rights theorists, Michael Ignatieff's description of the sacred as "some realm that is beyond human knowing or representation" (2001, 84) comes close, in both its substance and its use of spatial language, to Durkheim's.

114. It is true that some Jewish commentary about exhumation is centrally concerned with avoiding humiliation of the dead, an issue of honor and respect more than boundaries. However, other texts focus on the "confusion" experienced by the dead person who, "trembling at God's judgment," is suddenly called back into the world of the living (Geller 1996, 414). This second concern is very much about the boundary between the sacred and the profane. The dead person, who is on the threshold of a full and permanent entry into the sacred, experiences a disorienting return to a realm in which he no longer belongs. There is thus a double-intrusion: the person who dug him up has intruded on a sacred space, and in turn has forced the dead person to intrude on the profane world of the living.

115. International Committee of the Red Cross 2003, 113.

116. MacDonald 2004.

117. Doretti and Burrell 2007, 48.

118. See Cougill.

119. For example, the survivor community in Guatemala constitutes a long-oppressed indigenous *majority* with an ardent desire to counteract the official denial of recent atrocities. The resurgent Jews of Poland, meanwhile, represent a small minority that faced near-total extinction. As observed earlier, an exhumation of sixty-year-old graves could easily (and, to an important extent, *did*) upset apparently peaceful, and

sometimes even affectionate, relations with mainstream Polish culture. Do these different types of precariousness explain why one community was more inclined to be flexible in its religious interpretations than the other?

120. The Documentation Center of Cambodia, or DC-Cam, seems to have been particularly effective and persistent at granting some concessions to anti-exhumation royalists while also mobilizing allies among the government, clergy, and populace to make it clear that their views represent a minority (Cougill).

Chapter 4

1. Snow, personal interview with author.

2. Gorner 1991.

3. Though a "humanitarian" perspective on forensic investigations and the needs of families of the missing, described in Chapter 1, has been on the rise in the past decade and is now interwoven in complex ways with the human rights discourse that was more visible in Argentina, Guatemala, Rwanda, the former Yugoslavia, and other major forensic projects of the 1980s and 1990s.

4. See Stacy 2009, 76–108; "A Solution from Hell" 2011.

5. See Wilson 1997; Dawes 2007.

6. See International Committee of the Red Cross 2003; Stover and Shigekane 2004; Wagner 2010.

7. Domanska 2005, 403.

8. Verdery 1999.

9. Congram and Bruno 2007, 47.

10. See Gewirth 1983.

11. Etzioni 2010, 191. Etzioni does not make it entirely clear whether, in his view, the "self-evident" nature of human rights extends only to those classically liberal, "negative" rights specifically mentioned in the text—"that human beings have a right not to be killed, maimed, or tortured" (2010, 189)—or to the entire corpus laid out in the Universal Declaration of Human Rights and ensuing international covenants and treaties, which includes a fairly ambitious set of "positive" economic and social arrangements to which all people are entitled (the right to food, shelter, education, rest and leisure, marriage with a freely chosen partner, the right to join a trade union, and so on). The absence of such a discussion seems unfortunate, since the many critics who have contended that human rights are not "self-evident," but rather inflected with the values of Western, capitalist societies, have tended to focus less on the basic protections against physical harm in the declaration than on the economic and social arrangements it promotes.

12. Perry 1998, 28–29.

13. Arendt 1976, 290–302.

14. Ibid., 295.

15. See Mulgan 1999.

16. For a more detailed study of arguments about the agency, dignity, and rights of the dead, see Rosenblatt 2010.

17. Qtd. in Dawes 2007, 18–19.

18. See Aviv 2014.

19. Scott 2012, 114.

20. However, even this presumption, as we have seen in earlier chapters, is subject to some doubts and cautions. Some of the dead, in life, may have shared the views about the sacredness and untouchable status of graves described in Chapter 3. Others, by contrast, may have been atheists who would now be surprised, if not angry, to find themselves buried in a religious manner as the constellation of post-conflict national identities is reordered (see Wagner 2008, 216)—or to be posthumously remembered as martyrs for a political movement with which their living relationship was much more ambivalent. To the extent that exhumation is just the beginning of a process that continues through identification, recognition by the living, and memorialization, there are numerous places where the needs and desires of the living, as well as the identities they craft for the dead, may differ radically from the desires and identities the dead themselves would have recognized.

21. Barnett 2011, 216.

22. Qtd. in Tippet 2009.

23. See Smolensky 2009.

24. Herodotus's *The History* contains a useful anecdote: Darius, the king of Persia, asked two groups of men—one made up of Greeks and one of "Callatian" Indians—if they would, for any price, trade customs regarding the dead. The Greeks would have to cannibalize their dead fathers, and the Callatians would burn their fathers' bodies (no one seems terribly concerned about mothers in this story). Both groups wept at the thought of such "horrors" and refused (1998, 228). Herodotus's point, which has been called an early example of cultural relativism, is not just that every culture privileges its own customs, but that customs apparently motivated by the same sentiment can wind up seeming, when viewed through the eyes of others, completely contrary to the original sentiment—blasphemies against it, even.

25. Cohen Salama 1992, 233–34.

26. See Koff 2004; Stover and Shigekane 2004; Wagner 2008.

27. See Etzioni 2010, 194–95.

28. See Asad 2000, para. 28.

29. Arendt 1976, 295–96.

30. For this reason, according to James Ingram, Arendt herself was actually seeking not to dispense with the idea of human rights, but rather to emphasize the importance of "expand[ing] the conditions for participation in political life" as a way of bringing human rights from a lofty ideal to a lived reality (2008, 412).

31. See Callahan's 1987 argument that even rights of this sort actually belong to living heirs rather than dead benefactors.

32. See S. Anderson 2014; Wagner 2008.

33. Qtd. in Bustamante and Ruderer 2009, 51.

34. Ignatieff 2001, 18.

35. On the meaning of hope versus expectation, in a response to Ignatieff, see Cohen 2004, 191.

36. It is also one of the key differences between human rights and humanitarianism. Human rights, taken seriously, ask us to remake our existing models of governance, disrupt national sovereignty and the boundaries of citizenship, and radically rethink the economic and social arrangements in which we live. Humanitarianism, in the meantime, "claims to redeem . . . largely in the limited sense that in a world so disfigured by cruelty and want it intervenes to save a small proportion of those at risk of dying, and to give temporary shelter to a few of the many who so desperately need it" (Rieff 2002, 91–92).

37. Wagner 2008, 56–57.

38. See Dawes 2007, 70.

39. For a historical study of the development of these norms in Western culture, see Ariès 1974.

40. Holy Bible Gen. 47:29–30.

41. See V. Sanford 2003, 228.

Chapter 5

1. Hamington 2004, 59.

2. Koff 2004, 48–49.

3. Ibid., 49.

4. Koff, telephone interview with author.

5. See Congram and Steadman 2008, 166; Connor 2009; Pearlman 2008; Rosenblatt 2012; Simmons and Haglund 2005, 171.

6. Wagner 2008, 13.

7. See Hunter and Simpson 2007, 288; Steele 2008.

8. Thornton 2002, 18.

9. Ayau and Tengan 2002, 178. For a broader philosophical investigation of the connection between care and place, see Noddings 2002, 150–75.

10. Sant-Cassia 2005; Wagner 2008.

11. Wagner 2008.

12. A famous exception is the third volume of Michel Foucault's writings on the history of sexuality, *The Care of the Self*.

13. Meyeroff 1971.

14. Noddings 1984.

15. Meyeroff 1971, 41.

16. Caring *for* is much more demanding than caring *about*. It is hard to lie about caring for children, or paintings, or dogs: you either live a life that involves these things or you do not. We speak much more freely about things we care *about*. Ultimately, however, caring *about* usually has to be backed up by specific acts of caring *for*—if I really care *about* the environment, I should probably care *for* it by composting, refusing to eat factory-farmed meat or dairy, or other concrete practices. Otherwise, the caring *about* is at best a half-truth.

17. For classic discussions of the distance between citizens of industrialized societies and their dead, and the rise of professional handling of death and burial, see Ariès

1974; and Mitford 1983. Also see Drew Gilpin Faust's 2008 fascinating examination of the importance of the American Civil War in changing Americans' attitudes toward and experiences of death.

18. Meyeroff 1971, 21.

19. Some values lauded by feminist care theorists also have a long history outside of the feminist tradition. Scottish Enlightenment thinkers (Tronto 1993, 25–60), the English "father of conservatism" Edmund Burke, and some contemporary political commentators have all argued, in different ways, "for the relative importance of emotion over pure reason, social connections over individual choice, moral intuition over abstract logic, perceptiveness over I.Q." (Brooks 2011, 27)—ideas that are among the most basic tenets of care ethics. Interestingly, then, care ethics is one area where significant convergence of ideas can be found between some feminist scholarship and a particular brand of conservatism—one that emphasizes tradition, culture, and social ties over, for example, the purity of free-market economics.

20. Care theory also has its own internal divisions, including long-running conversations about the relationship between care ethics and other schools of thought, such as liberalism, communitarianism, pragmatism, virtue ethics, and many others. For excellent introductions to these discussions, see Engster 2007, 1–15; Hamington 2004, 9–37.

21. Most scholarship on care owes a debt to Carol Gilligan's book, *In a Different Voice: Psychological Theory and Women's Development*, which was based on her study of differences in the way men and women approach ethical decision-making. In the book, Gilligan leveled criticism at earlier theories of moral development that accorded higher status to impartial, abstract reasoning about principles than other types of moral thought. Gilligan's research showed that the supposedly inferior forms of moral reasoning were more predominant among women than men; she thus argued that women's "different voice" had been both marginalized and infantilized. What does this "different voice" amount to? According to Joan Tronto, care ethics place an emphasis on "responsibilities and relationships," and on "concrete circumstances" rather than conflicts between principles (1993, 79). Care—and ethical life more broadly—is conceived of as an ongoing activity rather than an argument that is won or lost (see Gilligan 1982, 19–20).

22. See Tronto 1993, 113–15.

23. Hamington 2004.

24. The relationship between gender and care ethics is an area of controversy. Some recent studies have seemed to illustrate that Gilligan's "different voice" is nearly as present among men as women (see Engster 2007, 13). Yet the project of care ethics continues to be identified, in moral psychology, with specifically "feminine" or even "maternal" thinking (see Noddings 1984; Ruddick 1995), and as a political and philosophical project with feminist, though not exclusively *feminine*, viewpoints (Engster 2007, 13). Arguments against care ethics, and also between different authors working in the tradition, have focused on whether it is accurate or advisable to cast women as "naturally" nurturing—or whether, on the contrary, this view amounts to gender essentialism or even "crypto-separatism" (Walker, qtd. in Tronto 1993, 86) since it may reinforce the idea that a woman's place is in the home, and not in public life.

25. Haglund 2005, 3.

26. See Houck 2006.

27. See MacKinnon 1994; Klein 2007, 140–42.

28. In many early accounts, care ethics were presented as an alternative to rights, an ethical foundation more likely to aid in the creation of a truly peaceful, just, and egalitarian society. More recent scholarship has largely abandoned this stark dichotomy, now defining care ethics as both complementary to and categorically different from the idea that people possess basic rights (see, for example, Engster 2007, 163–74; Hamington 2004, 2, 29; Held 2006, 68; Noddings 2002, 35–36, 53–57; Tronto 1993, 161).

29. See Antkowiak 2001; Cordner and McKelvie 2002, 872.

30. In this respect I agree with Maurice Hamington, who contrasts care ethics— "a self-contained theory of ethics that can be compared and contrasted with other theories"—with his own embrace of care as "an approach to morality that is basic to human experience . . . and therefore can be woven into traditional theories" (2004, 2).

31. Yoo 2003, 38.

32. See Gawande 2009.

33. Of course, there may be times when the obstacles to full participation in the life of the world come from institutional failures to provide equitable access to public spaces—for example, when wheelchair ramps are not available, or the wall text in a museum is not offered in nonvisual formats such as braille or audio tours. In these cases, issues of basic rights once again come to the forefront, and political advocacy is a necessary compliment to medical care.

34. Barnett 2011, 11.

35. Ibid., 34.

36. Cole 2012.

37. Barnett 2013.

38. See, for example, International Committee of the Red Cross 2003; Nesiah 2002; Stover and Shigekane 2004; Vollen 2001.

39. The Argentine Forensic Anthropology Team continues to insist on having the same investigators accompany mourners from the initial search and antemortem data collection stages all the way through identification and reburial (Center for Human Rights Science, Carnegie Mellon University 2011). During my visit to South Africa in March 2012, I witnessed the Missing Persons Task Team—which operates with a very small staff—operating in much the same fashion.

40. Wright 2006, emphasis added.

41. Renshaw 2011, 123.

42. Ibid., 124.

43. Tidball-Binz 2007, 438.

44. Haglund, telephone interview with author, 13 Apr. 2009.

45. Kirschner and Hannibal 1994; qtd. in Cordner and McKelvie 2002, 867.

46. In another recent article, Vesuki Nesiah reports that the International Committee of the Red Cross "has identified three principle categories of family needs and priorities: information, accountability, and acknowledgement" (2002, 823). Here is another

list of important outcomes that nevertheless leaves out a number of tactile, embodied experiences that might be crucial to mourners.

47. Barnett 2011, 216.

48. Nesiah 2002, 840.

49. See Wagner 2008, 180; Stover and Peress 1998, 173.

50. Koff 2004, 180.

51. This is not to imply that the "bodily reality" of forensic work stands in opposition to its scientific, technical, or rational sides. Forensic touches are rarely purely instinctive, but rather involve careful planning and thought. For example, Elizabeth Neuffer, observing an exhumation at a mass grave in Cerska, near Srebrenica, in the mid-1990s, observed, "An arm might lie at the surface of the grave, but the torso and legs could be buried deep in it, underneath other bodies. You couldn't just pull at the arm to release the body; the bodies were so decomposed it would come apart in your hands. [Bill] Haglund spent hours just gazing into the grave, puzzling out what limb connected to which body and at what angle and where next to dig" (2001, 235).

52. Tronto 1993, 107–8.

53. Held 2006, 36.

54. See Renshaw 2007, 241.

55. See Wagner 2008, 145.

56. Koff 2004, 228–29.

57. di Giovanni 2010.

58. Silver 2013.

59. This notion of a disembodied and purely technical identification process is, as I described earlier, an impossibility: there are still cases, especially when DNA samples from relatives are not available, where anthropological methods hold out more possibility than DNA matching. Furthermore, there is always the irreducibly physical task of exhumation, and of assembling the discreet dead body of each victim.

60. Nesiah 2002, 823.

61. Crossland 2002, 152.

62. This final task, though rarely identified as part of international forensic investigations, is a well-defined priority in the repatriation of indigenous remains and artifacts (see Watkins 2002).

63. *Stands in* for, but does not replace: care is, as stated earlier, both a response to violence and a reminder of the permanence of certain forms of damage.

64. For an exploration of the complex ways in which created objects mimic, substitute for, and express the needs of human bodies, see Scarry 1985, 278–326.

65. Zanetta 2009, 342.

66. Arendt 1976, 232.

67. See Hunter and Cox 2005, 220.

68. Koff 2004, 57.

69. Ibid., 296.

70. Ibid., 299.

71. Ibid., 54.

72. Koff, telephone interview with author.

73. Ibid.

74. Ibid.

75. Ibid.

76. In the same interview, Koff remarked, "I think that every step in the forensic process is an important one, and that it is a step, and that there is a reason for following the steps . . ." (ibid.).

77. Carter 1998, 199.

78. It is interesting to compare Koff's view with that of the cultural anthropologist Sarah Wagner, when the latter describes forensic experts taking samples from victims in Bosnia for DNA analysis: "The missing person has lost yet again a part of his body, but this time the violence—the sawing away of a tiny section of the bone sample—works to counter the brutality that the missing person experienced at the hands of the Bosnian Serb forces" (2008, 111). Wagner is simultaneously blunter than Koff—calling the practice "violence" without hesitation—and more forgiving. To Wagner, the extraction of samples is not just less "horrific" than the violations inflicted on the dead, but a reversal of those violations.

79. Here, too, Koff is drawing on her own experience. In 2005, she founded a now-defunct nonprofit organization called The Missing Persons Identification Resource Center (MPID), whose mission was essentially the same as the one headed by her fictional anthropologists, Jayne Hall and Steelie Lander.

80. Koff 2001, ch. 31, para. 48.

81. Ibid., ch. 18, paras. 55–67.

82. Ibid.

83. A "virtual autopsy," for example, uses radiation to create a high-resolution image of the body's interior without any invasive cutting (Bland 2009).

84. Hunter and Cox recommend, as a partial solution, that any part of the body removed for sampling ultimately be buried along with the body from which it was removed (2005, 218).

85. Qtd. in Dawes 2007, 212–13.

86. Siebert 2010, 48.

87. Wright 2006.

88. Congram and Bruno 2007, 41.

89. Koff 2004, 275–76.

90. Brkic 2005, 253–54. The exhumations in Bosnia were particularly tough on the various experts who participated: "It was impossible for team members to keep an emotional distance from the bodies. Yet they had little psychological support, cut off from their own families, their bosses in The Hague, even the families whose loved ones they were trying to uncover. [In contrast to Argentina, Guatemala, and other places, security issues and the displacement of survivor communities made it difficult for relatives to be present at the gravesite (Stover and Peress 1998, 156)]. And they were laboring to preserve evidence for a case that might never come to trial unless NATO troops began arresting war criminals" (Neuffer 2001, 243–44).

91. Renshaw 2011, 153.

92. Koff 2004, 314.

93. Cohen Salama 1992, 147, my translation.

94. See, for example, International Committee of the Red Cross 2003; Tidball-Binz 2007.

95. Qtd. in Noddings 2002, 127.

96. Carver 1996, 294.

Appendix

1. A longer, highly informative profile of most of the organizations listed here (and others) can be found in Kristen Juhl's "The Contribution by (Forensic) Archaeologists to Human Rights Investigations of Mass Graves" (2005, 24–33).

2. Argentine Forensic Anthropology Team 2014. See also http://eaaf.typepad.com

3. See http://equitascolombiablog.wordpress.com (in Spanish)

4. See http://epafperu.org

5. See Juhl 2005, 26–27.

6. See http://www.fafg.org/Ingles/paginas/FAFG.html

7. International Commission on Missing Persons 2014.

8. See Wagner 2010, 35–41.

9. See http://www.ic-mp.org

10. See http://www.icrc.org/eng/what-we-do/forensic/index.jsp

11. See http://physiciansforhumanrights.org/justice-forensic-science/ifp/

Works Cited

Allen, Michael J. *Until the Last Man Comes Home: POWs, MIAs, and the Unending Vietnam War.* Chapel Hill: University of North Carolina Press, 2012. Print.

"Amnesty and Immunity." *TRIAL: Track Impunity Always.* 6 June 2012. Web. 20 June 2012.

An-Na'im, Abdullahi Ahmed. "The Interdependence of Religion, Secularism, and Human Rights: Prospects for Islamic Societies." *Common Knowledge, Symposium: Talking Peace with Gods* 11.1 (2005): 56–80. Print.

Anderson, Barbara Cage. *Parturition Scarring as a Consequence of Flexible Pelvic Architecture.* PhD diss., Simon Fraser University, 1986. Web. 28 Feb. 2012.

Anderson, Jon Lee. "Lorca's Bones." *The New Yorker,* 22 June 2009: 44–48. Print.

Anderson, Scott. "Life in the Valley of Death." *The New York Times Magazine.* 1 June 2014: 25–33, 40–41, 46–47. Print.

Antkowiak, Thomas M. "Truth as Right and Remedy in International Human Rights Experience." *Michigan Journal of International Law* 23 (2001): 977. Print.

Anti-Defamation League. "Anti-Semitism Resurfaces At Jedwabne." *Anti-Defamation League.* 1 Sept. 2011. Web. 23 Jan. 2014.

Appiah, Kwame Anthony. *Cosmopolitanism: Ethics in a World of Strangers.* W. W. Norton & Company, 2007. Print.

Arditti, Rita. *Searching for Life: The Grandmothers of the Plaza de Mayo and the Disappeared Children of Argentina.* Berkeley: University of California Press, 1999. Print.

Arendt, Hannah. *The Origins of Totalitarianism.* New York: Harcourt Brace Jovanovich, 1976. Print.

———. *Eichmann in Jerusalem: A Report on the Banality of Evil.* New York: Penguin Books, 1992. Print.

"Argentina's Videla and Bignone Guilty of Baby Theft." *BBC.* 6 July 2012. Web. 6 July 2012.

Argentine Forensic Anthropology Team. "1996–7 Bi-Annual Report." 1997. Web. 7 June 2013.

———. "Annual Report: 1998." 1998. Web. 7 June 2013.

———. *EAAF Annual Report, Special Section: The Right to Truth.* 2002. Print.

———. "Press Release: The Argentine Forensic Anthropology Team (EAAF) Begins

Genetic Processing on 2,800 Blood Samples and 600 Bone Samples to Identify Argentine Disappeared." July 2008. Web. 8 July 2013.

———. "EAAF Recommendations." Web. 12 May 2010.

———. "EAAF Work by Region and Country." Web. 18 Mar. 2011.

———. "History of EAAF." Web. 29 May 2014.

Ariès, Philippe. *Western Attitudes Toward Death: From the Middle Ages to the Present.* Baltimore, MD: Johns Hopkins University Press, 1974. Print.

Aronson, Jay. "The Strengths and Limitations of South Africa's Search for Apartheid-Era Missing Persons." *International Journal of Transitional Justice* 5.2 (2011): 1–20.

Asad, Talal. "What Do Human Rights Do? An Anthropological Enquiry." *Theory & Event* 4.4 (2000). Web. 16 Mar. *2010.*

Aspillaga, Eugenio. Personal Interview with Author. 14 Dec. 2012.

Asociación Madres de Plaza de Mayo. "¡Hasta la victoria, siempre! Algunos hitos en la relación entre Néstor Kirchner y las Madres." *Asociación Madres de Plaza de Mayo.* 29 Oct. 2010. Web. 25 June 2012.

"Augusto José Ramón Pinochet Ugarte y el Patio 29: '¡Pero qué economía más grande!'" Online video clip. *YouTube.* 6 Sept. 2011 (1991). Web. 4 Dec. 2013.

Aviv, Rachel. "Wrong Answer." *The New Yorker.* 21 July 2014. Web. 14 Oct. 2014.

Ayau, Edward Halealoha, and Ty Hawika Tengan. "Ka Huaka'i O Na 'Oiwi: The Journey Home." *The Dead and Their Possessions: Repatriation in Principle, Policy, and Practice.* Ed. Cressida Fforde, Jane Hubert, and Paul Turnbull. Vol. 43. London: Routledge, 2002. 171–89. Print.

Baraybar, José Pablo. Personal Interview with Author. 24 May 2011.

Baraybar, José Pablo, Valerie Brasey, and Andrew Zadel. "The Need for a Centralised and Humanitarian-based Approach to Missing Persons in Iraq: An Example from Kosovo." *The International Journal of Human Rights* 11.3 (2007): 265–74. Print.

Barnett, Michael N. *Empire of Humanity: A History of Humanitarianism.* Ithaca, NY: Cornell University Press, 2011. Print.

———. "Humanitarian Governance." *Annual Review of Political Science* 16.1 (May 2013): 379–98. Web. 14 Oct. 2014.

Barry, Colleen. "Polish Exhumation Begins." *Jerusalem Post,* 31 May 2001: 6. Lexis-Nexis Universe. Web. 26 June 2012.

———. "Exhumation of Massacred Jews Raises Visible Divisions in Poland." *Laredo Morning Times,* 11A. 1 June 2001. Web. 27 June 2012.

Baxi, Upendra. *The Future of Human Rights.* New Delhi and New York: Oxford University Press, 2002. Print.

Beitz, Charles R. "Human Dignity in the Theory of Human Rights: Nothing But a Phrase?" *Philosophy & Public Affairs* 41.3 (2013): 259–90. *Wiley Online Library.* Web. 28 Jan. 2014.

Berkofsky, Joe. "Survivor Sues over Camp Memorial." *JTA.* 30 Nov. 1999. Web. 14 June 2010.

Berman, Daphna. "Zaka Takes Terror Bus to Hague." *Haaretz.* 30 Jan. 2004. Web. 25 Mar. 2011.

Bernardi, Patricia, and Luis Fondebrider. "Scientific Documentation of Human Rights Violations." *Forensic Archaeology and Human Rights Violations.* Ed. Roxana Ferllini. Springfield, IL: Charles C. Thomas, 2007. 205–32. Print.

Birkby, Walter H., et al. "Report of the Oversight Committee." Nov. 1997. Print.

Bland, Eric. "Virtual Autopsies Offer Clues Without the Knife." *Discovery News.* 21 Dec. 2009. Web. 7 Apr. 2011.

Blau, Soren. "The Powerful Evidence of the Bodies: Ethical Considerations for the Forensic Anthropologist Involved in the Investigation of Mass Graves." *VIFM Review* 6.1 (2008): 2–7. Print.

Boehnke, Megan. "New Program Will Expand UT Department's Focus in International Human Rights." *Knoxville News Sentinel.* 14 Apr. 2013. Web. 15 July 2013.

Bouvard, Marguerite Guzmán. *Women Reshaping Human Rights: How Extraordinary Activists are Changing the World.* Lanham, MD: Rowman & Littlefield, 1996. Print.

———. *Revolutionizing Motherhood: The Mothers of the Plaza de Mayo.* Lanham, MD: SR Books, 2002. Print.

Bradley, Chris. "Where Is Julio Lopez?" *New Statesman.* 31 Oct. 2008. Web. 4 Nov. 2010.

Brkic, Courtney Angela. *The Stone Fields: Love and Death in the Balkans.* New York: Picador, 2005. Print.

Brooks, David. "Social Animal: How the New Sciences of Human Nature Can Help Make Sense of a Life." *The New Yorker,* 17 Jan. 2011: 26–32. Print.

Browne, Malcolm W. "Computers Help Chilean Dead Tell Their Tales." *The New York Times.* 14 Jan. 1992. Web. 13 June 2012.

Bryner, Jeanna. "Forensics Helps ID Victims of Murderous Dictator Pinochet." *LiveScience.* 14 Sept. 2010. Web. 15 Oct. 2010.

Bustamante, Javiera, and Stephan Ruderer. *Patio 29: Tras la Cruz de Fierro.* Santiago, Chile: Ocho Libros, 2009. Print.

Bustos, Patricio. Personal Interview with Author. 2 Dec. 2012.

Cáceres, Iván. Personal Interview with Author. 19 Dec. 2012.

Caiozzi, Silvio. *Fernando ha vuelto.* Andrea Films, 1998. Film.

Callahan, Joan. "Harming the Dead." *Ethics* 97.2 (1987): 341–52. Print.

Carter, Albert Howard. *First Cut: A Season in the Human Anatomy Lab.* New York: Picador, 1998. Print.

Carver, Raymond. *All of Us: The Collected Poems.* London: The Harvill Press, 1996. Print.

Center for Human Rights Science, Carnegie Mellon University. "Conference Program: Workshop on the Ethics of Post-Conflict and Post-Disaster DNA Identification." Sept. 2011. Web. 9 July 2013.

Chacón, Alejandra. "Patio 29: El dolor de verlos desaparecer dos veces." *La Nación.* 22 Apr. 2006. Web. 13 June 2012.

Ciocca, Luis. Personal Interview. 20 Dec. 2012.

Chodakiewicz, Marek Jan. *The Massacre in Jedwabne, July 10, 1941: Before, During, After.* Boulder, CO: East European Monographs, 2005. Print.

Cohen, Joshua. "Minimalism About Human Rights: The Most We Can Hope For?" *The Journal of Political Philosophy* 12.2 (2004): 190–213. Print.

Cohen Salama, Mauricio. *Tumbas Anónimas: Informe sobre la identificación de restos de víctimas de la represión ilegal.* Buenos Aires: Equipo Argentino de Antropología Forense, Catálogos Editora, 1992. Print.

Comisión de Derechos Humanos, Nacionalidad y Ciudanía. "Informe de la Comisión de Derechos Humanos, Nacionalidad y Ciudadanía acerca de las eventuales irregularidades cometidas en el Servicio Médico Legal, las que condujeron a la errónea identificación de los cuerpos humanos hallados en el 'Patio 29' del Cementerio General de la Ciudad de Santiago." Oct. 2006. Web. 10 June 2013.

Committee on Identifying the Needs of the Forensic Sciences Community, National Research Council. *Strengthening Forensic Science in the United States: A Path Forward.* Washington, DC: The National Academies Press, 2009. Web. 28 Mar. 2011.

Committee on Missing Persons in Cyprus. "Bi-Communal Teams." Web. 28 June 2013.

CONADEP (National Commission on the Disappearance of Persons). "Nunca Más." 1984. Web. 30 May 2013.

Congram, Derek. Telephone Interview with Author. 30 July 2013.

———. "Cognitive Dissonance and the Military Archaeology Complex." *Ethics, Archaeology, and Violence.* Ed. Alfredo González-Ruibal and Gabriel Moshenka. New York: Springer, 2014: 199–213. Print.

———. "Re: publications." Message to Author. 8 Aug. 2013. Email.

Congram, Derek, and Dominique Austin Bruno. "[Don't] Smile for the Camera: Addressing Perception Gaps in Forensic Archaeology." *Archaeological Review from Cambridge* 22.2 (2007): 37–52. Print.

Congram, Derek, and Ariana Fernández. "Uncovering Trauma: The Exhumation and Repatriation of Spanish Civil War Dead." *Anthropology News* 51.3 (2010): 23–24. Print.

Congram, Derek, and Dawnie Wolfe Steadman. "Distinguished Guests or Agents of Ingérence: Foreign Participation in Spanish Civil War Grave Excavations." *Complutum* 19.2 (2008): 161–73. Print.

Connor, Melissa. "Forensic Science." Ed. David P. Forsythe. *Encyclopedia of Human Rights* 2009: 248–55. Print.

Constable, Pamela, and Arturo Valenzuela. *A Nation of Enemies: Chile Under Pinochet.* New York and London: W. W. Norton & Company, 1991. Print.

Cordner, Stephen, and Robin Coupland. "Missing People and Mass Graves in Iraq." *The Lancet* 362.9392 (2003): 1325–26. Print.

Cordner, Stephen, and Helen McKelvie. "Developing Standards in International Forensic Work to Identify Missing Persons." *International Review of the Red Cross* 84.848 (2002): 867–84. Print.

Cornet, Philippe. *The Seeker.* Filmoption International, 2007. Film.

Cougill, Wynne. "Buddhist Cremation Traditions for the Dead and the Need to Preserve Forensic Evidence in Cambodia." *Documentation Center of Cambodia (DC-Cam).* Web. 1 June 2010.

Cole, Teju. "The White Savior Industrial Complex." *The Atlantic,* 21 Mar. 2012. Web. 18 Sept. 2012.

Cox, Margaret et al., eds. *The Scientific Investigation of Mass Graves*. Cambridge: Cambridge University Press, 2008. Print.

Crossland, Zoë. "Buried Lives: Forensic Archaeology and the Disappeared in Argentina." *Archaeological Dialogues* 7.2 (2000): 146–59. Print.

———. "Violent Spaces: Conflict over the Reappearance of Argentina's Disappeared." *Materièl Culture: The Archaeology of Twentieth Century Conflict*. New York: Routledge, 2002. 115–31. Print.

Cuff, Abbie. "Evidence vs. Identification—The Role of Humanitarian Players in the Balkans 1992–2002." PhD diss., Bournemouth University, 2005. Print.

Damas, Sergio, et al. "Forensic Identification by Computer-Aided Craniofacial Superimposition: A Survey." *ACM Computing Surveys* 43.4 (2011): Article 27. *ACM Digital Library*. Web. 6 Dec. 2013.

Darewicz, Krzysztof. "We Trusted Each Other: Jedwabne Rabbi Jacob Baker." Trans. Peter K. Gessner. *Rzeczpospolita*. 10 Mar. 2001. Web. 5 July 2012.

Dawes, James. *That the World May Know: Bearing Witness to Atrocity*. Cambridge, MA: Harvard University Press, 2007. Print.

Dawson, Alexander. *Latin America Since Independence: A History with Primary Sources*. New York: Routledge, 2011. Print.

de Bonafini, Hebe. "Conference Given by the President of the Association 'Mothers of Plaza de Mayo' in Liber/Arte." Marguerite Guzmán Bouvard Papers, International Institute of Social History, Amsterdam. 8 July 1988. Print.

———. Interview by Marguerite Guzmán Bouvard. Marguerite Guzmán Bouvard Papers, International Institute of Social History, Amsterdam. 1989–90.

———. "Discurso De Hebe de Bonafini." *Debate sobre la posición de Hebe de Bonafini ante el 11 de septiembre del 2001*. Dec. 2001. Web. 21 June 2012.

de Bonafini, Hebe, and Hebe Mascia. "Mensaje de las Madres de Plaza de Mayo desde Belgrado." *Asociación Madres de Plaza de Mayo*. 7 Apr. 1999. Web. 9 July 2010.

de Mascia, Hebe. Interview by Marguerite Guzmán Bouvard. 1990. Marguerite Guzmán Bouvard Papers, International Institute of Social History, Amsterdam.

de Young, Mary. "Collective Trauma: Insights From a Research Errand." *American Academy of Experts in Traumatic Stress*. 1998. Web. 4 Oct. 2010.

Desbois, Father Patrick. *The Holocaust by Bullets: A Priest's Journey to Uncover the Truth Behind the Murder of 1.5 Million Jews*. New York: Palgrave MacMillan, 2008. Print.

Dirkmaat, D. C., et al. "Mass Graves, Human Rights and Commingled Remains: Considering the Benefits of Forensic Archaeology." *Proceedings of the 54th American Academy of Forensic Sciences*. Vol. 11. 2005. 316. *Google Scholar*. Web. 9 July 2013.

Dolan, Jill. "Critical Generosity." *Public: A Journal of Imagining America* 1.1–2 (2012). Web. 1 Nov. 2013.

Domanska, Ewa. "Toward the Archaeontology of the Dead Body." Trans. Magdalena Zapedowska. *Rethinking History* 9.4 (2005): 389–413. Print.

Doretti, Mercedes, and Jennifer Burrell. "Gray Spaces and Endless Negotiations." *Anthropology Put to Work*. Ed. Richard G. Fox and Les Field. Oxford: Berg Publishers, 2007. 45–64. Print.

Doretti, Mercedes, and Luis Fondebrider. "Science and Human Rights: Truth, Justice, Reparation and Reconciliation: A Long Way in Third World Countries." *Archaeologies of the Contemporary Past.* Ed. Victor Buchli and Gavin Lucas. London: Routledge, 2001. 138–44. Print.

Dostoevsky, Fyodor. *The Brothers Karamazov.* Trans. Richard Pevear and Larissa Volokhonsky. New York: Farrar, Straus and Giroux, 2002. Print.

Douglas, Mary. *Purity and Danger.* London and New York: ARK Paperbacks, 1989. Print.

Dres, Jérémie. *We Won't See Auschwitz.* Trans. Edward Gauvin. London: SelfMadeHero, 2012. Print.

Durkheim, Emile. *The Elementary Forms of Religious Life.* Trans. Joseph Ward Swain. New York: The Free Press, 1965. Print.

Dworkin, Ronald. *Life's Dominion: An Argument About Abortion, Euthanasia, and Individual Freedom.* New York: Vintage, 1994. Print.

Edkins, Jenny. *Missing: Persons and Politics.* Ithaca, NY: Cornell University Press, 2011. *Kindle* ebook file.

Encarnación, Omar G. "Pinochet's Revenge: Spain Revisits its Civil War." *World Policy Journal* 24.4 (2008): 39–50. Print.

Englander, Nathan. *The Ministry of Special Cases.* New York: Alfred A. Knopf, 2007. Print.

Engster, Daniel. *The Heart of Justice: Care Ethics and Political Theory.* Oxford and New York: Oxford University Press, 2007. Print.

Epelbaum, Renée. Letter to Marguerite Bouvard. 21 Jan. 1993. Marguerite Guzmán Bouvard Papers, International Institute of Social History, Amsterdam.

Equipo Peruano de Antropología Forense. "EPAF entrena a investigadores en Nepal." 16 Apr. 2010. Web. 17 May 2010.

———. "International Projects." Web. 29 May 2014.

Etzioni, Amitai. "The Normativity of Human Rights Is Self-Evident." *Human Rights Quarterly* 32.1 (2010): 187–97. Print.

Faust, Drew Gilpin. *This Republic of Suffering: Death and the American Civil War.* New York: Alfred A. Knopf, 2008. Print.

Federación Estatal de Foros por la Memoria. "Ideario de la Federación Estatal de Foros por la Memoria." *Foro por la Memoria.* Mar. 2007. Web. 9 Nov. 2010.

Feinberg, Joel. "Some Conjectures About the Concept of Respect." *Journal of Social Philosophy* 4.2 (1973): 1–3. Print.

Feitlowitz, Marguerite. *A Lexicon of Terror: Argentina and the Legacies of Torture.* New York: Oxford University Press, 1998. Print.

Ferguson, Sam. "Former Argentine President, Human Rights Champion Raúl Alfonsín Dies." *truthout.* 1 Apr. 2009. Web. 13 Sept. 2010.

Ferllini, Roxana, ed. *Forensic Archaeology and Human Rights Violations.* Springfield, IL: Charles C. Thomas, 2007. Print.

Ferrándiz, Francisco. "The Return of Civil War Ghosts: The Ethnography of Exhumations in Contemporary Spain." *Anthropology Today* 22.3 (2006): 7–12. Print.

Fforde, Cressida, Jane Hubert, and Paul Turnbull, eds. *The Dead and Their Possessions: Repatriation in Principle, Policy, and Practice.* Vol. 43. London: Routledge, 2002. Print.

Figueras, Marcelo. "Los Exhumadores de Historias." 2005. Web. 4 Oct. 2010.

Fisher, Josephine. *Mothers of the Disappeared*. Cambridge, MA: South End Press, 1989. Print.

Fletcher, Laurel, and Harvey M. Weinstein. "A World Unto Itself? The Application of International Justice in the Former Yugoslavia." *My Neighbor, My Enemy: Justice and Community in the Aftermath of Mass Atrocity*. Ed. Eric Stover and Harvey M. Weinstein. Cambridge: Cambridge University Press, 2004. 29–48. Print.

Fondebrider, Luis, Lance Gima, Ute Hofmeister, and Thomas Parsons. "Forensic Investigations and New Methods and Technologies." Soul of the New Machine: Human Rights, Technology, and New Media. University of California, Berkeley. 5 May 2009. Panel.

"Forensic." *Oxford English Dictionary*. Web. 22 Mar. 2011.

Forsythe, David P. *The Humanitarians: The International Committee of the Red Cross*. New York: Cambridge University Press, 2005. Print.

Foucault, Michel. *The History of Sexuality, Vol. 3: The Care of the Self*. New York: Vintage, 1988. Print.

Fox, Frank. "Return to Jedwabne." *East European Jewish Affairs* 32.2 (2002): 97–107. Print.

French, Howard W. "Congo Not Alone in Ending Massacre Inquiry." *The New York Times*. 7 May 1998. Web. 18 Dec. 2009.

Gallardo, Eduardo. "ID Mistakes Rile Missing Chileans' Kin." *The Washington Post*. 7 May 2006. Web. 27 Apr. 2011.

García-Lorca, Laura. "The Mail: Making a Memorial." *The New Yorker*, 6 July 2009: 5. Print.

Gawande, Atul. "Hellhole." *The New Yorker*, 30 Mar. 2009. *The New Yorker*. Web. 11 Feb. 2014.

Geller, Rabbi Myron S. "Exhuming the Dead." *Responsa of the CJLS 1991–2000* YD 363 (1996): 413–17. Print.

Gewirth, Alan. *Human Rights: Essays on Justification and Applications*. Chicago: University of Chicago Press, 1983. Print.

Ghani, Ashraf, and Clare Lockhart. *Fixing Failed States: A Framework for Rebuilding a Fractured World*. New York: Oxford University Press, 2008. Print.

Giannelli, Paul C. "Daubert and Forensic Science: The Pitfalls of Law Enforcement Control of Scientific Research." *University of Illinois Law Review* 2011.1 (2011): 53–90. Print.

Gilligan, Carol. *In a Different Voice: Psychological Theory and Women's Development*. Cambridge, MA: Harvard University Press, 1982. Print.

di Giovanni, Janine. "So Many Unanswered Questions for the Mothers of Srebrenica." *The Times*. 20 Apr. 2010. Web. 6 May 2010.

Girard, René. *Violence and the Sacred*. Trans. Patrick Gregory. Baltimore, MD: Johns Hopkins University Press, 1977. Print.

Glendon, Mary Ann. *A World Made New: Eleanor Roosevelt and the Universal Declaration of Human Rights*. New York: Random House, 2001. Print.

Glück, Louise. *Meadowlands*. Hopewell, NJ: The Ecco Press, 1996. Print.

Goldhagen, Daniel Jonah. *Hitler's Willing Executioners: Ordinary Germans and the Holocaust*. New York: Vintage, 1997. Print.

Goldman, Francisco. "Children of the Dirty War." *The New Yorker*, 19 Mar. 2012: 54–63. Print.

Gómez de Aguilera, María Estela. Interview by Marguerite Guzmán Bouvard. Marguerite Guzmán Bouvard Papers, International Institute of Social History, Amsterdam.

Gómez López, Ana María, and Andrés Patiño Umaña. "Who Is Missing? Problems in the Application of Forensic Archaeology and Anthropology in Colombia's Conflict." *Forensic Archaeology and Human Rights Violations*. Ed. Roxana Ferllini. Springfield, IL: Charles C. Thomas, 2007. 170–204. Print.

Goni, Uki. "Argentina's Campaigning Grandmother Finds Grandson Born to Death Camp Mother." *The Guardian*. 5 Aug. 2015. Web. 7 Oct. 2014.

Goobar, Walter. "Felipe y Marcela, a la Hora de la Verdad." *Waltergoobar.com.ar*. 30 Dec. 2009. Web. 14 Oct. 2010.

Goodale, Mark. *Surrendering to Utopia: An Anthropology of Human Rights*. Stanford, CA: Stanford University Press, 2009. Print.

Goodale, Mark, and Sally Engle Merry, eds. *The Practice of Human Rights: Tracking Law Between the Local and the Global*. Cambridge: Cambridge University Press, 2007. Print.

Goodman, Amy. "Obama Calls for Probe into 2001 Massacre 2,000 Suspected Taliban POWs by U.S.-Backed Afghan Warlord." *Democracy Now!* 13 July 2009. Web. 13 Oct. 2014.

Gorner, Peter. "Grisly Topic Makes a Fascinating Book." *Chicago Tribune*. 30 Jan. 1991. Web. 5 May 2011.

Graybill, Lyn. "To Punish or Pardon: A Comparison of the International Criminal Tribunal for Rwanda and the South African Truth and Reconciliation Commission." *Human Rights Review* 2.4 (2001): 3–18.

Gross, Jan Tomasz. *Neighbors: The Destruction of the Jewish Community in Jedwabne, Poland*. Princeton, NJ: Princeton University Press, 2001. Print.

———. "Critical Remarks Indeed." *The Neighbors Respond: The Controversy over the Jedwabne Massacre in Poland*. Ed. Antony Polonsky and Joanna B. Michlic. Princeton, NJ: Princeton University Press, 2004. 344–70. Print.

"Grupo de Antropología Forense." *Censo-Guía de Archivos de España e Iberoamérica*. 2005. Web. 19 Nov. 2010.

Gueler, Diego. "La Línea Fundadora, Las 'Otras' Madres." *Perfil.com*. 24 Mar. 2011. Web. 9 Jan. 2014.

Gupta, Neha. "Local Communities, National Governments and Forensic and Archaeological Investigations of Human Rights Violations." *Archaeologies* (2013): 1–26. Print.

H.I.J.O.S. "Historia." *H.I.J.O.S.: Por la Identidad y la Justicia Contra el Olvido y el Silencio*. 2010. Web. 13 Oct. 2010.

Haglund, William D. "Photo Summary: Scene Investigation Relating to the July 10, 1941 Massacre of Polish Jews in Jedwabne, Poland." 2002. MS obtained from author.

———. Telephone Interview with Author. 13 Apr. 2009.

———. Telephone Interview with Author. 17 Nov. 2009.

———. Telephone Interview with Author. 1 Mar. 2011.

Haglund, William D., and Marcella H. Sorg, eds. *Advances in Forensic Taphonomy: Method, Theory, and Archaeological Perspectives.* Boca Raton, FL: CRC, 2001. Print.

Haglund, William D., Melissa Connor, and Douglas D. Scott. "The Archaeology of Contemporary Mass Graves." *Historical Archaeology* 35.1 (2001): 57–69. Print.

Hamington, Maurice. *Embodied Care: Jane Addams, Maurice Merleau-Ponty, and Feminist Ethics.* Champaign: University of Illinois Press, 2004. Print.

Harroff-Tavel, Marion. "Principles Under Fire: Does it Still Make Sense to Be Neutral?" *ICRC Resource Center.* Dec. 2003. Web. 29 Mar. 2011.

Hart, H. L. A. *Essays on Bentham: Studies in Jurisprudence and Political Theory.* Oxford and New York: Clarendon Press; Oxford University Press, 1982. Print.

Hawley, Thomas M. *The Remains of War: Bodies, Politics, and the Search for American Soldiers Unaccounted for in Southeast Asia.* Durham, NC: Duke University Press, 2005. Print.

Hefner, Joseph T. "The Statistical Determination of Ancestry Using Cranial Nonmetric Traits." University of Florida, 2007. *Google Scholar.* Web. 20 Feb. 2014.

Heilman, Samuel C. *When a Jew Dies: The Ethnography of a Bereaved Son.* Berkeley and Los Angeles: University of California Press, 2001. Print.

Held, Virginia. *Feminist Morality: Transforming Culture, Society, and Politics.* Chicago: University of Chicago Press, 1993. Print.

———. *The Ethics of Care: Personal, Political, and Global.* New York: Oxford University Press, 2006.

Herodotus. *Herodotus: The History.* Trans. David Grene. Chicago: University of Chicago Press, 1988. Print.

Hinman, Kristen. "CSI: Iraq." *Riverfront Times.* 13 Sept. 2006. Web. 23 Mar. 2011.

———. "CSI: IRAQ Goes to Court." *Riverfront Times.* 29 Nov. 2006. Web. 23 Mar. 2011.

"History of the ICRC." *icrc.org.* 29 Oct. 2010. Web. 11 Sept. 2012.

Hofmeister, Ute. "ICRC Recommendations for Missing-Person Investigations in Conflict-Related Contexts." *Katyn and Switzerland: Forensic Investigators and Investigations in Humanitarian Crises, 1920–2007.* Ed. Delphine Debons, Antoine Fleury, and Jean-François Pitteloud. Geneva: Georg Editions, 2009. 351–57. Print.

The Holy Bible: Containing the Old Testament and the New. Philadelphia, PA: Thomas, Cowperthwait & Co., 1841. Print.

Hopgood, Stephen. *Keepers of the Flame: Understanding Amnesty International.* Ithaca, NY: Cornell University Press, 2006. Print.

Houck, Max M. "CSI: Reality." *Scientific American* 295.1 (2006): 84–89. Print.

Hubert, Jane, and Cressida Fforde. "Introduction: The Reburial Issue in the Twenty-First Century." *The Dead and Their Possessions: Repatriation in Principle, Policy, and Practice.* Ed. Cressida Fforde, Jane Hubert, and Paul Turnbull. Vol. 43. London: Routledge, 2002. 1–16. Print.

Hunt, Lynn Avery. *Inventing Human Rights: A History.* New York: W. W. Norton & Co., 2007. Print.

Hunter, John, and Margaret Cox, eds. *Forensic Archaeology: Advances in Theory and Practice.* New York: Routledge, 2005. Print.

Hunter, John, and Barrie Simpson. "Preparing the Ground: Archaeology in a War Zone." *Forensic Archaeology and Human Rights Violations.* Ed. Roxana Ferllini. Springfield, IL: Charles C. Thomas, 2007. 266–92. Print.

Hunter, Wendy. "Continuity or Change? Civil-Military Relations in Democratic Argentina, Chile, and Peru." *Political Science Quarterly* 112.3 (1997): 453–75. Print.

Ignatieff, Michael. *Human Rights as Politics and Idolatry.* Princeton, NJ: Princeton University Press, 2001. Print.

Ignatiew, Radoslaw J. "Jedwabne Tragedy: Final Findings of Poland's Institute for National Memory." *Info Poland.* 9 July 2002. Web. 25 May 2010.

Inforce. "Iraq Capacity Building Project—October 2004." 2006. Web. 10 Sept. 2009.

Ingram, James D. "What Is a 'Right to Have Rights'? Three Images of the Politics of Human Rights." *American Political Science Review* 102.4 (Nov. 2008): 401–16. Web. 13 Feb. 2014.

Institute of National Remembrance. "Manslaughter of Jewish Inhabitants of Jedwabne." *Institute of National Remembrance.* 8 Feb. 2001. Web. 15 Jan. 2014.

———. "Beginning of the Search in the Jedwabne Site." *Institute of National Remembrance.* 31 May 2001. Web. 15 Jan. 2014.

———. "Official Statement of the Institute of National Remembrance—Commission for the Prosecution of Crimes Against the Polish Nation on the Manslaughter of Jewish Inhabitants of Jedwabne, July 10th, 1941." *Institute of National Remembrance.* 14 Mar. 2001. Web. 15 Jan. 2014.

International Commission on Missing Persons. "Mandate." *International Commission on Missing Persons.* Web. 30 May 2014.

International Committee of the Red Cross. "ICRC Report: The Missing and Their Families." 19 Feb. 2003. Web. 5 May 2009.

———. "Missing Persons: A Hidden Tragedy." *International Committee of the Red Cross.* Aug. 2007. Web. 27 Apr. 2011.

———. "Customary IHL—Rule 113. Treatment of the Dead." *International Committee of the Red Cross.* Web. 24 Jan. 2014.

International Committee of the Red Cross et al. "Management of Dead Bodies after Disasters: A Field Manual for First Responders." *International Committee of the Red Cross.* 2006. Web. 11 July 2013.

Intriago, Marisol. Personal Interview with Author. 2 Dec. 2012.

Jayaprakash, P. T., G. J. Srinivasan, and M. G. Amravaneswaran. "Cranio-Facial Morphanalysis: A New Method for Enhancing Reliability While Identifying Skulls by Photo Superimposition." *Forensic Science International* 117.1–2 (2001): 121–43. Web. 18 June 2012.

Jessee, Erin. "Promoting Reconciliation Through Exhuming and Identifying Victims in the 1994 Rwandan Genocide." *Africa Portal.* 17 July 2012. Web. 20 Sept. 2012.

"Joe Hill—Murderer or Martyr?" *BBC.* 19 Feb. 2002. Web. 9 Feb. 2011.

Jones, D. Gareth. *Speaking for the Dead: Cadavers in Biology and Medicine.* Burlington, VT: Ashgate, 2000. Print.

Joyce, Christopher, and Eric Stover. *Witnesses from the Grave: The Stories Bones Tell.* New York: Ballantine Books, 1992. Print.

Juhl, Kirsten. "The Contribution by (Forensic) Archaeologists to Human Rights Investigations of Mass Graves." *Arkeologisk Museum.* 2005.

Juhl, Kirsten, and Odd Einar Olsen. "Societal Safety, Archaeology and the Investigation of Contemporary Mass Graves." *Journal of Genocide Research* 8.4 (2006): 411–35. Print.

"Justicia entregó identidad de DD.DD. encontrada en Cuesta Barriga." *Cooperativa.cl.* 22 Oct. 2012. Web. 20 Nov. 2013.

Kaplan, Temma. *Taking Back the Streets: Women, Youth, and Direct Democracy.* Berkeley and Los Angeles: University of California Press, 2004. Print.

Kateb, George. *Human Dignity.* Cambridge, MA: Belknap Press of Harvard University Press, 2011. Print.

Keck, Margaret E., and Kathryn Sikkink. *Activists Beyond Borders: Advocacy Networks in International Politics.* Ithaca, NY: Cornell University Press, 1998. Print.

Keely, Graham. "Archaeologists Dig for Remains of Spain's Federico García Lorca." *The Times.* 26 Oct. 2009. Web. 26 Jan. 2010.

Kennedy, David. *The Dark Sides of Virtue: Reassessing International Humanitarianism.* Princeton, NJ: Princeton University Press, 2004. Print.

Keough, Mary Ellen, Sara Kahn, and Andrei Andrejevic. "Disclosing the Truth: Informed Participation in the Antemortem Database Project for Survivors of Srebrenica." *Health and Human Rights* (2000): 68–87. Print.

Keough, Mary Ellen, Tal Simmons, and Margaret M. Samuels. "Missing Persons in Post-Conflict Settings: Best Practices for Integrating Psychosocial and Scientific Approaches." *Journal of the Royal Society for the Promotion of Health* 124.6 (2004): 271–75. Print.

Kim, Jaymelee, and Amanda Reinke. "The Whole Is Greater than the Sum of Its Parts: Anthropology of Disasters, Displacement, and Human Rights." *Anthropology News* 54.11–12 (2013): 14–15. Print.

King, Elizabeth B. Ludwin. "A Conflict of Interests: Privacy, Truth, and Compulsory DNA Testing for Argentina's Children of the Disappeared." *Cornell International Law Journal* 44.3 (2011): 536–68. Print.

Kinnell, Galway. *The Book of Nightmares.* Boston and New York: Houghton Mifflin, 1971. Print.

Kirschner, Robert H., and Kari E. Hannibal. "The Application of the Forensic Sciences to Human Rights Investigations." *Medicine and Law* 13.5–6 (1994): 451–60. Print.

Klein, Naomi. *The Shock Doctrine: The Rise of Disaster Capitalism.* New York: Metropolitan Books, 2007. Print.

Kleiser, Andreas. Telephone Interview with Author. 10 Mar. 2009.

Klinkner, Melanie. "Forensic Science for Cambodian Justice." *International Journal of Transitional Justice* 2.2 (2008): 227–43. Print.

Koff, Clea. *The Bone Woman: A Forensic Anthropologist's Search for Truth in the Mass Graves of Rwanda, Bosnia, Croatia, and Kosovo.* London: Atlantic Books, 2004. Print.

———. *Freezing.* Sutton, UK: Severn House Publishers, 2011. *Kindle* ebook file.

———. "No problem." Message to the Author. 13 June 2013. Email.

———. Telephone Interview with Author. 9 July 2013.

———. "Re: Thanks." Message to the Author. 10 July 2013. Email.

Kohen, Ari. *In Defense of Human Rights: A Non-Religious Grounding in a Pluralistic World.* New York: Routledge, 2007. Print.

Komar, Debra. "Variables Influencing Victim Selection in Genocide." *Journal of Forensic Sciences* 53.1 (2008): 172–77. Print.

———. "Ten Years On: Problems Relating to Victim Identification in Timor Leste." *Proceedings of the American Academy of Forensic Sciences* (2010): Item H117, 410–11. Abstract.

Kovras, Iosif. "Unearthing the Truth: The Politics of Exhumations in Cyprus and Spain." *History and Anthropology* 19.4 (2008): 371–90. Print.

Kwon, Heonik. *Ghosts of War in Vietnam.* Cambridge and New York: Cambridge University Press, 2008. Print.

Laqueur, Thomas W. "The Dead Body and Human Rights." *The Body.* Ed. Sean T. Sweeney and Ian Hodder. Cambridge: Cambridge University Press, 2002. 75–93. Print.

Lasseter, Tom. "As Possible Afghan War-Crimes Evidence Removed, U.S. Silent." *McClatchy.* 11 Dec. 2008. Web. 2 Sept. 2009.

Lawyers for Human Rights, and Aim for Human Rights. "Conference Proceeding Report on the Conference on the United Nations Convention for the Protection of all Persons from Disappearances." *International Coalition Against Enforced Disappearances.* Feb. 2008. Web. 25 Apr. 2011.

Leebaw, Bronwyn. "The Irreconcilable Goals of Transitional Justice." *Human Rights Quarterly* 30.1 (2008): 95. Print.

Lerner, Jessica Zwaiman. "Rabbi Michael Schudrich on the Opportunity for Renewed Jewish Life in Poland." *Jewish Times Asia.* Dec. 2010. Web. 3 Mar. 2011.

Lipman, Steve. "The Revival of Jewish Life in Poland." *Jewish World.* 11 Aug. 2010. Web. 9 July 2012.

Lonardo, Ana Maria Di, et al. "Human Genetics and Human Rights: Identifying the Families of Kidnapped Children." *American Journal of Forensic Medicine & Pathology* 5.4 (1984): 339. Print.

Lucas, Douglas M. "The Ethical Responsibilities of the Forensic Scientist: Exploring the Limits." *Journal of Forensic Science* 34.3 (1989): 719–24. Print.

MacDonald, G. Jeffrey. "Justice Clashes with Culture as Dead Are Exhumed." *The Christian Science Monitor.* 10 Nov. 2004. Web. 4 Aug. 2009.

MacKinnon, Catharine A. "Rape, Genocide, and Women's Human Rights." *Harvard Women's Law Journal* 17 (1994): 5–16. Print.

Madre de Plaza de Mayo (name unknown). Interview by Marguerite Guzmán Bouvard. Aug. 1989. Marguerite Guzmán Bouvard Papers, International Institute of Social History, Amsterdam.

Madres de Plaza de Mayo-Línea Fundadora. "Quiénes Somos." *Madres de Plaza de Mayo-Línea Fundadora.* 11 Sept. 2008. Web. 18 Oct. 2010.

———. "Discurso 24 de Marzo de 2010." *Madres de Plaza de Mayo-Línea Fundadora: Documentos*. 24 Mar. 2010. Web. 4 Nov. 2010.

———. "Origen de las Madres de Plaza de Mayo Línea Fundadora." *Madres de Plaza de Mayo-Línea Fundadora*. 8 July 2010. Web. 13 Oct. 2010.

———. "Identificados los restos de la joven Lila Epelbaum, hija de Renée 'Yoyi' Epelbaum." *Madres de Plaza de Mayo-Línea Fundadora*. 27 May 2014. Web. 10 June 2014.

Malik, Charles. "Talk on Human Rights." Nov. 1949. Web. 2 July 2012

Marchesi, Aldo. "Old Ideas in New Discourses: 'The War Against Terrorism' and Collective Memory in Uruguay and Argentina." *Social Science Research Council*. Web. 7 Oct. 2010.

Maykuth, Andrew. "Rebels Murder Hundreds of Refugees in Congo." *Philly.com*. 5 June 1997. Web. 6 June 2013.

McSherry, Patrice J. *Predatory States: Operation Condor and Covert War in Latin America*. Lanham, MD: Rowman & Littlefield, 2005. Print.

Mellibovsky, Matilde. *Circle of Love over Death: Testimonies of the Mothers of the Plaza de Mayo*. Trans. Maria and Matthew Proser. Evanston, IL: Curbstone Press, 1997. Print.

Meyer, Bill. "Bosnia: Tips on Mass Graves Traded for Cash." *MSNBC.com*. 10 July 2008. Web. 30 Mar. 2011.

Meyeroff, Milton. *On Caring*. New York: HarperCollins, 1971. Print.

Michel, Nicolas. "The Missing: Action to Resolve the Problem of People Unaccounted for as a Result of Armed Conflict or Internal Violence and to Assist their Families." *International Review of the Red Cross* 85.849 (2003): 185–93. Print.

Mihesuah, Devon A., ed. *Repatriation Reader: Who Owns American Indian Remains?* Lincoln: University of Nebraska Press, 2000. Print.

Minow, Martha. *Between Vengeance and Forgiveness: Facing History after Genocide and Mass Violence*. Boston: Beacon Press, 1998. Print.

Mitford, Jessica. *The American Way of Death Revisited*. New York: Vintage, 2000. Print.

Morales, Julio Aiub. "Dos madres de desaparecidos la cruzaron a Hebe de Bonafini." *Clarin.com*. 23 Dec. 2013. Web. 29 Dec. 2013.

Morsink, Johannes. *The Universal Declaration of Human Rights: Origins, Drafting, and Intent*. Philadelphia: University of Pennsylvania Press, 2011. Print.

Moyn, Samuel. "Dignity's Due." *The Nation*. 15 Oct. 2013. Web. 28 Jan. 2014.

Mulgan, Tim. "The Place of the Dead in Liberal Political Philosophy." *Journal of Political Philosophy* 7.1 (1999): 52–70. Print.

Muliero, Vicente. "Los organismos de derechos humanos: senderos que se bifurcan." *Clarín*, 24 Apr. 1992: Print. Marguerite Guzmán Bouvard Papers, International Institute of Social History, Amsterdam.

Musial, Bogdan. "The Pogrom in Jedwabne: Critical Remarks about Jan T. Gross's Neighbors." *The Neighbors Respond: The Controversy over the Jedwabne Massacre in Poland*. Ed. Antony Polonsky and Joanna B. Michlic. Princeton, NJ: Princeton University Press, 2004. 304–43. Print.

Nagar, Yossi. "Bone Reburial in Israel: Legal Restrictions and Methodological Implications." *The Dead and their Possessions: Repatriation in Principle, Policy, and Practice*.

Ed. Cressida Fforde, Jane Hubert, and Paul Turnbull. Vol. 43. London: Routledge, 2002. 87–90. Print.

Nesiah, Vasuki. "Overcoming Tensions Between Family and Judicial Procedures." *International Review of the Red Cross* 84 (2002): 823–44. Print.

Neuffer, Elizabeth. *The Key to My Neighbor's House: Seeking Justice in Bosnia and Rwanda.* New York: Picador, 2001. Print.

Noddings, Nel. *Caring: A Feminine Approach to Ethics and Moral Education.* Berkeley: University of California Press, 1984. Print.

———. *Starting at Home: Caring and Social Policy.* Berkeley and Los Angeles: University of California Press, 2002. Print.

Nowak-Jezioranski, Jan. "A Need for Compensation: *Rzeczpospolita,* 26 January 2001." *The Neighbors Respond: The Controversy over the Jedwabne Massacre in Poland.* Ed. Antony Polonsky and Joanna B. Michlic. Princeton, NJ: Princeton University Press, 2004. 88–92. Print.

Nussbaum, Martha. *For Love of Country?* Ed. Joshua Cohen. Boston: Beacon Press, 2002. Print.

Orentlicher, Diane F. "Settling Accounts: The Duty to Prosecute Human Rights Violations of a Prior Regime." *The Yale Law Journal* 100.8 (1991): 2537–2615. Web. 30 Mar. 2011.

Osorio, Víctor. "El escándalo del Patio 29: Los errores de identificación." *Revista Ercilla.* May 2006. Web. 22 Nov. 2010.

Oster, Marcy. "Poland's President Asks for Forgiveness at Jedwabne Memorial." *Jewish Telegraphic Agency.* 11 July 2011. Web. 23 Jan. 2014.

Ousley, Stephen, Richard Jantz, and Donna Freid. "Understanding Race and Human Variation: Why Forensic Anthropologists Are Good at Identifying Race." *American Journal of Physical Anthropology* 139.1 (2009): 68–76. Print.

de Pablo, Ofelia, Javier Zurita, and Tracy McVeigh. "Congo Examines Mass Graves to Find Proof of Revenge Genocide on Hutus." *The Observer.* 12 Sept. 2010. Web. 30 Mar. 2011.

Padilla, Elias. Personal Interview with Author. 19 Dec. 2012.

Paperno, Irina. "Exhuming the Bodies of Soviet Terror." *Representations* 75.1 (2001): 89–118. Print.

Parry, Marc. "A Polish Historian's Accounting of the Holocaust Divides His Countrymen." *The Chronicle of Higher Education.* 25 June 2012. Web. 26 June 2012.

Parsons, Thomas. Personal Interview with Author. 5 May 2009.

Pasikowski, Władysław. *Aftermath.* Meneshma Films, 2013. Film.

"Patricio Bustos Streeter asumirá como nuevo director de SML." *piensaChile.com.* 31 Mar. 2007. Web. 28 Dec. 2013.

Pearlman, Adam. "Digging for Truth, Justice, or the Humanitarian Way: Priorities in Post-Genocide Transitional Justice and Exhumations of Mass Graves." *Vermont Law School.* 2008. Web. 9 July 2013.

Pedreño, José. "Apoyar a la ARMH es enterrar la memoria." *Foro por la Memoria.* 23 Jan. 2004. Web. 27 Dec. 2013.

Peluffo, Ana. "The Boundaries of Sisterhood: Gender and Class in the Mothers and Grandmothers of the Plaza de Mayo." *A contra corriente* 4.2 (2007): 77–102. Print.

Pereira, Pamela. Personal Interview with Author. 18 Dec. 2012.

Perry, Michael J. *The Idea of Human Rights: Four Inquiries.* New York: Oxford University Press, 1998. Print.

Petras, James F., and Henry Veltmeyer. *What's Left in Latin America? Regime Change in New Times.* Farnham, UK: Ashgate, 2009. Print.

Physicians for Human Rights. "Iraq: PHR Documentation of Chemical Weapons Attacks Against Kurds by Hussein Regime's Anfal Campaign." *Physicians for Human Rights.* 24 Aug. 2006. Web. 23 July 2013.

———. "Deadly Delays: Maternal Mortality in Peru: A Rights-Based Approach to Safe Motherhood." *Physicians for Human Rights.* 2007. Web. 5 May 2011.

———. "Mission of the International Forensic Program." *Physicians for Human Rights.* 2009. Web. 11 Sept. 2009.

———. "Libyan Human Identification Needs Assessment and Gap Analysis." Mar. 2013. Web. 20 Nov. 2013.

Pierce, Steven, and Anupama Rao, eds. *Discipline and the Other Body: Correction, Corporeality, Colonialism.* Durham, NC: Duke University Press, 2006. Print.

Plotkin, Mariano Ben. *Freud in the Pampas: The Emergence and Development of a Psychoanalytic Culture in Argentina.* Stanford, CA: Stanford University Press, 2001. Print.

Polak, Joseph A. "Exhuming Their Neighbors: A Halakhic Inquiry." *Tradition* 35.4 (2001): 23–43. Print.

———. Telephone Interview with Author. 3 July 2012.

"Polish Investigators Exhume Bodies of Nazi Victims." *Amarillo Globe News.* 5 June 2001. Web. 27 June 2012.

Polish Radio 1. "Poland: Minister to Consult Jewish Leader About Exhumation of Pogrom Victims." *BBC Monitoring Europe: Political.* 21 May 2001. Web. 3 Mar. 2011.

"The Politics of Memory: Genocide Memorials in Rwanda." *LookingGlassLand.* 24 Mar. 2006. Web. 5 June 2009.

Polonsky, Antony, and Joanna B. Michlic, eds. *The Neighbors Respond: The Controversy over the Jedwabne Massacre in Poland.* Princeton, NJ: Princeton University Press, 2004. Print.

"Prosecutor Versus Georges Anderson Nderubumwe Rutaganda (Judgment and Sentence)." 6 Dec. 1999. Web. 30 Aug. 2013.

"Prosecutor Versus Vujadin Popović et al." 15 Mar. 2007. Web. 2 Feb. 2010.

Puenzo, Luis. *La historia oficial (The Official Story).* Almi Pictures; MK2 International, 1985. Film.

Purcell, Julius. "The Memory That Will Not Die: Exhuming the Spanish Civil War." *Boston Review,* Aug. 2009: 31–34. Print.

Raino, Juha, Kaisa Lalu, and Antti Sajantila. "International Forensic Investigations: Legal Framework, Organisation, and Performance." *Forensic Archaeology and Human Rights Violations.* Ed. Roxana Ferllini. Springfield, IL: Charles C. Thomas, 2007. 55–75. Print.

Rauschenbach, Mina, and Damien Scalia. "Victims and International Criminal Justice: A Vexed Question?" *International Review of the Red Cross* 90.870 (2008): 441–59. Print.

Rawls, John. *A Theory of Justice*. Revised ed. Cambridge, MA: Belknap Press of Harvard University Press, 1999. Print.

Rebolledo, Javier, and Luis Narváez. "Patio 29: Muertos sin nombre." *La Nación*. 30 Apr. 2006. Web. 13 June 2012.

Reichs, Kathleen. "Report on the Forensic Investigations at the Amgar Garage and Nearby Vicinity, Kigali, Rwanda, by William Haglund, Ph.D." 18 Jan. 1999. Web. 11 Sept. 2013.

Renshaw, Layla. "The Iconography of Exhumation: Representations of Mass Graves from the Spanish Civil War." *Archaeology and the Media*. Ed. Timothy Clack and Marcus Brittain. Walnut Creek, CA: Left Coast Press, 2007. 237–51. Print.

———. *Exhuming Loss: Memory, Materiality and Mass Graves of the Spanish Civil War*. Walnut Creek, CA: Left Coast Press, 2011.

Renteln, Alison Dundes. "The Rights of the Dead: Autopsies and Corpse Mismanagement in Multicultural Societies." *South Atlantic Quarterly* 100.4 (2001): 1005–27. Print.

Republic of South Africa. "Constitution of the Republic of South Africa: Bill of Rights." *South Africa Government Online*. 4 Dec. 1996. Web. 8 Mar. 2011.

Reveco, Isabel. Personal Interview with Author. 23 Dec. 2013.

Rieff, David. *A Bed for the Night: Humanitarianism in Crisis*. New York: Simon & Schuster, 2002.

Robben, Antonius C.G.M. "The Assault on Basic Trust: Disappearance, Protest, and Reburial in Argentina." *Cultures Under Siege: Collective Violence and Trauma*. Ed. Antonius C.G.M. Robben and Marcelo M. Suárez-Orozco. Cambridge: Cambridge University Press, 2000a. 70–101. Print.

———. "State Terror in the Netherworld: Disappearance and Reburial in Argentina." *Death Squad: The Anthropology of State Terror*. Ed. Jeffrey A. Sluka. Philadelphia: University of Pennsylvania Press, 2000b. 91–113. Print.

Robins, Simon. "Towards Victim-Centred Transitional Justice: Understanding the Needs of Families of the Disappeared in Postconflict Nepal." *The International Journal of Transitional Justice* 5 (2011): 75–98. Print.

Rodríguez Arias, Miguel. "El trabajo del Equipo Argentino de Antropología Forense llega al cine." *Télam*. Web. 11 Dec. 2013.

Rosen, Michael. *Dignity: Its History and Meaning*. Cambridge, MA: Harvard University Press, 2012. Print.

Rosenblatt, Adam. "International Forensic Investigations and the Human Rights of the Dead." *Human Rights Quarterly* 32.4 (2010): 921–50. Print.

———. "Humanitarianism and Human Rights in the Context of Post-Conflict Forensic Investigations." Abstract. *Proceedings of the American Academy of Forensic Sciences*. Atlanta, GA: American Academy of Forensic Sciences, 2012. 223–24. Print.

———. "Exhuming Equality: The Forensics of Human Rights." *Boston Review.* 2 Dec. 2013. Web. 4 Dec. 2013.

———. "The Exhuming State: Identifying the Disappeared in Democratic Chile." Knoxville, TN. 2013. Conference presentation.

Rotberg, Robert I., and Dennis Thompson, eds. *Truth v. Justice: The Morality of Truth Commissions.* Princeton, NJ: Princeton University Press, 2000. Print.

Rotella, Sebastian. "Second Ex-Leader Held in Argentina Baby Kidnappings." *Los Angeles Times.* 25 Nov. 1998. Web. 25 June 2012.

Ruddick, Sara. *Maternal Thinking: Toward a Politics of Peace.* Boston: Beacon Press, 1995. Print.

Sacchetti, Maria. "The Unforgotten." *Boston Globe.* 27 July 2014. Web. 10 Oct. 2014.

Salaheddin, Sinan, and Lee Keath. "U.S. Forensic Scientist Testifies at Saddam Genocide Trial." Associated Press. 28 Nov. 2006. Web. 7 Oct. 2014.

Sanford, George. *Katyn and the Soviet Massacre of 1940: Truth, Justice and Memory.* London and New York: Routledge, 2005. Print.

Sanford, Victoria. *Buried Secrets: Truth and Human Rights in Guatemala.* New York: Palgrave MacMillan, 2003. Print.

Sant-Cassia, Paul. *Bodies of Evidence: Burial, Memory, and the Recovery of Missing Persons in Cyprus.* New York and Oxford: Berghan Books, 2005. Print.

Sassòli, Marco, and Marie-Louise Tougas. "The ICRC and the Missing." *International Review of the Red Cross* 848 (2002): 727–50. Print.

Sauer, Norman J. "Forensic Anthropology and the Concept of Race: If Races Don't Exist, Why Are Forensic Anthropologists so Good at Identifying Them?" *Social Science & Medicine* 34.2 (1992): 107–11. Print.

Scarry, Elaine. *The Body in Pain: The Making and Unmaking of the World.* New York: Oxford University Press, 1985. Print.

Schudrich, Michael. "Jewish Descent on the Rise." 2012. *TedxWarsaw.* Web. 10 July 2012.

Schüller G., Patricia. "Caso de forense en estado vegetal: entregan antecedentes al Senado." *Nación.cl.* 14 July 2011. Web. 27 Dec. 2013.

———. "Patricia Hernández, forense de los peritajes del Patio 29." *Vea.* Web. 13 June 2012.

Scott, James C. *Two Cheers for Anarchism: Six Easy Pieces on Autonomy, Dignity, and Meaningful Work and Play.* Princeton, NJ: Princeton University Press, 2012. Print.

Sen, Amartya. "More Than 100 Million Women Are Missing." *The New York Review of Books.* 20 Dec. 1990. Web. 25 Mar. 2011.

———. "Elements of a Theory of Human Rights." *Philosophy & Public Affairs* 32.4 (2004): 315–56. Print.

Sepúlveda Ruiz, Lucía. "Proponen a Bachelet uso de técnicas de ADN mononuclear para identificar a detenidos desaparecidos del Patio 29." *Archivo Chile.* May 2005. Web. 23 Apr. 2011.

Servicio Médico Legal. "Identificación y DD.HH." Web. 21 Feb. 2014.

———. *Memorías: Programa de Derechos Humanos 2007–2010.* Chile: Servicio Médico Legal, 2010. Print.

Sherwell, Philip. "Haiti Earthquake: Thousands of Bodies Are Dumped in Stench-filled Mass Graves." *The Telegraph.* 6 Feb. 2010. Web. 1 Mar. 2011.

Shin, Laura. "On The Job: Grave Testimony." *Stanford Magazine.* 2005. Web. 26 Oct. 2010.

Siebert, Charles. "The Animal-Cruelty Syndrome." *The New York Times Magazine,* 13 June 2010: 42–51. Print.

Silver, Marc. "Bodies on the Border." *The New York Times,* Op-Docs. 17 Aug. 2013. *NYTimes.com.* Web. 13 Feb. 2014.

Simmons, Tal, and William D. Haglund. "Anthropology in a Forensic Context." *Forensic Archaeology: Advances in Theory and Practice.* Ed. Margaret Cox and John Hunter. New York: Routledge, 2005. 159–76. Print.

Simons, Marlise. "Dutch Peacekeepers Are Found Responsible for Deaths." *The New York Times,* 6 Sept. 2013. *NYTimes.com.* Web. 1 Nov. 2013.

Skinner, Mark. "Hapless in Afghanistan: Forensic Archaeology in a Political Maelstrom." *Forensic Archaeology and Human Rights Violations.* Ed. Roxana Ferllini. Springfield, IL: Charles C. Thomas, 2007. 233–65. Print.

Smillie, Ian, ed. *Patronage Or Partnership: Local Capacity Building in Humanitarian Crises.* Bloomfield, CT: International Development Research Centre/Kumarian Press, 2001. Print.

Smolensky, Kirsten Rabe. "Rights of the Dead." Arizona Legal Studies Discussion Paper No. 06–27. *SSRN eLibrary.* 9 Mar. 2009. Web. 4 June 2009.

Snow, Clyde Collins. Personal Interview with Author. 7 Feb. 2013.

Snow, Clyde Collins, and María Julia Bihurriet. "An Epidemiology of Homicide: Ningún Nombre Burials in the Province of Buenos Aires from 1970 to 1984." *Human Rights and Statistics: Getting the Record Straight.* Ed. Thomas B. Jabine and Richard Pierre Claude. Philadelphia: University of Pennsylvania Press, 1992. 328–63. Print.

Soler, Angela, Robin Reineke, and Bruce Anderson. "Crisis at the Border: Human Rights and Forensic Investigations at the Pima County Office of the Medical Examiner." Knoxville, TN. Unpublished conference paper, 2013.

"A Solution from Hell: The Perils of Humanitarian Intervention." Courtesy of *n+1* magazine. *Slate.com.* 17 Aug. 2011. Web. 17 Aug. 2011.

Sophocles. *Sophocles I: Oedipus the King, Oedipus at Colonus, Antigone.* Ed. David Grene and Richmond Lattimore. Trans. David Grene. Vol. 2. Chicago: University of Chicago Press, 1991. Print.

"Soul of the New Machine." *Human Rights Center, Berkeley Law, University of California.* Web. 17 July 2013.

Stacy, Helen. *Human Rights for the 21st Century.* Stanford, CA: Stanford University Press, 2009. Print.

Stadler, Nurit. "Terror, Corpse Symbolism, and Taboo Violation: the 'Haredi Disaster Victim Identification Team in Israel' (Zaka)." *Journal of the Royal Anthropological Institute* 12.4 (2006): 837–58. Print.

Steadman, Dawnie Wolfe, and William D. Haglund. "The Scope of Anthropological Contributions to Human Rights Investigations." *Journal of Forensic Sciences* 50.1 (2005): 23. Print.

Steele, Caroline. "Archaeology and the Forensic Investigation of Recent Mass Graves: Ethical Issues for a New Practice of Archaeology." *Archaeologies* 4.3 (2008): 414–28. Web. 22 May 2009.

Stern, Alex. "Science in the Service of Human Rights: Argentina 37 Years After the Coup." *Huffington Post*. 28 Mar. 2013. Web. 11 Dec. 2013.

Stiglmayer, Alexandra. *Mass Rape: The War Against Women in Bosnia-Herzegovina*. Trans. Marion Faber. Lincoln: University of Nebraska Press, 1994. Print.

Stover, Eric. Telephone Interview with Author. 28 June 2012.

Stover, Eric, William D. Haglund, and Margaret M. Samuels. "Exhumation of Mass Graves in Iraq: Considerations for Forensic Investigations, Humanitarian Needs, and the Demands of Justice." *Journal of American Medicine* 290 (2003): 663–66. Print.

Stover, Eric, and Gilles Peress. *The Graves: Srebrenica and Vukovar*. Zurich: Scalo, 1998. Print.

Stover, Eric, and Rachel Shigekane. "Exhumation of Mass Graves: Balancing Legal and Humanitarian Needs." *My Neighbor, My Enemy: Justice and Community in the Aftermath of Mass Atrocity*. Ed. Eric Stover and Harvey M. Weinstein. Cambridge: Cambridge University Press, 2004. 85–103. Print.

Suleiman, Nestor Antonio. *Saddam Hussein: Revolución y resistencia en Iraq*. Buenos Aires: Ediciones Madres de Plaza de Mayo, 2006. Print.

Syeed, Nafeesa, and Vanessa Hand Orellana. "Va. Lab IDs Argentine 'Dirty War' Victims by DNA." *Omaha.com*. 26 Dec. 2009. Web. 8 July 2013.

Teitel, Ruti. *Transitional Justice*. New York: Oxford University Press, 2002. Print.

Thornton, Russell. "Repatriation as Healing the Wounds of the Trauma of History: Cases of Native Americans in the United States of America." *The Dead and Their Possessions: Repatriation in Principle, Policy, and Practice*. Ed. Cressida Fforde, Jane Hubert, and Paul Turnbull. Vol. 43. London: Routledge, 2002. 17–24. Print.

Tidball-Binz, Morris. "Managing the Dead in Catastrophes: Guiding Principles and Practical Recommendations for First Responders." *International Review of the Red Cross* 89.866 (2007): 421–42. Print

Tippet, Krista. "Laying the Dead to Rest: Meeting Forensic Anthropologist Mercedes Doretti." *Speaking of Faith*. American Public Media. 19 Feb. 2009. Web. 27 July 2009. Radio Transcript.

Tremlett, Giles. "Spanish Archeologists Fail to Find Federico García Lorca's Grave." *The Guardian*. 18 Dec. 2009. Web. 13 May 2010.

Tronto, Joan C. *Moral Boundaries: A Political Argument for an Ethic of Care*. New York: Routledge, 1993. Print.

"U.N. Examiners on Atrocities Flee in Congo." *New York Times*. 24 Mar. 1998. Web. 6 June 2013.

United Nations. "Manual on the Effective Prevention and Investigation of Extra-Legal, Arbitrary and Summary Executions." *The Advocates for Human Rights*. 1989. Web. 11 July 2013.

United Nations General Assembly. "Convention on the Prevention and Punishment of the Crime of Genocide." *Prevent Genocide International.* 12 Jan. 1948. Web. 8 Nov. 2010.

"Universal Declaration of Human Rights." *United Nations.* 10 Dec. 1948. Web. 3 June 2009.

van der Ven, Johannes A., Jaco S. Dreyer, and Hendrik J. C. Pieterse. *Is There a God of Human Rights? The Complex Relationship Between Human Rights and Religion: A South African Case.* Trans. M. Manley. Lieden, Netherlands: Brill Academic Publishers, 2005. Print.

Van Schie, Kristen. "Archaeology Helps in Solving Atrocities." *iol scitech.* 27 Nov. 2013. Web. 4 Dec. 2013.

Vasagar, Jeevan, and Julian Borger. "A Jewish Renaissance in Poland." *The Guardian.* 6 Apr. 2011. Web. 23 Jan. 2014.

Verdery, Katherine. *The Political Lives of Dead Bodies: Reburial and Postsocialist Change.* New York: Columbia University Press, 1999. Print.

Vollen, Laurie. "All that Remains: Identifying the Victims of the Srebrenica Massacre." *Cambridge Quarterly of Healthcare Ethics* 10.03 (2001): 336–40. Print.

Wagner, Sarah E. *To Know Where He Lies: DNA Technology and the Search for Srebrenica's Missing.* Berkeley: University of California Press, 2008. Print.

———. "Identifying Srebrenica's Missing: The 'Shaky Balance' of Universalism and Particularism." *Transitional Justice: Global Mechanisms and Local Realities After Genocide and Mass Violence.* New Brunswick: Rutgers University Press, 2010. 25–48. Print.

Waldron, Jeremy. *Dignity, Rank, and Rights.* Ed. Meir Dan-Cohen. Oxford and New York: Oxford University Press, 2012. Print.

wWeiss, Avi. "A Tribute that Desecrates Rather than Sanctifies." *The Jewish Daily Forward.* 22 Aug. 2003. Web. 14 June 2010.

Weizman, Eyal, and Thomas Keenan. "Interview with Eric Stover." *Forensic Architecture.* 18 Nov. 2011. Web. 17 June 2013.

Wendt, Alexander. *Social Theory of International Politics.* Cambridge: Cambridge University Press, 1999. Print.

Wilson, Richard A. "Representing Human Rights Violations: Social Contexts and Subjectivities." *Human Rights, Culture and Context: Anthropological Perspectives.* Ed. Richard A. Wilson. 134–60. London and Chicago: Pluto Press, 1997. Print.

Wolentarska-Ochman, Ewa. "Collective Remembrance in Jedwabne." *History & Memory* 18.1 (2006): 152–78. Print.

Wright, Richard. "Tales of Atrocity from the Grave." *Srebrenica Genocide Blog.* 17 May 2006. Web. 8 July 2013.

Wyndham, Marivic, and Peter Read. "From State Terrorism to State Errorism: Post-Pinochet Chile's Long Search for Truth and Justice." *The Public Historian* 32.1 (2010): 31–44. Web. 11 June 2012.

Yoo, John. "Memorandum for William J. Haynes II, General Counsel of the Department of Defense Re: Military Interrogation of Alien Unlawful Combatants Held Outside the United States." *American Civil Liberties Union.* 14 Mar. 2003. Web. 3 Mar. 2011.

"ZAKA International Rescue Unit." *American Friends of ZAKA*. Web. 13 Mar. 2009.

Zanetta, Sabina. "Missing Persons: Scientific Methods for Investigating the Truth." *Katyn and Switzerland: Forensic Investigators and Investigations in Humanitarian Crises, 1920–2007*. Ed. Delphine Debons, Antoine Fleury, and Jean-François Pitteloud. Geneva: Georg Editions, 2009. 335–50. Print.

Index

Note: Page references followed by *f* refer to figures.

CPSIA information can be obtained
at www.ICGtesting.com
Printed in the USA
LVOW07s1731100817
544522LV00005B/941/P